T0158221

'Fiction has to be realistic, unlike real life…..'
Ian Rankin, 'A Question of Blood'

SARAH VALENTINE, NO GREAT EXPECTATIONS

PART 2

THE TRUE STORY OF HER TRAGIC LIFE IN DICKENSIAN LONDON

BY

PHILIP VALENTINE COATES

authorHOUSE®

AuthorHouse™ UK
1663 Liberty Drive
Bloomington, IN 47403 USA
www.authorhouse.co.uk
Phone: 0800.197.4150

Published by AuthorHouse 11/09/2016

ISBN: 978-1-5246-6413-8 (sc)
ISBN: 978-1-5246-6414-5 (hc)
ISBN: 978-1-5246-6417-6 (e)

THE AUTHOR

This is the second book for general public release written by Philip Valentine Coates. However it is certainly not the second written article he has produced. He spent many years as a highly qualified professional technologist specialising in advanced thermal imaging and image processing systems.

He has written many comprehensive technology papers for publication in specialist journals and has presented technical papers at many prestigious International Conferences. He even has acclaimed technical papers held in the British Library.

He is also the holder of many Patents registered in a wide variety of countries.

This experience has given him a unique skill in the in-depth researching of topics which has enabled him to produce a unique and revealing detailed insight into the remarkable life of a poor woman who was born 200 years ago in a deprived and dangerous Dickensian London.

He was born in Sheffield, England and attended The University of Surrey where he gained his Masters Degree.

He is married. He and his wife Jennifer have five children and fifteen unruly grandchildren who are the love of his life (if more than a little demanding!!)

INTRODUCTION

WHEN MY GRANDFATHER, Charles Valentine died, my mother and I visited my grandmother Florence Valentine regularly, at her home in East London, and when she was too old to live on her own, she came to live her last days with us. She was crippled with arthritis, but she was sharp as a tack and very talkative. Like most elderly people, her short term memory often failed her, but her memory of the past seemed to be enhanced, particularly about her husband's family, the Valentines'. Many times she regaled me, an impressionable schoolboy, with tales of old ancestors. One ancestor, in particular, intrigued me, as she clearly did my grandmother. This was my grandfather's grandmother, my great, great, grandmother, Sarah Valentine. She was born in the early 1800's in one of the roughest areas of East London. She came across as a dark and mysterious figure who lived a difficult, but colourful, life, in turbulent times, struggling against great adversity.

It was almost certainly these tales that prompted me, in later life, to look into my family history. When I located Sarah Valentine in the records I was astonished to find that the documents verified much of what I had been told. She was very much a woman of her time and as I uncovered more and more records a remarkable story unfolded.

One day, looking at the sterile pile of documents recording the individual events, I decided that I wanted to bring her, her family and her times, to life, making her more of a real person. I wanted to get a more complete picture of her day to day existence, to fill in the details between the documented facts. However, no one that was actually there survives today, so to do this I have combined family history, with evidence drawn from contemporary writers, such as Henry Mayhew and Edwin Chadwick, who have written extensively of people and conditions in the poor parts of East London during the 1800's.

I uncovered so much information that it was not possible to condense it into a single book so it became a trilogy of books.

Sarah Valentine and her family lived in a notoriously bad area of London at a time of great change and major influx of people of various nationalities, creating a local mass of deprived humanity. In addition, England was in a deep depression, along with the whole of Europe, brought on by the Napoleonic wars. These conditions are well documented by contemporary authors and journalists. In particular, the Essex Street, Rose Lane area of Whitechapel, where Sarah Valentine was born, is particularly well documented, being the scene of a major early slum clearance initiative resulting in, what we now know as, Commercial Street.

In putting this narrative together my role has not been that of an author devising a plot; history itself has fabricated the plot which has unravelled with each document uncovered and is there for all to see, written indelibly in the old documents of East London Parishes. My role has been that of a chronicler, and the truth is indeed both stranger and more compelling than any fiction I might have dreamed up. But, it has not been an easy task, in fact, I have re-written it several times as further startling information came to light. She has proved to be a complicated character and I would not be surprised if there were yet more unknown revelations waiting to be unearthed.

She clearly led a rich and interesting life with significant lows and some highs, which I have attempted to capture as faithfully as possible. The neighbours, work colleagues and friends are also drawn from actual records of real people living there at the time; we can be sure that the events are recorded with as high a degree of verisimilitude as possible.

I have all the records to support the people and locations described in this narrative. Most of these were obtained from the Public and

General Record Offices in London and Kew, the newspaper archives at Colindale and various libraries in East London. These are available to all.

This book is Part 2 of the trilogy and focuses on the single girl, Sarah Valentine, as she grows from her coming of age in 1837 to her regarding marriage.

As you read this account, you must keep in your mind that it is not some made up work of fiction, these events actually happened.

Philip Valentine Coates

LONDON IN THE
EARLY 1800'S

LIKE MOST MAJOR cities, London evolved around a major river, the Thames, which loops and curls through the city from west to east, exiting into the North Sea on England's East Coast. In the 1800's, as now, the geographical centre of the city could be regarded as being Charing Cross, with the Palace of Whitehall and the Houses of Parliament close by. The most built up areas lay to the north of the river in the old county of Middlesex. There was comparatively little to the south, which was in the county of Surrey.

From the city centre, on the north of the river, if we travelled east, along the Strand and Fleet Street, after about two miles we would have reached the Tower of London and the old London Bridge (replaced later by Tower Bridge). This marked the start of the East End. Just to the east of the Tower lay Wapping and the new docks. To the north of the docks was Whitechapel and the main thoroughfare to the east, the Whitechapel Road. Spitalfields was just to the north of the Whitechapel Road and in the early 1800's, Essex Street was a narrow alleyway running from the north side of the High Street end of the Whitechapel Road up into Spitalfields, leading to Rose Lane and Red Lion Street. This area was a rabbit warren of decrepit run down housing, some dating back to before the great fire of London in 1666. Rife with disease, teeming with thieves, footpads and paupers; it is in this area that Sarah Valentine was born, lived her life and died.

LONDON 1830 – KINGSLAND ROAD HACKNEY

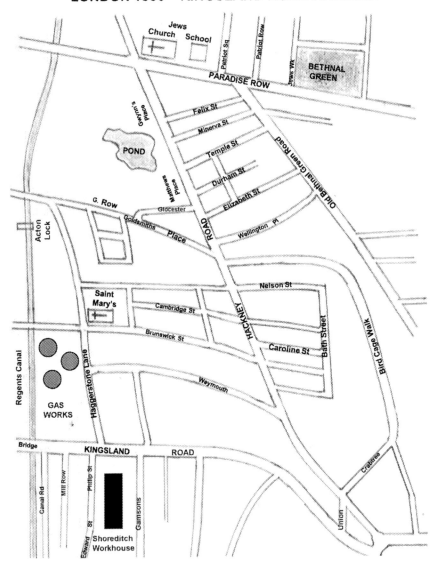

Cary's map of London 1837

PROLOGUE

SARAH VALENTINE WAS born on a cold December of 1819 in a slum in a run-down area known as the Essex Street, Rose Lane, rookery. It was just to the east of London town and bursting to overflowing with the masses of people who had flocked to London to get work. Most failed in this endeavour as they were living in an England that was deep in economic recession following the end of the Napoleonic wars. The wars had cost the Country dearly, even necessitating the first ever 'income tax' to be levied on the Nation. The Royal Family was universally hated; the King, George lll, was insane and his sons openly led a life of debauchery.

Her home was just off the High Street end of the Whitechapel Road, which was the main thoroughfare running west to east out of the city. It was an area that would gain notoriety in later years as the haunt of 'Jack the Ripper'. She and her parents and siblings lived in a court off Essex Street, which ran north from the Whitechapel High Street, up to Wentworth Street. The entrance to Essex Street was a small gap, no more than six feet wide, which ran under an arch through the buildings on the north side of the High Street. It could barely admit a small cart. This was, of course, in the time of Charles Dickens and he would have known the area well.

Her parents were Sarah Valentine and James Valentine who worked at the nearby docks, as a porter. She was the oldest and had a slightly younger brother James, who was a chimney sweep. She also had brothers and sisters; Henry, Charlotte and Caroline. Her two younger brothers, both called Joseph, died young, succumbing to the many diseases rife at the time

Her story is filled with heartache and adversity. She suffered much anguish and sorrow; events that were amplified as her life touched that of other tragic people. The fact that she survived at all is quite remarkable.

In her early years she became a rebel and was regularly beaten by her father for misbehaving. She fell under the spell of a woman called Mary Barker who was a female 'Fagin' of the time. She ran a group of young boys and girls that she used mercilessly to rob innocent people walking the streets.

She was so much trouble that, at twelve-years-of-age, her parents threw her into the Shoreditch Workhouse where she was ill treated badly by the staff. The worst of these was a large evil woman known by the inmates as 'the Vixen'. There was another member of staff they called the 'thin woman' who treated Sarah a little better

After a time in the Workhouse, she left with another girl, called Ann Pluckrose, to try their luck on the streets. They managed a precarious existence doing casual work for a variety of people organized by an old woman in Kingsland Road that they both reported to on a daily basis. Over time they were given a wide variety of menial tasks. Mostly it was 'day work', working in local trades-peoples' premises or, in different houses, as a 'Girl Occasionally'.

Saturday was a particularly hard day as they were given a wide variety of jobs as a 'Saturday Girl'. The lower middle class people that could not afford a permanent, live-in servant girl, would frequently employ a Saturday Girl to carry out the messy tasks that they dare not be seen doing by their neighbours. This would invariably involve scrubbing the outside step, washing the windows, cleaning and polishing the grate and many other tiresome jobs. The trouble was that, in order to maximise her income, the old lady who employed them, farmed each of the girls out to several clients on the same Saturday. She would say to them. "You spend no more than two hours at each house. That way you will easily get them all done in the day."

That was easily said. The problem was that the 'clients' were clearly not aware of this 'rule' and piled on the work. Also, a hastily scrubbed step that was not 'up to the mark', would have to be done again. The girls dare not upset a client, any complaint would get straight back to the old lady and lead to a beating from her husband, or worse, no further work offered to them. During that time they were given work at a Taylor's shop in the Hackney Road where Sarah met a young lad called Freddy Linford, who clearly liked her very much.

However, the girls fell on hard times and Sarah was forced to go back into the Shoreditch Workhouse once again. Whilst in the Workhouse, she fell foul of a number of feral girls, who were quite happy to inflict serious harm to any who got in their way.

The worst of these were Sophia Crafts, a big girl with pig like eyes and thick lips, not one to mess with. Elizabeth (Liz) Weston, broad and heavily built, with a prominent scar on her face and Eliza Waghorn, with dark black eyes and an evil temper.

The Workhouse was run, on a day to day basis, by the 'Workhouse Master' who was based in the 'House'. Entry to the House was organised from the Parish Offices in Worship Street by the Relieving Officer of the Parish of St Leonards Shoreditch, one John Coste. There was frequent trouble and John Coste was very friendly with the district Beadle who lived in the local Police house. They frequently drank together in a local Ale House.

Then, in the Shoreditch Workhouse, approaching her 18th birthday, things took a bad turn for the worst for Sarah Valentine when she was transferred from a girls ward to a womens' working ward.

CHAPTER 18

The End of Part 1, 1839

IT WAS ONE day, in early February, just after supper, the thin woman came up to Sarah Valentine and told her to follow her. She trailed behind the thin woman as they mounted the stairs to the next floor. The Workhouse was built over three stories, but this was the first time Sarah had been above the ground floor. She was led down a long corridor to a door. The thin woman paused and told Sarah that she was now of an age to be transferred from the girls' ward to a womens' working ward and that she had been instructed to take her to ward 14. At this, Sarah was in two minds; she had been concerned about the arrival of Liz Weston in ward 12 and a change of ward might not be such a bad thing and her face lit up a little, but the thin woman's eyes narrowed at Sarah's look. "I wouldn't look so happy if I was you girl," she said meaningfully.

Sarah's look faded and she was a little apprehensive as she followed the thin woman to the new ward. Inside, at first sight, it was much the same layout as ward 12 with many beds set against the walls on either side of the length of the room. But, on a second look, it was immediately apparent that this ward was entirely different; she first noticed that there were no young girls at all. Most of the occupants were much older than Sarah, some as old, if not older, than her parents. Then she became aware of an unpleasant odour that stung the nostrils, it seemed to be an indeterminate mixture of shit, urine and some powerful chemical. More worrying was the distinct impression that struck Sarah as she and the thin woman walked down the ward. It seemed that there was a palpable tension among the women, she felt dozens of eyes looking her over as she was led to a bed half way down one side; she chose to ignore them, sat on her bed and watched the thin woman as she exited the ward. It was with some apprehension and not a little fear that she saw the door close behind her and heard the key turn in the lock. She was now in a strange ward in which she knew no one. She felt alone, abandoned and vulnerable; warily, she tried a casual glance round.

That evening, a bitter cold wind was coursing down Worship Street. The Beadle and the Shoreditch Relieving Officer, John Coste, had taken their seats at the front of the fire roaring in the hearth of the Cock and Magpie Tavern on the corner of Worship Street and Wilson Street. The Beadle was gulping his ale down whilst listening to John Coste regaling him with his latest gripes.

"That Chadwick fellow has been bending my ear again," he said.

"Yes, there's not much round here he doesn't stick his nose in, what's his problem now?" asked the Beadle.

"Well," said the Relieving Officer, "he has taken exception about our paupers in the Workhouse. He is of the opinion that we have too many lunatics in the working wards and should separate them from the rest of the inmates."

"Does he have an opinion on where you should put them?"

"Ha! He does not concern himself with practicalities of that nature, nor indeed with any extra cost involved, or where such extra funding should come from. Do you know that in the last December and in January of this year we admitted nearly 300 people, of which 50 or 60 could be termed as lunatic. At any one time we have 150, or more, lunatics in the House. He is right in that many of these lunatics are unclean and many have disease and disability which we find impossible to treat. Any medication or dressings applied will be torn off and discarded. It is truly a frightful accumulation of human failures, but what the devil does he expect us to do with them?"

"What does happen to them now?" asked the Beadle.

2

"Well, some of them are bedridden and are in the male and female sick wards. As far as the others are concerned, the Master does try to keep them together; the male lunatics are mainly in ward 3 and the females in the womens' working ward 14," replied John Coste.

"You mean you put them in a ward with normal people!" exclaimed the Beadle, "I would have thought that's a recipe for big trouble. Would it not be better to spread them out a bit? spread the pain so to speak"

"The Master and I have discussed that issue many times. Certainly it causes a great deal of trouble in ward 3 and ward 14, and the healthy and normal inmates in those wards suffer greatly, but there is much less trouble elsewhere."

"Mmm," said the Beadle, "I certainly would not want to be in either of those wards!"

A silence settled whilst they supped their ales and contemplated the roaring fire.

Back in ward 14, Sarah had completed her surreptitious glance round and was not happy with what she saw. Several of the inmates had watched her arrival with the thin woman and they were all staring at her with wide eyes and unfriendly faces. It occurred to her that they did not look to be quite right. This impression was reinforced when one of them let out a manic screech that made Sarah jump out of her skin. Some of the women sitting on the beds opposite to her had been staring fixedly at her, they now started to cackle, like old witches. Others were standing in groups scattered about the wards. As she looked more closely at them she was startled to see that many of them were undressed, with wasted figures and pendulous hanging empty breasts. She could see that their skin was parchment like, many covered with a multitude of red marks. Her blood ran cold at the sight and a shiver ran up her spine. She was so intent on looking at the gibbering women opposite that she did not see the figure approaching her bed from the side. Suddenly, a heavy hand clamped down on her shoulder; a startled cry escaped from her before she could prevent it and the hand gripped her shoulder more tightly. As she looked up she became aware of a bad smell. The sight that greeted her made her cry out again, in terror. A fearsome looking woman was staring down at her. Her face was covered in open sores, some weeping pus. The source of the bad smell became apparent when Sarah looked at her thin emaciated legs down which brown watery diarrhoea was running. She retched uncontrollably, the sight and smell overcoming her. The hideous woman started to climb into her bed pushing her face into Sarah's; she had a grin on her face as she put an arm round Sarah's neck, pulling her closer. Now in an abject panic, Sarah screamed, wrenched herself away from the woman and leaped from the bed. She ran desperately down the ward towards the exit to get away from the hideous woman. With the cackling laughter of scores of women ringing in her ears, she finally reached the door and pulled at the handle. But it was locked, ready for the night bell; there was no way out! She fell to her knees sobbing, shoulders heaving, her heart pounding; she was terrified and started hammering on the door shouting to be let out. Nobody answered the door. She gripped the door handle with white knuckles and pressed her head against the door panel, tears streaming down her face.

After a few minutes, her panic started to subside, her heart stopped pounding. She regained a little control and, wiping the tears from her eyes with the back of her hand, she took a tentative glance round. It looked as if the whole ward was watching her, waiting to see what she would do next. She felt foolish, humiliated, but she couldn't stay where she was, kneeling at the door, so she rose unsteadily to her feet. She stood at the door, swaying slightly, considering her options. Eventually, the realisation dawned on her that she had no real choice but to walk back to her bed. As she moved back down the ward she felt all the eyes upon her; reaching her bed she was relieved to see that the hideous woman had gone, but she had left her mark. Pulling back the rough straw cover, the stench rose up, and Sarah saw with dismay the diarrhoea staining the already dirty mattress. As she stood there, she could hear the women sitting on the beds opposite cackling inanely. There was no way she could sleep on that mattress, so she replaced the cover. Just then the night bell sounded for the candles to be extinguished and a short while later the thin woman opened the door. She walked down the ward carrying her own candle and ensuring that the ward candles were put out. Then she noticed Sarah standing by her bed and she shouted at her to get into the bed. Sarah pulled the cover back to reveal the soiled mattress; the thin woman wrinkled her nose and glared at Sarah.

"I didn't do that!" Sarah shouted then, more meekly, "what kind of hell have you put me in?"

For a moment the thin woman pursed her lips. "I can't help where you are," she snapped, "you'll just have to grin and bear it. You're in the House fer Gawds sake. What do yer expect?"

With that she turned away and exited the ward, locking the door behind her. One small candle had been left burning at the end of the ward near the door. Sarah stood by her bed in the dim flickering light, unsure what to do; the women opposite were still cackling. With a sob of despair, she curled up on top of the cover across the bottom of the bed; the smell of shit assailed her nose. The candle at the end of the ward flickered once, then died, darkness descended.

Sarah spent a fitful night. The women opposite kept up a non-stop cackling, occasionally there was a manic screech, from someone down the ward. At one point she heard people walking down the ward towards her, mumbling to themselves. In pitch darkness, she kept absolutely still, fear making her heart pound. With immense relief, she heard the footsteps continue on down the ward. The hours seemed endless, the noises relentless; she had just eventually dozed off when the morning bell sounded. She felt completely drained as she dragged herself unsteadily to her feet.

The women in the beds opposite were still cackling and when she looked round the ward she noticed that the women either side of her were both sitting on their beds with their backs towards her and that several of the women on her side of the ward were avoiding her looks, pointedly turning away. This puzzled her.

When the thin woman opened the door to lead them to breakfast she noticed that there was no roll call. She was also surprised to see that the cackling women opposite did not accompany them out of the ward. As she followed the others down the stairs to the womens' dining room, she was conscious that the other women were giving her odd looks, as if she shouldn't be there. One of them, a small older woman, whispered something to the thin woman who shook her head and told her to get a move on.

She spent her day in the kitchen, as usual, but the lack of sleep was taking its toll and she found the work much more difficult than usual. When she returned to the ward in the evening after supper, she collapsed on top of her bed, ignoring the strong smell of shit and the raucous jabbering from the women opposite. She had almost dozed off when she felt a tap on her shoulder; she jerked herself up, startled and fearful at what she would encounter. But, when she turned to look round, all she saw was a small old woman with a heavily lined face and apprehension in her dark little eyes standing at the side of her bed. After a moment Sarah recognised her as the woman who had whispered to the thin woman that morning on their way to breakfast.

They looked at each other for a few moments then the old woman addressed her. "Hello," she said, in a quiet voice "my name's Mary, what's yours?"

"Sarah," she said meekly, not knowing what to expect.

"Your not mad, are you?" she said, then pointing across the ward, "like them."

"No!" exclaimed Sarah, now alarmed.

"It's alright," said the old woman soothingly, "we were not sure, after what you did last night."

Sarah's face fell, she realised that she must have seemed mad, running down the ward and hammering on the door to be let out. She looked at the woman. "What is this place?" she asked, her eyes now wet with the beginning of tears.

The old woman had a sad expression on her face; she sat down on Sarah's bed, beside her. She then told Sarah about the lunatics in ward 14 that the sane occupants had to contend with. Sarah exclaimed with horror. It transpired that the old woman was Mary Caddy; she did not know her exact age but was over 70 and had been in the House for six years, all spent in ward 14. She told Sarah that the woman with the face covered in sores, who had approached her last night, was called Jane and had severe incontinence. She was in constant pain from her sores, which she would not stop scratching. Nurses had applied dressings, but she pulled them off to continue her scratching. She was getting worse day by day and would probably not last long. She was continually seeking attention from anyone she could accost and was just one of the many lunatics that the sane had to endure. As Mary Caddy continued to point out the terrible occupants of ward 14, Sarah became more and more distressed. After all, there was no escape, everyone was locked in with them.

Mary pointed out that there was a rough demarcation line down the centre of the ward between the sane and the insane. Sarah was relieved to note that she was on the side of sanity. The lunatics caused so much trouble at meal times that they were fed in the ward. In fact, none of them were capable of working, even at the most menial tasks, so they spent all day, and night, in the ward, moping about in herds causing endless trouble to all the sane occupants.

Over the next few days Sarah had managed to clean her bed. But it was necessary to keep it continually looked after as the lunatics were always ready to foul it. In the day Sarah was at work in the kitchen and could not keep it in view, so frequently when she returned in the evening she would find it in a terrible state. It was pointless complaining to the thin woman, who could do little about it anyway. She spent most evenings sleeping on the cold floor.

As the days went by she was becoming more depressed with her life in ward 14. It was the constant smell of the mostly incontinent and diseased lunatics that oppressed her most. One inmate was particularly bad, suffering with a fearful and extensive sore, in a state of absolute putridity; the exposed buttocks were covered with a filth and excoriated. In an attempt to mask her smell, dry chloride of lime was strewed on the floor under, and around, her bed. This was the source of the intense chemical smell she had encountered on her first admission to ward 14. It was difficult to decide which smell was the most abhorrent, the shit or the chloride of lime.

Any sleep was impossible, the dark nights being frequently broken by an epileptic fit or the gibbering and fitful laughter of the more excitable lunatics. Sarah was descending into a terrible state. She was tired and exhausted; out on her feet, virtually unable to walk in a straight line. Her life was becoming completely unbearable.

She was just 18, but her coming of age was no cause for celebration. Late at night, as she contemplated her surroundings, her heart sank, she felt completely abandoned. Her lips quivered and despite her attempts to prevent it, she burst into tears. She buried her face in her hands, her sobs wracking her body, her tears streaming between her fingers. She was shattered and had relinquished all hope. At her lowest ebb, it seemed her life could not get any worse and she had no idea what her future could possible hold for her. As she collapsed, exhausted, onto the cold, hard floor it seemed to her that all was lost and there was no future worth living for.

CHAPTER 19

Freddy Linford Turns Up, 1839

It was at this time that the recently established Board of Guardians set up a workshop in the Shoreditch Workhouse where the women could make clothing for the local retailers. It was basically a slop house where Workhouse girls would work at sewing garments together. It was a hangover from the original plan that the Workhouse inhabitants would make their own clothing. This proved to be a dismal failure as the Workhouse inmates were unskilled and failed to produce usable garments. The new idea was that local retailers would visit the Workhouse, inspect the work and instruct the women. On paper it seemed a good idea, in that the women would learn a trade, albeit a very poorly paid one and, in return, the local retailers would get cheap clothing to sell on.

One day Sarah found herself assigned to the workshop, but she found the work difficult; she had no formal training in needlework and was constantly pricking her fingers, getting blood on the fabric. Local traders visited, from time to time, and usually rejected her efforts as being well below par.

Then, one morning, who should breeze into the workshop but Freddy Linford. He, his father George Linford and brother Edwin Linford worked in a tailors shop just off the Hackney Road. Sarah had worked at the shop for a short while keeping the shop clean, sweeping the floor, cleaning the counters, washing the front windows and, of course, keeping the front step immaculate and the front door clean and polished.

Freddy, was quite the dandy with bright shirts and colourful cravats; his personality matched his loud clothing and it was during the period Sarah worked at the shop that he often flirted with her. Sarah did not discourage him, finding his attentions not unpleasant. However, when she left her employment at the tailors shop she had seen little of him. But now, here he was!

They spotted each other immediately, he walked over and smiling, knelt down beside her and pretended to inspect her work. He squeezed her leg and she did not object. He chatted to her for a while, but could not dally in case anyone suspected that they knew each other. He whispered in her ear that he would be sure to come back and walked over to talk with the workshop administrator.

Whilst Sarah Valentine was wasting away in the Shoreditch Workhouse, her family, with the encouragement of their friend and neighbour Nell had arranged a dual baptism. It was Sunday 14 April 1839 and Sarah's parents, together with brother Jimmy and sister Caroline were ushering young three-year-old Mary down Essex Street to the Whitechapel High Street. Jimmy was carrying his four-month-old brother, Henry, whom Sarah as yet knew nothing about. They were followed by Nell and her children: Beth, Ellen, Margaret and Julia. On reaching the High Street, they turned left and marched en-mass to the imposing Church of St Mary Matfelon. There the two young children: Mary and Henry Valentine, were baptised. Following the ceremony, they all walked out of the church and Jim suggested that they cross the road to the Two Bells Tavern and have a celebratory drink. Sarah's mother excused herself and said that she would join them shortly. With a quizzical look at his wife, Jim led the band across the road and into the tavern. Sarah's mother walked slowly round to the Church Yard and made her way to the far corner; a spot she knew well. She kneeled down on the grass and her eyes watered over as she recalled the awful day that they buried her baby son Joseph, in this very spot. After a few minutes with her private thoughts, she rose to her feet and walked back across the Church Yard and exited through the big iron gates. She wiped her eyes with the back of her hand as she crossed the Whitechapel Road and entered the Two Bells.

They had been drinking and chatting for some time when Jimmy found himself thinking about his absent sister Sarah. He was very fond of her and could not help wondering how she was. Was she all right? Or was she in trouble? He dearly wished that he knew the answer.

Meanwhile, Freddy Linford had managed to visit the workshop in the Shoreditch Workhouse every week. Each time he devoted as long as he could with Sarah. He whispered sweet nothings in her ear and took every opportunity to touch her; he flattered her constantly and on one occasion he even managed to steal a kiss whilst no one was looking their way. He told her what a wonderful woman she was turning into. The contrast between the dismal Workhouse and Freddy's courting was exhilarating; Sarah was enthralled by his attentions and could not get enough. He had lifted her spirits and life took on a different aspect for her; it was as if she had crawled out of a dark place and finally found the light. Even the horrible ward 14 was becoming almost bearable.

Then, on 24th May 1839, Sarah was sitting on her bed awaiting the night bell. A new girl was led into the ward by the thin woman; the ward was becoming quite crowded and the new girl was led up to Sarah. She looked up and saw a tousle haired, fresh, freckle faced, individual with a smile on her face. It was Sarah Murray! Jumping up Sarah embraced her old friend.

"Your to share a bed again," said the thin woman, then turned and exited the ward.

They both sat down on the bed and it was not long before Sarah Murray noticed the cackling lunatics on the other side of the ward. She, like Sarah Valentine, was now a little older and it was the first time she had been in any ward other than the girls' ward 12. Sarah explained the situation to her and enlightened her as to what they would have to put up with. But Sarah Murray shrugged her shoulders, demonstrating her usual acceptance of whatever life could throw at her.

She proved to be her old cheerful and garrulous self and was soon chatting with Sarah who wanted to know what had happened since they shared a bed together, back at the end of January. Sarah Murray explained that they had found her a position in service with a very nice old lady. Unfortunately, the old lady had died and she had found herself out on the street. She decided to try Crossing-Sweeping as she had seen children doing it before. She begged two pence and bought a broom. After walking about for a while she came across a young girl sweeping at a crossing and found out from her what to do. But the girl would not let her sweep at her crossing saying she had to find one of her own. Eventually she found a large crossing being swept by two boys. She asked if she could sweep there, They said yes, but she had to give them half what she got for using their crossing. She stayed there for a few weeks and learned the ropes. If she saw a gentleman coming she would call out and he would be hers; then she would sweep the road for him to cross and beg a halfpenny. But the boys were very careful to watch what she was getting. They were bigger than her and would gang up on her at the end of the day and take at least half, sometimes more, of what she had. Her hands were sore and bleeding from the sweeping and, with the boys taking most of her money, together with having to replace a worn out broom every few days, she was earning so little it was not possible to live on it, so she came back to the Workhouse.

The arrival of Sarah Murray and meeting up with Freddy Linford again had considerably bucked Sarah Valentine up. Her will to do something with her life was now returning. She started to wonder about her family. Thoughts that had not entered her head for many months now bubbled to the surface. How were her brother Jimmy and sister Caroline doing, and her little sister Mary? by heavens, Mary would be a grown up three-year-old, running around by now. These feelings, together with her dislike of the conditions in ward 14, started to instil in her a growing desire to be out of the Workhouse.

There was, at this time, a steadily increasing movement within the Parish to try and find work outside the Workhouse for the, more able, inmates. The local Church Wardens were becoming quite active in this respect. Their view was that it was better they work for a living than sponging off the local rate-payer's. So it was that Sarah found herself with several other girls, including Sarah Murray, called into the Master's office. They were interviewed by members of the local church, who wanted to know what work experience they had. Sarah said that she had done some domestic service, so they said that they would try to find her some work in that field. That evening, she discussed the work prospects with Sarah Murray. Both hoped that it would present an opportunity to get out of the dismal Workhouse. For the first time in nearly two years Sarah found herself lying awake contemplating a brighter future.

When Freddy Linford visited the Workhouse workshop, he had a surprise for her, he declared that he loved her dearly and wanted to marry her. Sarah was stunned by this revelation and found herself speechless; she was concerned that it was all too sudden. But, Freddy continued his endearments and she felt compelled to restrain his enthusiasm. To change the subject, she mentioned what the Church Wardens had told her. Freddy immediately seized on the opportunity and said that he would try to get her a job at the tailor's shop as it appeared that the shop girl had upped and left, so there was a potential position for her.

That evening she discussed Freddy's unexpected proposal with Sarah Murray who congratulated her and said that one 'should not look a gift horse in the mouth' to which she laughed and said that Freddy did not look in the least like a horse.

On Wednesday 26th June, Sarah Murray was called into the Master's office and told she was going into domestic service as a live-in 'Slavey', starting tomorrow. Slaveys were employed in poorer households that could not afford proper servants. They were paid next to nothing, but they at least had a roof over their head and the prospect of their next meal. For Workhouse girls like Sarah Murray, they represented a significant step up. That evening she discussed it with Sarah Valentine, who agreed that it was a good opportunity. The next morning, Sarah Murray departed the Workhouse and Sarah Valentine now had the bed to herself. She felt the loss of the bubbly and invigorating company of her recent friend. She felt quite lonely, but that was not going to last long.

On Saturday the 29th June 1839, Sarah had just finished breakfast and was on her way to the kitchen, when the thin woman walked up to her. "Come with me!" she said in a stern voice.

"Oh dear, what have I done now," mumbled Sarah under her breath, as she trailed along behind.

She was still pondering the nature of her misdemeanour, when the thin woman spoke again. "You have been found work at a local tailor's shop and they have come to collect you."

Sarah held her breath, a tailor's shop! Could it be Freddy's doing? Her heart was pounding as she went through the ritual of changing into her own clothes and collecting her meagre belongings. She was escorted to the Master's office and, after knocking, the thin woman opened the door and pushed her in, closing it behind her. When she saw Freddy standing in front of the Master's desk, she felt like running across the room and throwing her arms around him. But she restrained the urge and walked up to the Master's desk, attempting a clumsy curtsey. The Master grunted, filled in the formalities of the discharge and sent them both on their way.

Outside the Workhouse Freddy took her in his arms and spun her round till she was dizzy. Finally, he put her down and laughed as she staggered about. When she had her head back in order she punched him on the arm and admonished him, but in a friendly laughing manner. Then he got serious and produced a poesy ring with a red stone and engraved with a heart emblem. Solemnly, he presented it to her and asked her to be his wife. Her eyes watered and tears ran down her cheeks; she took the ring and it was the most beautiful thing that she had ever owned in her entire life. He helped her to put it on her finger; it fitted perfectly and she felt incredibly happy.

She was in seventh heaven as they walked down the road, arm in arm. She was not really aware of the direction they were taking until they passed Goldsmiths Place where the tailor's shop was situated. "Am I not supposed to be working there?" she asked.

Freddy laughed, "no, not today, we have things to do."

She gave him an old fashioned look, but chose to keep her thoughts to herself for the time being. They reached the end of the Hackney Road and turned right, walking past the Jews' school and the Bethnal Green. Just past the Green they turned left down Chester Place towards the district known as Globe Town. This was not an area that Sarah was familiar with, but the houses looked bigger and better than those she had been used to. After a short walk they turned right into Green Street and then right again into Charles Street. After a few minutes walk they stopped outside No. 6 Charles Street. Freddy looked down at Sarah and said. "This is our new home."

Sarah looked up at him, "oh it is, is it?" she said.

He laughed, "you think I want to make a dishonest woman out of you. We are only here to drop off your things. Then," he said mysteriously, "we have somewhere else to go."

Still confused, she followed him into the house. They walked up some narrow stairs to the second floor; after walking a short distance down a dark corridor Freddy stopped outside a door. He produced a key and opened the door. Sarah walked into a clean, sparsely furnished room. It had a couch set against the far wall and a small table, with two chairs, under a window with intact glass and real cloth curtains which let in a welcoming light; there was even a small carpet on the floor. To Sarah, it was a magnificent residence indeed, far above her expectations. She walked across the room, it even smelled nice.

Freddy watched her, a smile on his face. At the far end was a door; she opened it into a small bedroom. Inside was a double bed, she turned and looked at Freddy, but before she could say anything, he piped up. "That is where you sleep, I sleep on the couch in this room."

"Yes," she said, holding his eyes for a moment, "that will be acceptable."

Laughing at her serious expression he walked over and put his arms around her. "Come on," he said, "we have more business to attend to."

His cheeky grin and bubbly personality won her over again and she allowed herself to be led out of the house. They walked down Charles Street and cut through North Street to Globe Road and walked to the bottom junction with the main road. They spent a little time trying to cross the Mile End Road. It was packed with traffic: horse drawn carts, trams, horses and all manner of people. Eventually, reaching the other side, they set off down George Street. Sarah was mystified as to their destination, but had to admit that she was curious as to Freddy's intentions. Her curiosity intensified when they arrived outside the Stepney Parish Church of Saint Dunstan's. Smiling at her odd expression, Freddy took her arm and led her down a pathway across a grassy expanse to a door at the side of the church. Pushing it open, he entered pulling her along behind him. He walked down a side isle and stopped outside a stout studded wooden door. He knocked, and after a few moments a voice invited them to 'come in'. They entered a small office with dark wood panelled walls; behind an old leather covered desk sat a middle aged man in a clerical gown. He smiled up at them and Sarah got the distinct impression that they had been expected.

Freddy spoke first. "Reverend James, this is my betrothed, Sarah Valentine."

The Reverend rose to his feet and proffered his hand to Sarah. Still in a state of shock, Sarah meekly took the Reverend's hand. "Please be seated," he said pointing at two chairs in front of his crowded desk.

For the first time Sarah noticed that his large desk was completely covered with masses of paper; untidy and precariously balanced piles of large, leather bound, books and a variety of boxes of quills and official looking stamps looked ready to spill over onto the floor. She and Freddy took the proffered seats.

The next twenty minutes went by with Sarah in a daze. She vaguely registered the fact that they were arranging to get married. Their banns were set to be posted on the 7th, 14th and 21st of July 1839, with the wedding to be performed on the Monday the 22nd of July. She was still in a daze when the Reverend was shaking her hand and congratulating her as they were ushered out the door. Standing in the church grounds she tried to pull herself together. She clung to Freddy as he led her back to their new home; was this all happening a little too fast she asked herself?

That evening Freddy took her to an eating house on the Mile End Road. It was the first time that she had ever been in such a place and she felt a little uncomfortable eating in the presence of such obviously middle class clientele, who she perceived to be watching her every move. When they arrived back at their new home in Charles Street, Sarah was surprised to bump into one of the seamstresses from the tailor's shop in the hallway. Freddy tried to take her upstairs to their room, but she resisted and started to talk to the seamstress. Her name was Ann Patients and it transpired that she was also living in the same house with her brother and mother, also called Ann Patients. They had been living there for some time and found the neighbourhood to be very acceptable; she expressed some surprise at her and Freddy being there. It seemed to Sarah that there had been no mention at the tailor's shop of her and Freddy's forthcoming marriage, but perhaps that should be no surprise, bearing in mind the gossiping nature of the seamstresses.

When they entered their rooms, Freddy immediately cuddled and kissed her, declaring his love. She accepted his attentions until it was time to retire. He followed her into the bedroom and embraced her again. She gently pushed him away, saying that they were not yet married. She was a little concerned, but despite her misgivings, Freddy duly spent the night on the couch in the adjoining room.

The next day, a Sunday, they spent arm in arm walking around. They strolled down the Hackney Road where they turned off down Wolverly Place towards the Regents Canal. They turned off before the Hackney Footpath Bridge and joined the towpath at the Acton Lock. It was a bright sunny summer's day, sunbeams glittered off the ripples in the canal. She watched a group of ducks swimming in formation across the water; she held on tightly to Freddy's arm. They wrinkled their noses as they passed the Imperial Gasworks and, laughing, stepped up their pace to exit the towpath at the Agostone Bridge. After a short walk down Brunswick Street they found themselves back in the Hackney Road. It was now early evening and Freddy suggested a drink in the Globe. Sarah was a little apprehensive, but when they entered there was no sign of Martha Herbert, her husband John was serving.

They were just finishing their third drink and Sarah was about to suggest they walk home, when in walked Freddy's brother Edwin Linford with a young lady in tow. Freddy jumped up and, with his customary exuberance, invited them to join him and Sarah. When their drinks had been procured they sat down at Freddy and Sarah's table. Sarah was interested in the young lady with Edwin and it was soon explained that she was called Susan Smith and she and Edwin had been 'walking out together' for a number of weeks now. Observing them together, it was very clear to Sarah that they were quite enamoured of each other. Susan Smith turned out to be a very nice well mannered girl and it occurred to Sarah that she and Edwin were well suited. After a few more drinks Edwin and Susan said they must go; Sarah took the opportunity to stand up and encourage Freddy to do likewise. He seemed a little reluctant, but eventually agreed, and they all left the tavern together.

Freddy and Sarah made their way back to Globe Town whilst Edwin and Susan set off down the Hackney Road in the opposite direction. Sarah and Freddy were both meandering a little, with the effects of the alcohol. They passed the Bethnal Green and turned left into Chester Place but, to Sarah's surprise, Freddy did not turn right down North Street to get back to their home in Charles Street. Instead he took the next turning down Globe Road; Sarah looked up at him quizzically, but he ignored her and they marched on. When they reached the corner with Devonshire Street, Sarah gave a gasp of dismay as Freddy ushered her through the door of the Prince Regent Tavern.

The bar was quite full with the evening crowd, but Freddy elbowed his way to the counter and shouted at a woman standing behind the bar. "Come on Martha! We're dying of thirst here!" As Freddy ordered two large measures of gin, Sarah lightly squeezed his arm and whispered that she had really had too much to drink already. He shushed her into silence. "We have a wedding to celebrate!" he said, "here's to us!" And with that he downed the gin and ordered another two. Sarah was staring in dismay at the two drinks in front of her when a voice sounded just behind her.

"Hello love, fancy seeing you here."

She turned round to see the seamstress Ann Patients standing there with a young man beside her; the young man was introduced as her brother John Patients. Freddy seemed a little annoyed at them being there, but grudgingly engaged them in conversation. After a few more drinks, Ann Patients and her brother said they must go home as her brother worked as a porter at the docks and needed an early start. Taking the opportunity Sarah rose and said that they were going home as well; she gave Freddy a stern, meaningful look. With poor grace, Freddy downed his drink, then the one that Sarah had left and followed the trio out of the door. When they reached No. 6 Charles Street, they said goodbye to Ann and John Patients in the hallway and, after staggering up the stairs to the second floor, Freddy made several attempts to unlock the door before finally succeeding.

When they got indoors, Sarah made for the bedroom and kicked off her shoes; she sat down on the bed and lay back on the pillow, quite exhausted and much the worse for the drink. She was just dozing off when she became aware of Freddy on the bed beside her, he was undoing her clothing. Startled into wakefulness, she tried to push him away, but he was not to be deterred in his purpose, he ripped her dress open at the front and climbed on top of her, pushing her down on the bed underneath him. "No! No! No! Freddy, please! Please! Don't!" she pleaded

"Come on Sarah!" he shouted, "It's alright. We're to be married!"

She realized that her breasts were exposed where he had torn open her dress. She put her hands over her chest to cover herself up. Then she felt his hands pulling at her drawers, she reached down to stop him. Next thing, she felt a sharp pain between her legs and Freddy's hands were squeezing her breasts. She sobbed as she felt him pushing into her. The sharp pain caused her to cry out, but Freddy seemed oblivious to her distress and forced himself into her more urgently. The effects of the drink had left her weakened and she had no strength to push him off. It seemed to go on for an age then, eventually, he slowed down and she felt him withdraw. She took a deep breath and, as she felt him relax, she brought her knee up as hard as she could into his exposed groin. He howled like a wounded bear and rolled over onto his side. Seizing her opportunity, she rolled off the bed and staggered through the door into the adjoining room. Without pause, she rushed to the front door; there was a moment of panic as it wouldn't open. Then she realized that it was locked, but the key was in the door. She turned the key and pushed the door open. As she walked through the opening she glanced back and saw Freddy, his face a mask of fury, limping towards her. Pulling the key out, she slammed the door and locked it from the outside. Leaving the key in the lock she tottered down the stairs, staggered down the hallway and out into the street. As she hobbled up Charles Street, she could hear Freddy shouting her name and hammering on the door.

Her first instinct was to get as far away as possible and, in her desire to do so, she took little note of the direction she was taking. Then she became aware that she was retracing her earlier steps and was now walking past Bethnal Green. She continued on and turned left into the Hackney Road. She clasped her torn dress to her body against the chill of a light evening breeze; it was then that she noticed Freddy's poesy ring, still on her finger where he had placed it. Anger rising up in her, she pulled it off and was about to throw it away, when she changed her mind and put it in her pocket intending to return it to him.

It was the early hours of the morning and the streets were strangely quiet. As she walked on down the Hackney Road, she glanced over and saw the tailor's shop, now in darkness. She half thought of knocking on the door, but quickly dismissed the idea. When she reached the end of the Hackney Road she became aware of a throbbing pain between her legs; she could feel a warmth that she felt must be blood and she knew that she could not go much further. There was really only one choice; she turned up the Kingsland Road and, fifteen minutes later, was standing outside the massive door to the Shoreditch Workhouse, which at that time of night was firmly shut. She knew that the Worship Street Parish Office and the Court House would also be shut. She also knew that she could gain entry to the House without visiting them, if she could convince the Master of her need, as he had the power to admit people directly. She sat down on the step outside and leaned back against the door. She felt a light drizzle of rain brush her face; it was not unpleasant. As the early flush of dawn lightened the sky, she fell into a disturbed slumber where she dreamed that she was running as hard as she could, away from a dark sinister shape, hot on her heels.

The next morning was the 1st of July 1839 and when the Workhouse door was opened, a slumbering Sarah fell back onto the feet of a startled gatekeeper, one John Smith. He took in her ripped dress, the blood on her legs and immediately went for the Matron. The Matron, Louisa Slee, came running at his shout and knelt down beside Sarah. One look at her torn dress and the blood between her legs was enough to tell her exactly what had befallen this girl. At her instruction Sarah was taken immediately to the sick ward, where nurse Eliza Ribnell cleaned her up and placed her in a bed.

The sick ward was packed with masses of women, old and young. The beds were jammed tightly together with not an inch between them. All were occupied by sick and chronically ill inmates. The old women in the beds either side of Sarah were running high fevers, coughing and spitting up phlegm. There was no ventilation in the ward and the stench was repulsive in the extreme; a mixture of sick sweaty bodies, many lying in their own urine and excreta.

It was Sunday 7th July and after seven horrendous days in the sick ward Sarah was contemplating the fact that her wedding banns would be posted that very day at St Dunstan's in Stepney. She found herself grimacing at the thought. She really was not yet ready for marriage, although she did wonder what Freddy was doing and if he had any regrets about what he had done to her. She felt well enough recovered physically, but still somewhat taken aback mentally by Freddy's attack on her. She had a visit from the Workhouse Master, William Thomas, who asked who had attacked her. She half thought of naming Freddy, but then decided against it. Instead, she claimed that an unknown drunken man had accosted her on the street and ran off afterwards. The Workhouse Master grunted at this and gave her an old fashioned look which indicated that he did not believe her.

The following Sunday, the 14th July, the date that the second of her wedding banns would be posted, the old woman in the bed next to Sarah died. The body was unceremoniously wheeled out and another unfortunate installed almost immediately. The new occupant was old with grey, parchment like skin, and clearly running a very high fever. Sarah climbed out of her bed and approached the nurse Eliza Ribnell.

She pleaded with her that she was quite recovered and wanted to get out of this terrible ward. Eliza summoned the Matron, Louisa Slee, and Sarah repeated her plea to her. As it was patently obvious that the ward was massively overcrowded and Sarah seemed well enough, she readily agreed. So, Sarah was ensconced back in the usual Workhouse garb and was placed in the women's working ward 16. Next day, she found herself back in the slop workshop ripping her fingers to shreds trying to sew garments together. Ward 16 was mainly full of normal people and Sarah was grateful not to have been placed in ward 14. However, she immediately recognised Sophia Crafts in a bed further down and decided that meant trouble; she made a point of keeping clear of her.

It should not really have come as a surprise when, later that week, she looked up from her work to see Freddy Linford standing in front of her, after all it was here that she had met him before. She looked at his face, she could see mixed emotions: the first was surprise, he had clearly not expected to see her here, then she saw shame and maybe a tinge of regret. Well, she was not going to make anything easy for him, she turned away and carried on with her work.

It was more than an hour later and Sarah still had her head down, focused on her work, when she became aware of a figure standing behind her, she ignored it. Then a voice, barely above a whisper, said. "I know I don't deserve it, but could you please find it in your heart to forgive me for the terrible thing that I did to you." There was a pause, "don't answer now. I will be back." Then he was gone.

The next day found Sarah contemplating Freddy's words. Should she forgive him? She had quite recovered from his attack, but did he deserve forgiveness? She was not sure on that point, but she would hear what he had to say when he next visited the Workhouse slop shop.

Freddy duly visited during the week and for most of the time he was there, instructing some of the women, he just looked at her from time to time as if he was afraid to approach her. He had such a hang-dog expression, in stark contrast to his usual cheeky grin, that she found herself actually feeling a little sorry for him; after all, up until the attack he had always been very kind to her. She watched him instructing one of the more ham-fisted women in how to hold the needle. He glanced up at her and, as their eyes met, almost involuntarily she found herself flashing him a quick slight smile. The result was startling, his jaw dropped open and he stabbed himself in his finger with the needle; he yelped in pain as a drop of blood dripped onto the garment the woman had been sewing. The woman Freddy had been instructing was looking in dismay at the blood on her fabric and giving him a verbal assault, the net upshot of which informed him, in no uncertain terms, that he made a far more effective butcher than tailor. Sarah could not help herself, she burst out laughing, then quickly disguised it by pretending to have a coughing fit.

Just before he left Freddy came past her and whispered in her ear again. "I am so sorry for what happened, please, please, forgive me. I promise I will make it up to you," Then he was gone again.

CHAPTER 20

The Abduction

THE FOLLOWING SUNDAY, the 21ˢᵗ July 1839, Sarah was walking to St Mary's Haggerstone in the Workhouse crocodile, to attend the weekly service. She had felt a little dizzy when she woke up and found herself swaying from side to side as she walked. Dismissing the feeling, her thoughts turned to the last of her wedding banns, which would be posted that very day. The thought stayed with her as she slumped down on the pew in the church. As she listened to the Reverend droning on, she contemplated the fact that tomorrow would have been her wedding day. A part of her felt a deep regret, after all doesn't every girl secretly want to get married? And what of Freddy, what did he mean by 'I promise I will make it up to you?' How could he possibly do that?

She fell asleep that night wondering what her wedding day would have been like? Would Freddy have made her a special dress? She had already decided that she would forgive Freddy and do her best to put the memory of that terrible interlude behind her, all she wanted to do now was get on with her life.

However, the next day, Monday 22ⁿᵈ July, her proposed wedding day, Sarah woke up feeling quite ill; she felt like her whole body was on fire. Her bed was soaked with her sweat, her hair was matted to her head and perspiration was running down her forehead into her eyes. She tried to get up from the bed, but a dizzy spell overcame her and she fell heavily onto the hard stone floor. Her head hit the wall behind her bed and she lost consciousness.

When she woke up, her head was hurting badly and she could barely focus her eyes. After a few moments she could just make out her surroundings. Panic filled her body when she realised that she was back in the dreaded sick ward! But this time she was running a high fever; she began falling in and out of consciousness. Time had no meaning, one day merged into the next. She had no desire for food and as each day passed she grew weaker.

Meanwhile, Freddy had noticed that Sarah no longer attended the slop shop. In response to his enquiries, the thin woman told him that she had fallen ill and was in the sick ward. Alarmed, he asked if he could visit her. He was told to speak with the sick nurse, Eliza Ribnell. He found his way to the sick ward where he located Eliza Ribnell. She proved to be quite unhelpful until he produced a shiny shilling piece, following which he was escorted to Sarah's bedside. He was horrified when he beheld her, she was covered in sweat, eyes sunk in her head, mouth drooling saliva. She gave no response to his voice and did not respond to his touch. Badly shocked, he went back to the nurse Eliza, who gave him little hope; her opinion was that, left in here she would just fade away. Freddy knew that he had promised to make it up to Sarah for what he had done to her, he also knew that he wanted her. He felt sure that if he could get her to his home he could have her; she would be grateful to him. After some thought, he hatched a plan. He returned to Eliza Ribnell to discuss it. Shortly afterwards they both met with the gatekeeper: terms were agreed.

The next evening, at midnight, Freddy arrived at the Workhouse in a coach. As prearranged, the gatekeeper admitted him. Eliza Ribnell was waiting in the shadows, supporting an almost comatose Sarah Valentine. The three of them helped her into the coach. Freddy boarded the coach and it departed; the gatekeeper locked up after them. Freddy took her back to No. 6 Charles Street in Globe Town and put her to bed. The next day he consulted with an apothecary who came round, examined Sarah and prescribed medication.

Sarah spent the next few days virtually comatose, oblivious to the world around her. But no longer festering in an unhealthy environment and not surrounded by sick and chronically ill inmates, she started to recover. The fever gradually diminished and her coma lifted. Then, one morning, she woke up, feeling much better; her head was much clearer. She opened her eyes and slowly became aware of her surroundings. She was lying in a bed and she could see the sun shining through a window illuminating the room. She lay there for a while trying to remember where she was. Then, she recalled the Workhouse sick ward where she had laid. This was clearly not it, but it did look familiar. Then she became conscious of someone lying beside her. Suddenly becoming alarmed, she turned her head to see Freddy's face, on the bed next to her; he was deep in slumber. Shocked, she turned away, put her feet over the side, onto the floor, and slipped out of the bed. To her astonishment, she crumpled to the floor; she had been off her feet for so long that she had lost all strength in her legs. She crawled to the door and into the next room. She now knew where she was; she was back in Globe Town, in Freddy's home. She crawled to the couch that Freddy had promised to sleep on when he assaulted her. She pulled herself onto the couch and rested. She wasn't sure how she had got here, but she was very worried about what Freddy might do to her; moreover, her legs were too weak for her to make an escape this time.

She must have dozed off, because the next thing she was aware of was a hand on her shoulder which startled her into wakefulness. Her eyes sprang open and she found herself staring straight into Freddy Linford's face.

"How are you feeling Sarah?" he asked, smiling at her.

"What am I doing here?" she demanded.

Freddy looked at her for a while, then slowly explained to her what had happened and how he had taken her from the Workhouse sick ward. On hearing this Sarah became very alarmed.

"Freddy!" she shouted, "I can't just run away from the Workhouse, they will put me before a Magistrate!"

"Don't fret my love," he said, "it's all taken care of, no one will speak of it, you are quite safe."

Sarah fell silent unsure what to say or what to do.

Over the next few days an uneasy atmosphere settled over them. Sarah explained that she was grateful that Freddy had nursed her back to health, but she could not remain there. He begged her to give it a try, but she was adamant. He tried to get her back to bed, but she remained on the couch. He went to work at the tailor's shop during the day and brought food back in the evening. She was beginning to regain her strength. But she still did not trust him.

She had left the Workhouse barefoot in the Workhouse garb. Freddy had provided her with a dress, shawl, bonnet and serviceable shoes; they had disposed of the Workhouse uniform. It was then that she remembered Freddy's poesy ring. She wanted to return it to him, but she realised that she had taken it off when he first attacked her and had put it in her dress pocket; it was back in the Workhouse with her original clothing, left there when she was taken in. Still, no matter, she had little use for it now.

She approached Freddy one evening and said she needed to get a job, find accommodation and would pay him back for the garments. He told her that her job at the tailor's shop was still open to her. Apparently, they had been employing a casual Day Girl who would not be required if Sarah took up her position. This pleased her greatly, it meant her independence.

So after a few days, with her strength much improved, she took her leave; not without some effort as Freddy continued to plead with her to stay. Having left, she decided that it would be better to find accommodation as far away from Globe Town as feasible. So, she walked back to the Hackney Road and walked its full length to St Leonards Church. She stood on the corner of Kingsland Road and contemplated her options. She needed a, not too expensive, place to live. The only area she was familiar with was the Philips Street tenements, where she and Ann had stayed. So, she walked up the Kingsland Road and turned into Philips Street. After trying all the tenements in Phillips Street with no luck at all, she carried on walking further and found herself in an area built as an extension to Philips Street, called Edward Street. It was more run down and overcrowded, with as many as three or four families living in one 10 foot square room.

But, after an hour of searching, she located a young coster couple who were struggling to make ends meet and were prepared to share their room with her. He was short and stocky with thick black curly hair and called Tom Freestone; his fair haired wife was called Jane. He sold fruit and vegetables that he bought from a wholesale green market. Unable to secure a 'permanent pitch' or stationary stall in the street, he was obliged to carry his wares round with him, in a small barrow. Most days he would walk for many hours through streets crowded with the poor of the East End of London, trying his hardest to part them from the meagre sums of money they possessed. His father, now dead, was a coster too, and his father's father before him. Of late, trade had been poor, with the result that they were behind with the rent. It was agreed that Sarah would contribute one shilling and three pence a week to share their room. She was given a small straw mattress in one corner, with a little curtain strung across, to give her some privacy.

She was up bright and early on the following morning, to start work at the tailor's shop and was soon making her way down the Hackney Road. It was quite crowded with people, mostly heading to their work and, like her, they were pulling their clothes tightly round themselves against the chilly morning mist. She was adjusting her shawl, when a tousle haired girl burst out of the side alley of a large house and bundled right into her, nearly knocking her off her feet.

She was about to shout out angrily at this clumsy female, when she recognized the face. "Sarah Murray!" she shouted, "what are you doing here?"

The clumsy girl looked at her for a moment, then a smile spread across her face. "Sarah Valentine!" she exclaimed, "why, I could ask you the same."

"Well, I'm on my way to work," Sarah said.

"Where do you work?"

"In the tailor's shop, just down the road, in Goldsmiths Place" Sarah replied.

"Ha," she said, "with that dapper man of yours. Now what was his name? Don't tell me! Yes Freddy!" she shouted in triumph. "You were to be married weren't you?"

Sarah had to smile at her friend's statement. She then proceeded to tell her about her adventures since they last parted in the Workhouse. Sarah Murray listened in awed silence as the story unfolded. Her eyes widened when Sarah told her of Freddy's attack on her.

At the end she looked Sarah straight in the eyes. "You be very careful of that man she said," in a serious voice that Sarah had never heard her use before. She found herself a little unnerved by her friend's serious expression.

To change the subject she asked her original question again. "What are you doing here, in the Hackney Road?"

"I work here," Sarah Murray said, pointing at the big house she had just left. "And bloody slave drivers' they are!" she added with venom. "I'm supposed to get the fresh bread, and I'm late."

With that a huge woman with thick arms and massive breasts, wearing a dirty apron, came waddling out of the alley. "What yer doin' dawdling 'ere girl?" The woman shouted at Sarah Murray, "I told yer ter get the bread. Nah get a move on!"

"Hell! That's the cook. Gotta get going!" shouted Sarah Murray, dashing off down the road; she immediately collided with a gentleman and knocked his hat off. She stopped and stepped back to retrieve the hat, stepping on it as she did so, crushing it underfoot. She picked the crumpled hat up and gingerly held it out to the gentleman. He snatched it from her hand, calling her a clumsy wretch. Sarah Valentine was convulsed with laughter as her friend apologised and tried a travesty of a curtsy, then stumbled on her way, down the Hackney Road, to the baker.

She was still giggling to herself when she arrived at the tailor's shop. She made her way down the side alley to the back entrance and was surprised to see Freddy standing in the yard outside the back door. He walked up to her and smiled. "Thought I'd catch you before you went in."

"Yes," said Sarah, standing in a confrontational pose, with her hands on her hips, "and why is that?"

"Well," said Freddy, a little uncertainly, "no one knows what happened between us."

"What!" said Sarah, "how come? Doesn't even Edwin know?"

"No," said Freddy, looking sheepishly down at his feet, "I was too ashamed."

There was a prolonged silence whilst Sarah contemplated what he had just said. On the one hand it was a deceitful lie. But, on the other hand, it would make both their lives a little easier at the tailor's shop; and after all they did have to work together.

"Fine," she said and turned on her heel and walked to the back door.

Freddy followed her through the back door and down the corridor to the workshop. She walked into the workshop and saw many familiar faces from her previous time working there. Then she spotted Edwin at the cutting table. He turned and smiled at her. She walked over to him and kissed him lightly on the cheek. He flushed a deep red. She laughed and asked him about Susan Smith, the nice girl she had seen him with. He shyly stated that they were still 'stepping out together'. Smiling at him, she walked out into the shop and started polishing the counter.

Her first day went surprisingly well, the Jewish owner, William Snelgrove, was happy to see her again and she found out that he now had two sons and his wife was pregnant with their third child. At the end of her working day, she went out into the shop. Edwin was closing up and putting the rolls of material away; she started sweeping the floor. She was at the front of the shop, looking out at the street scene, slightly distorted by the ripples in the imperfect glass window, when she saw a coach pull up outside. Intrigued, she watched as a girl stepped out of the coach, waved to the driver and approached the shop door.

With a start, she recognized the girl as Susan Smith, Edwin Linford's lady. She opened the door and Susan walked in. She looked at Sarah for a moment then, as recognition dawned, put her arms round her and hugged her. "Sarah!" she said, "wonderful to see you again!" And stepping back to look at her, "yer lookin' well."

"Thank you," responded Sarah, "You must be rich, I saw you turning up at the door in a posh coach an' all."

Susan laughed, "you silly girl! That's my dad! He's a coach driver. You don't think I can afford to travel about like that all day, do you. He was going my way and kindly dropped me off here."

Edwin walked over to them and Susan proffered her cheek to him, which he duly kissed. Susan linked arms with Sarah and pulled her to the door.

"Come on, lets go for a little drink, I want to hear all about what you've been doing with yourself."

Sarah looked at Edwin, he smiled and nodded. "Off you go," he said, "I'll join you shortly when I've finished here."

The two girls crossed the road arm in arm and entered the Globe. Whilst Susan ordered the drinks, Sarah noted that John Herbert was alone behind the bar. Susan was counting out the money for the drinks and, as she watched, Sarah's mind was racing. She knew that Susan would want some explanation as to where she had been for the last few weeks; what was she to say? And what about Freddy; what should she say of him? Her thoughts were still tumbling about in her head as she followed Susan to a table over in one corner. When they had sat down, Susan looked at her expectantly. Sarah took a small sip of ale to buy some more time, then made her mind up. She told Susan that she and Freddy had too much to drink and quarrelled, then she had stormed out. Susan asked her what they had quarrelled over, Sarah said that she really couldn't recall, probably something stupid. Susan looked her straight in the eye, it was clear that she did not believe a word of it. Sarah realized that it was not going to be so easy to pull the wool over this young lady's eyes. Then, Susan asked her where she had been. She hesitated a moment, she had been tempted to say that she had stayed with her family, but decided that Susan was too nice a girl to feed such a pack of lies to. So, she told her the truth, that she had ended up in the Shoreditch Workhouse, only omitting her stay in the sick ward. Susan's mouth fell open in horror at the thought of ending up in the dreaded House.

Sarah laughed at her horrified expression. "It's not really as bad as you think, at least you get three meals a day, a bed and a roof over your head."

Susan opened her mouth to ask something else, but at that moment, the door opened and in walked Edwin and Freddy. Sarah looked at Freddy in dismay, but then realized that she could not expect him to forgo his evening tipple just because she was there. The boys bought drinks for themselves and refills for Sarah and Susan, then joined them at the table. Edwin naturally sat next to Susan, leaving Freddy sitting next to Sarah. Sarah found herself wondering how on earth she had ended up in this situation. She would have stood up and left, but it would have been very bad manners towards Susan and Edwin; she liked them too much to want to offend them.

However, it did not go as badly as she expected, Freddy was courteous, polite and attentive to her without being overbearing. As the four of them chatted away, she found herself addressing Freddy. His cheeky smile was back and she was very aware of his, not unpleasant, slightly scented smell. After a few drinks, Susan and Edwin got up to leave, Sarah rose with them, she politely refused Freddy's offer of another drink and he rose up as well. The four of them walked down to the Hackney Road and after a few minutes of walking stopped opposite the corner of Caroline Street, where the Linford family lived. They said their goodbyes and Susan gave Sarah a peck on the cheek. As they crossed the Hackney Road to walk down Caroline Street, Sarah carried on down the Hackney Road. As she walked, it occurred to her that Freddy must have given up the room in Globe Town and moved back in with his parents.

Her first week passed quite well. She met with Sarah Murray in the mornings outside the baker and chatted to her whilst she waited for the bread. The evening drink, when the tailor's shop closed, had become a regular occurrence, with Susan giving Sarah no opportunity to refuse. Susan was still gently probing her for more information and Sarah was finding it more and more difficult to put her off. She was also becoming more comfortable in Freddy's presence; his cheeky smile and loud personality was starting to win her over. He even kissed her on the cheek on the Friday, when they parted at the corner of Caroline Street and she did not rebuff him.

The next day was Saturday, her day off, and she rose early and made her way down the Kingsland Road to Shoreditch. Her brother Jimmy had moved in with a sweep, George Ricketts and his wife Liz in Pidgeon Court, a small group of run down houses off Long Alley. She wanted to see her whole family; she knew her parents and other siblings lived in Martins Court off Essex Street, but she did not want to go straight there alone and risk a confrontation with her father and mother over them throwing her into the Shoreditch Workhouse. It was her hope to find her brother Jimmy in the hope that he would go with her to her parent's house. She had completely changed from the disrespectful rebel she was and had some better understanding of why they sent her away and did not want any more bad feelings with them.

As she walked into Pidgeon Court, she saw Liz and George Ricketts standing outside the door to their house. They were bidding goodbye to someone inside and it looked as if they were about to walk out. Sarah walked up to them and after looking at her for a few moments, Liz Ricketts face cracked into a smile. "It's Sarah Valentine, isn't it? Jimmy's sister," she said.

"Yes," said Sarah, "I'm looking for Jimmy, is he inside?"

It was George Ricketts who answered, "no love," he said, "day off, and he's gone to his mum's. You should find him there."

After thanking them, Sarah made her way down Long Alley and across Shoreditch to Whitechapel. As she turned off Whites Row into the top of Rose Lane she became aware of the increasingly bad smell. There was a wind in the air and as she got further down, it hit her solidly; the stench of the many slaughter houses wafting over her almost overwhelmed her. She had spent nearly two years in the Workhouse, where she had become accustomed to the smells there; apart from the lunatic Ward 14, mostly the place smelled of carbolic soap. Part of the work ritual had been the constant scrubbing of the floors; inmates on their hands and knees every day. After all, the establishment had a surfeit of labour to use at any task they desired. Now she was faced with the reality of the place she grew up in. She put the sleeve of her dress to her nose, but the smell could not be diminished. Surely it had not smelt as bad as this when she had lived here? Certainly she had no recollection of it smelling so bad. She increased her pace and trotted down Rose Lane to the junction with Wentworth Street.

She glanced at the Black Swan Tavern on the corner as she crossed Wentworth Street, there was a group of raggedly dressed youths lounging about outside; none of them had any shoes on and the sight of them made Sarah feel uneasy. They were looking directly at her and she became conscious of her smart tailored dress; she was very aware that she looked out of place in this area. She hurried on and reached the entrance to Essex Street, where she had been born. The entrance was narrower than she remembered and almost completely blocked by rubbish: fish bones and mounds of ash, dumped there by the residents. As she negotiated her way round the mess and stepped into Essex Street another unpleasant smell hit her nostrils. This was the unmistakable smell of raw sewage. As she walked down the street she tried to avoid stepping into the evil looking sludge and treading on the faeces. She was now retching with the horrendous stench. Filthy residents hanging about in the doorways of low lodging houses glared at her, immediately registering her disgust. She walked gingerly past rabid dogs with black matted fur, rooting through the piles of debris. With some relief she reached the Throwstik's Arms and passed under the low, narrow entrance into Martins Court. Here, as she gingerly stepped through the alleyway alongside the Throwstik's, she encountered more rubbish and sewage blocking the court; impossibly, the stench of sewage was worse in this dark enclosed space and she paused, holding her hand to her mouth. As she came level with the walled-off back yard of the tavern she saw a movement, it was a dog pawing at the rubbish in the court. As she watched it lifted a leg and relieved itself against a wall. Other than the dog, the court was deserted. She walked past the first house on her right. This was No. 1 Martins Court, where she knew that her mother's friend Nell and her family shared a small downstairs room with a further family of four; it was a tight squeeze. Another family of five and an old charlady shared the small upstairs room. She counted on her fingers as she walked past three more, ramshackle, back-to-back, two storey houses, all looking very run down and barely standing. They looked for all the world as if they were just about to fall down in a heap. She reached No. 5 where, some two years ago, Jimmy had told her that her parents had moved to. A sudden gust of wind sent ash and cinders billowing around her face and into her eyes. Squinting against the sting, her eyes watering, she raised her hand to knock on the door.

Suddenly, she heard a sound to her right; a young girl had just run into the court from Essex Street. Sarah recognised her immediately. It was Caroline, her sister, now quite a big six-year-old. "Caroline!" Sarah called out.

The girl stopped dead and looked at her for a second. Then recognition came. "Sarah!" she shouted, and ran up to her and flung her arms round her.

Sarah staggered back under the onslaught, laughing.

Releasing her hold, Caroline pushed the door to the house open and disappeared inside shouting, "its Sarah. Sarah's back!" At the top of her voice.

She followed Caroline through the door, into a dingy room about eight feet square; in one corner was a set of narrow steps leading up to the next floor. She had barely taken a few steps into the room when she came face to face with her brother Jimmy, black as ever. They embraced fondly. When they parted they stood and looked closely at each other. It was nearly two years since they last met and both had grown. Jimmy was now a fine strapping lad, a good three inches taller than her with strong features and a wiry frame, much like his father.

He smiled at her. "My, what a fine woman you are becoming," he said, admiring her dress.

Looking across the room, she saw her mother with Mary, now a robust three-year-old and a baby boy crawling across the floor. Astonished, she looked at the little boy: jet black hair, dark brown eyes. He was the image of Jimmy as a baby. "Who's he?" she exclaimed.

"Meet your new brother Henry," said her mother, "He'll be one-year-old soon."

Sarah went over and kissed her mother on the cheek, then bent down and picked up Henry. She held him in her arms; he looked at her, clearly curious. He reminded Sarah so much of Jimmy, when he was young. She put him back down on the floor. He crawled across to his mother and, gripping her legs, pulled himself unsteadily upright. From the safety of his mother he stared fixedly at Sarah.

"Anyways," said Sarah, looking at Jimmy, "I called in at Pidgeon Court on my way here and spoke to George and Liz Ricketts. They said you weren't working."

Jimmy laughed, "yes, just a couple of days off, we start on the chimneys of a big house on Monday. And what are you up to?"

"Working at a tailor's shop in Goldsmiths Place off Hackney Road," she said.

"Ha!" He replied, "that explains the posh dress!"

She stayed for a few hours, during which time she discovered that they shared the small two storey house with a couple and their ten-year-old daughter, who had the upstairs room. Unlike Factory Court, the whole of the downstairs, such as it was, was theirs alone. She noted a small coal scuttle next to an empty grate. If they could afford the coal, they would at least have some heat in the winter.

They brought each other up to date on what had happened in the intervening years. Sarah chose not to tell them of her affair with Freddy Linford, but did tell them of the curious incident at the Workhouse relating to her sister Charlotte. None of them knew what to make of it. Certainly no one had seen or heard of Charlotte. She had completely vanished.

It was just starting to get dark when Sarah took her leave and made her way back up to Shoreditch and her small corner in Edward Street. Lying on her mattress that night, her thoughts turned to her new brother Henry and how fine he looked. If he turned out like Jimmy, she could look forward to having two splendid brothers. She fell asleep with a smile on her face.

The next morning, Sarah was up early. As it was a Sunday morning, she met few people as she walked down the Kingsland Road. Turning into the Hackney Road, she encountered a cluster of cows in the street. This was not an unusual sight as there were still many cow houses in Hackney and it was a frequent practice to turn them out in the street. She carefully negotiated her way past the lumbering beasts, taking great care to look where she was treading. Having safely passed the obstacle, she continued on her way down the Hackney Road,

Even though it was a Sunday, the baker was still making bread and she met her friend Sarah Murray outside. After their customary chin wag, she continued on her way, turning down Goldsmiths Place, she reached the tailor's shop and walked down the side alley to enter through the back door. She went about her chores in a surprisingly happy mood. Freddy was very attentive, but careful not to crowd her too much, and his brother Edwin was wonderful in his natural charming way. The customary evening drink went well, Freddy was back to being his charming self and even put his arm round Sarah's shoulder; she did not object. Martha was absent, her husband serving behind the bar.

That evening, when she arrived back at her lodgings, she was in a happy mood. She found her roommates also in a happy mood, it seemed that Tom Freestone had had a particularly good day on his rounds and his goods had sold well, he was flush with the day's success. His wife was putting on her Sunday gown and explained that they were going to a local 'twopenny-hop' where a first rate professor of the 'clog-hornpipe' was performing. Sarah remained in the room, happy to be alone with her thoughts. They arrived back, around midnight, exhausted from their vigorous capering and merry from their drinking. They were carrying some penny meat pies and a jug of ale which they shared with Sarah. She tucked in greedily, thankful for the food. After consuming her food and drink, she retired to her corner and lay down on her straw mattress. She lay there, a little tipsy, and fell asleep thinking of Freddy and what she should do about him.

On the Monday evening, after work, Sarah went for a drink in the Globe with Freddy, Edwin and Susan. To her dismay Martha was behind the bar. She remembered Martha warning her about Freddy and pointedly ignored her. Her bad experience with Freddy was now only a dim memory and he was proving to be good company. As she left the Globe, with Freddy's arm around her, she glanced towards the bar and saw Martha staring at her with a sad expression on her face.

Without noticing it, she was falling under Freddy's spell again, to the extent that she now found herself happy being with him. After work, Freddy invited her out for a walk along the tow path of the Regent's canal. He was attentive, but not intrusive and he reminded her that he had rescued her from the Workhouse sick ward. On recalling that, she could not help but feel grateful to him. She did not realize that she was being lulled into a false sense of security in his company, all thoughts of her bad experience with him now completely forgotten.

CHAPTER 21

The Disaster

THEN, IN THE middle of September 1839, disaster befell her. It was their day off and Freddy persuaded her to spend the day with him. They took a walk down the length of the Hackney Road. At Freddy's insistence they called in several of the taverns along the way and during the course of the day, they consumed quite a few drinks. When they reached the eastern end of the Hackney Road, they were both a little unsteady, Sarah was leaning on Freddy, giggling as they swayed from side to side. As the weather was clement, they decided to sit on the Bethnal Green. Freddy chose a spot behind some bushes where they were screened from view. The autumn sunshine was still quite warm and Sarah lay back on the grass idly watching the birds flying from tree to tree; she started to doze off. Freddy leaned over to kiss her and, dulled by the drink, she did not resist him. Then, he started to caress her body and undo her clothing. Suddenly, she realized that it was now getting out of hand and tried to push him off, but he became more forceful and, weak with the drink, she could not resist him. For the second time, in her short life, she felt him force himself into her. It was not so painful this time, but it was not what she wanted. She tensed, but endured his forced attentions, until she felt him relax, then pushed him hard to one side and managed to roll out from underneath him. She clambered to her feet and staggered away sobbing in frustration at her foolishness in allowing herself to be assaulted by him again. She turned and looked back at him, worried that he might pursue her and harass her further. But he was still lying on the grass, a smirk on his flushed face. As she walked back up the Hackney Road, tears were running down her cheeks. She ignored the stares of the people she passed in the street. She bitterly regretted what she knew to be a grubby unwanted trespass on her body.

That evening, lying on her bed, in the corner of the small room, she felt regret that she had been so used, and a sadness that she had been so easily fooled into forgetting what Freddy Linford was really like. She finally fell asleep with tears stinging her eyes.

The next day, arriving at the tailor's shop, Sarah was a little apprehensive when she walked into the workroom. However, to her relief, she saw no sign of Freddy. Edwin was at the cutting table and he smiled sweetly at her as she walked past into the shop. She busied herself cleaning the shop and scrubbing the step. When she returned to the cutting room she was surprised to see that Freddy had still not put in an appearance. She dared not ask where he was.

After work, she firmly declined Susan's invitation to the customary drink in the Globe and took her leave. Susan wore a worried expression as she watched Sarah stride off. Sarah hurried straight back to her corner in the Freestone's room and fell on her mattress sobbing quietly behind her screening curtain.

For the next few days Freddy still did not put in an appearance at work. Sarah continued to refuse the evening drink and Edwin and Susan went over to the Globe together.

Finally, on the Friday, Freddy turned up at work. The owner called him upstairs immediately he arrived and, from the raised voices she heard through the ceiling, he was most displeased by his absence. Freddy was quiet and subdued when he walked back into the workshop. He avoided looking at Sarah and busied himself with the seamstresses. This suited Sarah fine and she ignored him, carrying on with her own work.

Over the next few weeks she did her best to cast Freddy out of her mind. It had now become accepted that she would not go for the evening drink. Susan sometimes tried to encourage her to come over with them, but Sarah was adamant. Susan was clearly curious as to the drastic change in her attitude and the obvious tension between her and Freddy. This had also not gone unnoticed by the seamstresses.

Her friend, Sarah Murray, with her bubbly personality, was a godsend at this time. Sarah had confided in her about what had happened with Freddy and she found herself looking forward to their brief daily meetings, which never failed to lift her sagging spirit.

She spent Christmas of 1839 with her family and her brother Jimmy significantly helped to buck her spirits up. She chose not to tell them about her experiences with Freddy Linford and resolved to do her utmost to cast it out of her mind, but this would prove to be easier said than done.

Left much more to her own devices, she started to take an interest in the ladies who frequented the tailor's shop. Most attended with their husbands, who were clearly expected to foot the bill for their extravagant clothing. The more well-heeled would have several fitting sessions until they were completely satisfied with their attire. She was curious about the costumes. It seemed that, with Queen Victoria's ascension to the throne, modern fashions were changing to dresses with increasing fullness. It occurred to Sarah that the ever more masses of crinoline must have made it very difficult for fine ladies to negotiate even the most simple obstacle. Seeing them struggle to get in and out of their coaches left her crying with laughter.

But, for her, the most astonishing spectacle was the evening wear. It was the case that ladies were virtually naked to the waist. A very small strip extended upwards to cover the nipples. Less endowed ladies were in real trouble. During the day they could cover their diminished charms with padding. But, in the evening, it was impossible to disguise what nature had given them. For once, Sarah was quite happy not to be rich and being obliged to enter this particular competition.

The year of 1839 drew to a close with a cold snap followed by heavy snow. Walking up the Hackney Road to work, she found herself dodging snowballs, as the children played in the snow. She envied their joy and found herself smiling at their happy antics.

The snow continued through January and her morning meetings with Sarah Murray outside the baker were frequently conducted against a heavy white backdrop. By mutual consent, Freddy was not mentioned. Their conversation focused on the major news of the day; wedding bells were in the air, there was to be a magnificent royal wedding.

It was Monday February 10th 1840 and the new Queen Victoria was to be married to her beau, Albert, at the Chapel Royal in St James's Palace. It was a public holiday and both Sarah Valentine and Sarah Murray had been given the day off. They were walking the streets of London with crowds of other people in celebratory mood. Bunting was everywhere, fun was in the air. Sarah Murray was joking about the fact that they had not been invited to the wedding, when she noticed that Sarah Valentine was looking a little subdued. She was concerned that there was something on her friend's mind, so she suggested that they have a little celebratory drink. This proved to be difficult as every tavern was bursting at the seams. Eventually, they found a space in a small drinking house off the beaten track and, after ordering their ales, settled down at a small corner table.

Sarah Murray was looking closely at Sarah Valentine, worry written on her face. "You look quite pale and sickly. Are you coming down with something?" she said, concern in her voice.

Sarah looked up at her. She was silent for a while. Then she realized that she couldn't keep a secret from her dearest friend and she badly needed someone to talk to. "I think I'm in trouble," she said in a quiet voice.

Her friend put her arms round her. "Come on love, what's the matter?" she said.

Sarah Valentine's eyes filled with tears, "I haven't had me monthly bleeding for three months now and sometimes I feel quite faint. I think I'm going to have a baby," she said sheepishly; the tears now running freely down her cheeks.

"Oh my Gawd!" said Sarah Murray, pulling her friend closer to her and letting her sob on her shoulder.

A few days later, Sarah Valentine was in the back room at the tailor's shop, when she felt a dizziness come over her. The room spun and she grabbed for the cutting room table. Her hand missed the edge and she collapsed on the floor, hitting her head on the side of the table as she fell.

One of the older seamstress ladies came over, helped her sit up and looked anxiously into her white face. "Are you alright dearie?" she said kindly.

"Yes," said Sarah weakly, "I'm alright, just a little dizzy that's all."

With the seamstresses help she stood upright. Still a little unsteady on her feet, she leant on the cutting table edge for support. The old lady stared into Sarah's face, her wise old eyes held a knowing look. "You're not expectin' are you love?" she said.

"No!" Protested Sarah, turning away. She saw the shop owner walking towards her.

"What's going on here?" he said. Then looking at Sarah and seeing the cut on the side of her head. "My dear, have you hurt yourself?" He took her hand in his.

"I'm alright sir," said Sarah. But it was clear to all that she was not.

The shop owner's wife bathed Sarah's head with water and she was told to take the rest of the day off to recover. She promised to return the next morning.

She stood outside the shop, the cool winter air clearing her head a little. She had made up her mind what she would do. She walked into the Hackney Road and set off towards Shoreditch. Turning left at St Leonard's Church, she made her way to Whitechapel and Essex Street.

Soon she was walking down Essex Street. At the Throwstik's Tavern she turned right into Martins Court. She found the door to No. 5 standing ajar and, after a slight hesitation, she took a deep breath and walked in. She was surprised to see the small downstairs room crowded to bursting point. Her mother was standing in the middle of the room talking with her friend Nell, Nell's two eldest daughters, Beth and Ellen were standing just inside the doorway, her third daughter, the ever effervescent little Julia, was running round in circles barely missing standing on baby Henry's little fingers as he crawled across the floor; Sarah embraced everyone.

It was Nell who spotted the cut on Sarah's face and her drawn, worried look. She immediately shooed the younger children out the door into the court to play. It left Sarah's mother, with baby brother Henry crawling round her feet, Nell, and her eldest daughter Beth still in the room.

Nell walked up to Sarah and put her arms round her. "What's up my love?" she said in her broad Irish brogue.

All four of them were looking intently at her, even baby Henry was quietly staring at her with his big brown eyes. Sarah burst into tears and was unable to say anything for several minutes. Then, her tears subsiding and with the four expectant faces turned towards her, she lowered her head.

"I think I'm going to have a baby," she said quietly.

The room went silent. Sarah could hear the children playing outside. After a minute, the silence was broken by Beth, who was hopping from one foot to the other in excitement. "How'd that 'appen?" she said.

Nell turned and glared at her daughter. "If yer got nothin' better'n that ter say, get out with the kids!" she stormed.

Sarah's eyes started to water again. She was surprised when her mother came over to her and put her arms round her. "Come and sit down," her mother said kindly, "tell us all about it."

"Who is he?" Beth wanted to know.

"Shut up girl!" shouted Nell.

So, sitting on a mattress in the corner of the room, Sarah told them all about Freddy. Her mother's mouth fell open when she told them about Freddy's proposal and the banns being set at Stepney Parish Church. "Why didn't you tell us?" she asked.

Sarah looked at her, "I was too ashamed of what had happened," she said.

When she explained that she had let him back into her life, after he took her from the Workhouse, Nell pursed her lips and muttered something under her breath. When she got to the bit about her indiscretion on Bethnal Green, she was interrupted by Beth starting to say something. But Beth was cut short by a withering look from her mother. When Sarah had finished, they all looked aghast.

"He's taken you for a fool!" Sarah's mother said angrily, "and how could you be so foolish as to trust him a second time! Did you not realize what he was like?"

Tears welled in Sarah's eyes again.

"Don't fret so," Nell said, dabbing Sarah's eyes with the hem of her dress, "we all do foolish things sometimes."

"What am I going to do?" wailed Sarah.

It was a question that no one could readily answer, so silence descended once again. For a few minutes all that could be heard was the muted squealing of the children playing outside. Then Nell got up and went outside. After a short while she came back indoors. "I've asked Ellen to look after the children," she said, "Lets go in the Throwstik's, I think we all need a drink."

They made their way to the nearby tavern on the corner and Sarah was given a good measure of gin. The others drank ale. When they left, Sarah's mother said she should stay with them for a while, but Sarah refused; she felt that she would not be able to look her father in the eye. So she walked back and settled onto her mattress in the corner of the small room she shared with the Freestones; life was now starting to look an awful lot bleaker.

Sarah settled into a routine of work, trying her best to ignore the child growing inside her. She struggled on through February and into March. She was lucky in that her pregnancy did not show too much on her slight figure, and she was able to disguise it by loosening the waist of her long dress. But it was clear to her that her condition would become all too apparent soon enough.

She got into the habit of visiting her mother on her Saturdays off work and one Saturday Nell brought up the topic of Freddy. Sarah had not informed him of her state and Nell thought this a serious mistake. They all discussed this at length and Sarah was becoming convinced that she should tell Freddy about the baby.

On the following Monday morning she discussed the issue with Sarah Murray, who fully supported Nell's viewpoint. She must tell Freddy that she was expecting his child. So, she resolved to do it, that very day.

On the Monday evening, at the end of the day's work and, with the tailor's shop closed, Sarah approached Freddy. They had few conversations these days and he was surprised to see her standing next to him. She was conscious of his perfumed smell. "Freddy," she started, "I have something that I need to tell you. Will you come for a walk with me?" she looked up at him expectantly.

"Yes, of course," he replied, a worried expression on his face. His cheeky smile had disappeared of late and his bubbly personality was held well in check.

They left the shop, turned left and walked down Goldsmiths Row. There was silence between them until they reached the end of the houses. Here they both stopped. It was the road they used to take down to the Regent's canal, to walk along the towpath. Memories came back to Sarah. She dismissed them. "Freddy," she said, "I have something important to tell you."

"I think I know," said Freddy in a quiet, barely audible voice.

Sarah stared into his face, looking closely into his eyes. He looked back at her.

"You're going to have my baby aren't you?" he whispered.

"Yes," said Sarah simply.

Freddy said nothing. He started to walk aimlessly towards the canal. Sarah walked in silence alongside him. Nothing was said. They reached the canal and started to walk along the southern towpath. A huge shire horse approached pulling a massive barge, by a thick rope. They were forced to step aside up the slight bank to give it room to pass. The bargeman, walking beside the horse, nodded to them. Sarah broke the silence. "How do you know?" she asked him.

"It's the talk of the seamstresses," he laughed, without any mirth, "you might be able to pull the wool over the eyes of the men," he added, "but not those hawk eyed bitches. They all know that you are expecting, and they also feel that they know the name of the father as well."

This last comment shocked Sarah and silence descended between them again.

"What are you going to do?" asked Freddy, "you see I'm not really ready for a family just yet. Do you want to get rid of it, it can be arranged you know. There are people....." He stopped, halted by the expression on Sarah's face.

"How dare you!" she screamed, slapping the side of his face with all her might, "I thought you wanted to marry me, or was that all a sham to get your wicked way with me?"

He staggered back under the blow. Instinctively raising his fist to strike back.

"Go on you lousy coward!" Sarah screamed, "hit a woman with child."

Freddy saw the heavily built bargeman turn at Sarah's words; he stared directly at Freddy, who lowered his arms to his side, shame written on his face. Silence descended between them once again. The bargeman turned back to his horse and continued on his way. Sarah looked away from Freddy and started to walk back along the towpath. Freddy stood there, watching her go. He made no attempt to follow.

The following Saturday, at her mother's house, Sarah recounted her interlude with Freddy at the canal. It was Nell who broached the subject on everyone's mind. "You want this baby Sarah?" she said softly.

Sarah looked at her, "it's my baby," she said, "I feel it growing in me. I don't know what I will do when it's born, but I will not knowingly have it harmed!" she finished loudly.

"Do you want Freddy to marry you and take up his responsibility?"

Sarah thought for a while before answering. "No," she finally said, "whatever happens, I could not face being with a man I couldn't trust."

Nell nodded her agreement.

The next few weeks went by with Sarah and Freddy pointedly ignoring each other, but Edwin was quite attentive and frequently asked if she was alright. Susan Smith always spoke with her when she turned up in the evening to accompany Edwin for a drink and usually asked Sarah to join them.

One evening she was a bit more insistent. "You needn't worry about Freddy coming," she said, "we seldom drink with him these days."

Seeing a slight weakening in Sarah's resolve at this statement, Susan took her arm and led her out the door and across the road. When they entered the Globe Tavern she sat Sarah down at their customary corner table and went and got their two drinks. Sarah watched her, noting that John Herbert was alone behind the bar.

When Susan returned, she wasted no time. "Your expectin' Freddy's child aren't you?"

Sarah felt the tears welling in her eyes, but said nothing.

Susan leaned across and put her arms round her. "There's something that you should know," she said, leaning back, "that Freddy....well, he's not very nice sometimes."

"What do you mean?" asked Sarah.

"He's alright most of the time, but he gets drunk and when he's drunk he gets nasty......especially with women."

"What are you saying?" Sarah said with some alarm.

"He has a history," Susan continued, "about two years ago, there was a seamstress. He beat her up badly in one of his drunken spats. She died and he was taken to Court for manslaughter, but he got off. I think people were paid to keep their traps shut. And that wasn't the first time he has beaten up on a woman."

Sarah was horrified, all manner of thoughts crashed through her head. It must be true, both times he assaulted her he had been the worse for drink. "How do you know this?" she asked.

"I got it out of Edwin last night. He didn't want to tell me, but I knew that there was something not right about Freddy and I pressed him. He finally gave in and blurted it out. It seems the family don't want to talk about it"

Sarah was stunned. She fell silent, staring at the wall, seeing nothing.

Susan was looking very closely at her, "he attacked you as well, didn't he?"

Sarah felt the tears well up again, she gave a slight nod.

Susan lent across and put her arms round her again and whispered, "I thought so."

Sarah was about to reply when she caught sight of Martha Herbert arriving behind the bar to assist her husband. She seemed to sense Sarah's presence and immediately looked over at her. Sarah quickly looked away.

"Is something the matter?" It was Susan, a worried expression on her face.

"No it's alright," said Sarah, then added, "it's just that Martha Herbert. She just walked in. She unnerves me somehow."

Susan laughed, "your not alone there, she's a strange one. Seems she's clairvoyant."

"What's that?" said Sarah, never having heard the word.

"Well," said Susan, glancing towards the bar, "she seems to know things we don't and can see what will happen, before it does....." She tailed off realizing that she was probably talking nonsense.

Sarah was staring at her, "she warned me off Freddy, a long time ago," she said.

Now Susan was staring at Sarah. She started talking softly, "Martha has said some remarkable things," then, after a pause for thought, "she told an old man to be very careful when he left the tavern. Turns out he was run down and killed by a coal cart moments later. She always seems to know when something bad is going to happen. People are scared to talk to her lest they find out something they don't want to know." An ominous silence descended between them.

Sarah glanced up towards the bar and was startled to see Martha staring fixedly straight at her, as if she knew she was the focus of their conversation, Sarah quickly looked away. Susan got up and went over to the bar to refill their glasses. She deliberately made for where John Herbert was standing.

Sarah was staring down at the table when she suddenly became aware of a presence beside her. She looked up and was aghast when she saw Martha Herbert standing there, her deep blue eyes fixed on hers. For a few seconds they stared at each other, then a faint enigmatic smile touched Martha Herbert's lips and she placed a hand softly on Sarah's shoulder. "Don't fret love," she said in a soft voice, "all will be well, your baby will be fine and healthy," then a serious expression crossed her face, "you will have difficult decisions to make, but I know you will make the right ones." Then she turned and was gone, as quickly as she had arrived. Sarah stared at her departing back.

Susan arrived with the drinks and Sarah told her of the mysterious conversation; how on earth did Martha know that Sarah was expecting?

They talked about it as they sipped their drinks, but could make little sense of it.

Sarah left the Globe before Edwin arrived and went straight home. As she lay on her mattress, her mind was buzzing, she was still trying to come to terms with what Susan had told her about Freddy killing a seamstress and puzzling over Martha Herbert's odd words. She shivered, but not with the cold.

The next morning, she told Sarah Murray about what Susan had told her of Freddy's past. She expressed no surprise on hearing this and told her to watch out for him as he was clearly bad trouble. But, in that, she was mistaken, for it was not Freddy who would attack her next.

Sarah spent the next few days avoiding Freddy, this was not difficult as he clearly wanted nothing to do with her. Most of her dialogue was with Edwin who was proving to be very supportive. She was not sure if Susan had told him about their conversation in the Globe, but from his attentive manner, she suspected that she had.

It was just after work, one evening, and Sarah was not feeling well enough for a drink in the Globe. As she left the tailor's premises and stepped out into the road, she was approached by a woman. The woman was not young, a little older than her own mother, but better dressed, with smart shoes and new bonnet. She was tall, broad shouldered, with a superior air about her. Sarah was startled to see a stern, almost angry, expression on her heavily lined face.

"Are you Sarah Valentine?" the woman asked in a clipped voice.

"Yes," said Sarah cautiously.

The woman quickly stepped up to Sarah and slapped her hard across the face. Sarah staggered back under the force of the blow and looked incredulously at the woman.

"You accuse my son falsely!" she shouted, "you Workhouse tramp! How dare you!" With that she made to strike Sarah again.

But Sarah was having none of that. She grabbed the woman's arm and held on tightly. A struggle broke out. Although older than Sarah the woman was taller and quite strong; she succeeded in pushing Sarah to the ground and moved forward to grind her heel into Sarah's face.

Then, arms grabbed her and pulled her back. It was Edwin, come from the shop, alerted by the commotion.

"Mother!" he shouted, "what are you doing here?"

"I'll teach that tramp to cast her false accusations!" the woman stormed, struggling in Edwin's grasp.

"Come with me mother," Edwin said softly and pulled her into the tailor's shop. He looked back at Sarah with a sad expression on his face.

Sarah picked herself up from the ground and after a few seconds of dizzy nausea, was able to make her way home. That evening, she had a troubled sleep. The woman was clearly Freddy's mother. What on earth had he told her to make her so angry?

That Saturday, at her mother's home, Sarah told them about her experience with Freddy's mother. They were horrified that she should be attacked, in her state. She also recounted Susan's comments about Freddy's drunken temper and how both Sarah Murray and Martha Herbert, the Landlady of the Globe, had warned her to watch out for him. As the women discussed this new occurrence, they were unaware of Jimmy standing in the court outside. He had heard Sarah's tale and his face was red with rage over what the Linfords were doing to his beloved sister.

It was Tuesday morning and Sarah arrived at the tailor's shop to start her chores. She was deep in thought and about to go into the rear entrance when a hand grabbed her arm in a tight grip. Startled, she whirled round to see Freddy, wearing an angry scowl on his face. "What do you mean by sending those thugs round to my house?" he hissed in her ear, still gripping her arm.

Sarah stared at him, "what are you talking about?"

"You know!" he said, "claimed to be your brother and in the company of a footpad the size of a mountain!"

Sarah was completely puzzled by this. "I don't know what house you live in, and neither does my brother," she said.

Seeing genuine puzzlement on her face, Freddy relaxed his grip. Sarah took the opportunity to pull her arm free and started to rub it where he had gripped it.

"You mean you really know nothing about this?" Freddy said doubtfully.

"I know nothing about any such nonsense!" Sarah stormed.

Then, she turned away from him and walked into the rear entrance and on through to the workroom. The stares from the seamstresses told her that they had probably heard her and Freddy arguing outside.

Sarah spent the day focused on her work. Each time she entered the workroom, she could feel the massed eyes of the seamstresses boring into her back. She was heartily grateful when the day's work was over and she could leave for home. As she opened the door to exit the premises, she looked carefully around to see if anyone was lurking about. Satisfied that she was not going to be accosted, she swiftly made her way down the Hackney Road.

Sarah was concerned about what Freddy had said to her that morning and was determined to get to the bottom of the matter. At the end of the Hackney Road, she turned left to Shoreditch and made her way to Pidgeon Court. Jimmy was not home, so she stood in the court and waited there until he put in an appearance.

Whilst she was waiting her mind was thinking of the words Freddy had said to her, 'a man claiming to be your brother in the company of a footpad the size of a mountain.' She started to have her suspicions; her father worked at the docks as a porter and he had a number of friends that he drank regularly with. One of them was massive with wide shoulders and huge arms; as a little joke he was nicknamed Tiny. She wondered if he might have something to do with it. But she needed to talk to her brother to find out the truth.

She had been waiting for nearly an hour when she saw him turn the corner into the court. She walked up to him. She was just going to ask him about Freddy's claims, when she saw the answer written in his face. "You went round to Freddy's house last night didn't you?" she said simply.

Jimmy hung his head. He looked so miserable that she put her hand on his arm. "I'm sorry Sarah," he said, "but I heard what they did to you and I was so angry I wanted to get back at them."

"What happened?" she asked.

"Well," said Jimmy, "I had a drink with dad and his friends Tom and Tiny, from the dockyard."

Sarah could not help a knowing smile briefly touch her face.

Her brother was continuing, "while dad and Tom were chatting, I told Tiny about what had happened to you. He was as angry as me, but he knew exactly what to do about it. Monday evening we waited on a corner just across the road from the tailor's shop, keeping an eye on it. When we saw Freddy come out, we followed him home. Then we knocked on the door. As it opened, Tiny gave it a kick and strode in."

"Oh my!" said Sarah, who knew how big Tiny was and what effect he would have had towering in their home.

"I swear Freddy shit his pants when he saw Tiny," said Jimmy.

Sarah could not suppress a giggle at the thought of Freddy messing his posh suit.

"What did you do?" asked Sarah.

"Nothing really," said Jimmy, "there was no need. Tiny's presence said it all. I told them I was your brother and that if anyone attacked you again we would be back, and in double quick time. Tiny bared his teeth, Freddy shit himself again. Then we left."

"I know you meant well Jimmy, but you can't go round threatening people like that. You'll just make things worse for me."

Jimmy looked crestfallen.

Sarah kissed him on his sooty cheek.

"Sorry Sarah," he said.

"You won't do it again will you?" she said

"No I won't," said Jimmy aloud then, quietly under his breath, "unless they try to harm you again."

Sarah took her leave. She had much to think about as she walked back up the Kingsland Road. She decided that she would have it out with Freddy the very next day.

On Wednesday morning, she met with Sarah Murray outside the baker and they discussed what Jimmy and Tiny had done at Freddy's house. They both giggled at Freddy pooping himself at the sight of Tiny. Sarah Murray was of the opinion that it was the correct thing to have done and that Jimmy had acted well, showing his rightful concern for Sarah. Certainly, it should ensure that there would be no further trouble from that quarter. But, it was agreed that she should have further words with Freddy.

At the end of work, she went looking for Freddy in the shop. She saw his father George Linford rolling up some material. She went over to him. "Do you know where Freddy is?" she asked.

He looked closely into her eyes. His face was not unkindly. "You know you can't do things like that," he said, "I know Jane was wrong in attacking you the way she did, but we are not footpads, we do not deserve to be treated that way."

"I know," said Sarah, "it was done without my knowledge. You must believe that. My brother acted rashly out of his love for me. I spoke with him last night. It will not happen again."

George Linford was looking intently at her. Her voice had the ring of truth and it was mirrored in her face.

"We must talk before this thing gets too out of hand," he said.

"That's what I want to do with Freddy," Sarah said. "Where is he?" she repeated.

"I am afraid he has sneaked out. Sometimes I think he is more coward than man. His mother has molly coddled him so. I'm afraid that your brother's enormous friend scared the wits out of him." Sarah couldn't help but smile at this, remembering her brother's description of the events of that night. She was about to turn away and go home, when George Linford spoke again. "If you would permit an old man buying a young lady a drink, I would like to talk with you. If I may."

Sarah looked at him. There was no guile in his face, so she agreed.

They left the shop and started walking down the Hackney Road, neither of them wished to use the Globe in Goldsmiths Row for their quiet talk. They soon found a small tavern just down a side street. Inside it was dark and uninviting, with low cracked ceilings, but there were few customers and it was quiet. George Linford bought two glasses of wine and they sat down in a far corner. Sarah had never drunk wine before, but after taking a tentative sip, found that she was pleased with the taste. She waited for him to speak.

"I'm afraid my wife Jane cannot come to terms with this…." he paused, looking for words, "er, situation." He paused again, then, mustering his thoughts, he continued. "She has doted on Freddy from his birth. As the first born she has spoiled him. He now feels that he should have anything he wants. I know he drinks and has a foul temper when he is drunk." He paused to take a sip of wine. "You see Jane has had a bad time of it. After Freddy was born she had a girl, Elizabeth, she died a baby. Then there was a stillborn birth. We even had twins, Henry and Mary Ann Adelaide. Henry ran off and we never found him. Mary Ann Adelaide is still with us, but she is a weak, sickly child and not expected to live long. Of course we have Edwin, a fine young man, so different from Freddy and we have a daughter, Caroline Amelia, more than ten years Freddy's junior. Lovely, dutiful girl, dotes on Freddy. But Jane gives her little attention, poor thing." He stopped again, and took another sip of wine before continuing. He turned troubled eyes on Sarah. "Please don't take this wrong," he paused, "I suppose that there is little doubt that Freddy is the father?"

Sarah felt a flash of anger at this remark. But it subsided when she saw the honest, pained look in the man's eyes. He was not trying to insult her. "There is absolutely no doubt!" she said very firmly. Then, added softly, "he is the only man I have ever been with."

He looked closely at her. Again, he saw the truth written in her eyes. "I am not sure what is to be done," he said, "marriage would be the usual outcome. But his mother Jane is adamant that Freddy will only marry a girl of her choice."

"You mean not a girl from the Workhouse," Sarah said bluntly. He did not answer and picked his glass up to take a sip of wine, so she continued. "Did you know that Freddy proposed to me and that our wedding banns were posted, with a wedding to take place last July?"

The glass stopped a few inches from his lips and he stared at her in disbelief, "where?" he asked

"Stepney Parish Church," she replied, then seeing his disbelieving look, "you can easily check with the Reverend James, he noted it in his ledger."

He unconsciously placed the glass back on the table without imbibing. "Why did the wedding not take place?" he asked.

Sarah paused for a moment, then decided the truth must out, so she told him about Freddy attacking her in the Globe Town tenement and her spell in the Workhouse. She also told him about his assault on her on the Bethnal Green.

He paused a moment, then asked, "was he drunk?"

"Yes," she replied, "both times."

He did not answer, but his face wore a deep frown. A few moments passed, then he picked up his glass again and this time he took a sip of his wine. Sarah did likewise. She was not sure where this conversation was heading, but felt that she needed to make a few points clear to him. "There are some things I need to say to you" she started. He nodded. "I want to make it clear to everyone that I will have this baby, and I pray to God that it'll be fine and healthy." She paused, then went on, "I don't want Freddy to marry me, I don't want to spend my life with a man like that, and I don't want any money. Please do not trouble yourself, we will get by."

There was silence between them. It was broken by George Linford. "Those are fine words young lady. And well spoken. But the child of which you speak is to be my grandchild. Moreover, it will be my first grandchild and I may have something to say of his, or her, upbringing."

Sarah was not sure whether to be comforted, or threatened, by those words. She chose to remain silent. There seemed to be nothing more to be said, so they finished their wine and left the tavern. They walked together, in silence, down the Hackney Road towards Shoreditch. At the junction with Caroline Street George Linford stopped. "I live down there," he pointed down Caroline Street. "Number nine". Then, turning towards her, "look, if you need someone to talk to. I'm always available."

She smiled at him. They separated and went their individual ways. He down Caroline Street, her on down the Hackney Road and up the Kingsland Road to her lodgings.

That night she thought long and hard about her conversation with George Linford. He seemed a fair man, genuinely concerned for his family. She could not hold that against him.

The following morning she discussed the issue with Sarah Murray. As they debated the various points, they began forming opinions: George Linford seemed, on the face of it, to be a good honest man, they were both sure of that, his wife Jane would be big trouble, and Freddy was a spoiled brat, who would do whatever he could to get his own way. But, of positive solutions, there was a distinct shortage. Sarah left her friend and carried on to work.

As the work-day wore on, Freddy had not shown up at the tailor's shop and the owner was furious. Neither George nor Edwin Linford offered any explanation.

That evening when the tailor's shop closed Susan Smith called in and whispered conspiratorially in Sarah's ear. "I have something important to tell you, come over the road to the Globe as soon as you can." With that she disappeared out the door.

Sarah was curious about Susan's statement and got away as soon as she could. When she walked into the Globe she saw Susan sitting at their usual table with two drinks in front of her. Glancing at the bar, she saw John Herbert standing there alone. He smiled a greeting at her and she waved back at him, making her way to Susan's table, where she sat down opposite her, facing the bar. Susan wasted no time, it was clear that she was bursting to tell Sarah something. The story that unfolded left Sarah open mouthed with astonishment. It seemed that after his conversation with Sarah, George Linford went home in a furious mood and confronted Freddy. After harsh words, Freddy finally admitted to making the wedding arrangements, knowing full well that it could be easily checked simply by visiting Stepney Parish Church. At first he accused Sarah of being a tramp, but George made it clear that he did not believe it. His wife Jane was staggered that Freddy would arrange a wedding without talking to her about it, and moreover, one that he had no intention of going through with. The net upshot was that Freddy got very angry and upped and left, taking all his things with him. George Linford's wife Jane and her daughter Caroline begged him to stay saying that it should be possible to sort things out. But, with one look at his father's enraged face, he stormed out the door. The Linford household was not a place to be at this time, the atmosphere was such that you could cut the air with a knife. Susan stopped and took a sip of her drink, watching Sarah take it all in. Sarah was staggered and remained silent for some time.

After a while Sarah got up and took their glasses to the bar for refills. Just as she walked over, a door opened behind the bar and Martha Herbert walked out, straight in front of her. She took the glasses from Sarah and proceeded to fill them. When she returned, Sarah nervously started to count out the money, dropping a halfpenny on the floor. She bent down and picked it up. As she rose and placed it on the bar, Martha Herbert smiled her enigmatic smile at her and said. "Don't look so worried. You have problems right now, but they will resolve themselves. You must be strong, you have good people who will stand by you. In time you will meet the right man, indeed you will set eyes on him soon, but his name will not yet be known to you."

Sarah was intrigued by this statement, recalling the discussion she had had with Susan about Martha being 'clairvoyant'. She contemplated these odd words as she made her way back to the table with the drinks. She discussed the conversation with Susan, but despite much comment, neither of them could understand what it might mean.

Further conversation was prevented by the arrival of Edwin. He had a worried expression on his face and Sarah felt quite sorry for him. He could not help having a drunken cad for a brother. She politely declined his offer of another drink and, after finishing hers, bid them farewell.

That night she had a troubled sleep wondering what on earth could happen next.

CHAPTER 22

The Birth, 1840

THE WEEKS ROLLED relentlessly on and Sarah's pregnant state was now clear for all to see. Not that it stopped the speculation and gossip amongst the seamstresses. Freddy had not turned up for work since the day Sarah had told George Linford about him assaulting her. It looked like he had disappeared for good. His father George Linford was courteous and often smiled at her whenever their paths crossed. He did not repeat his offer of a drink, but she felt more comfortable in his presence and felt sure that she would be able to talk with him should it become necessary.

Freddy's brother Edwin was very kind to her and occasionally she would go for an evening drink with him and Susan Smith, both of whom usually inquired into her health and offered her support if she needed it. At these times it struck her how different were the natures of these two brothers: one so genuine and helpful, the other an unmitigated cad. Her regular meetings with Sarah Murray, and her visits to her family were also helping to keep her spirits up, and she felt just about able to cope.

March, of 1840, arrived, and with it a surprise. The Freestones, with whom Sarah was sharing a room, were clearly aware of her condition, but did not pry. It was a Monday evening and Jane Freestone came over to Sarah and invited her out for a drink with them. This was a little unusual, as, typical of costers, they generally kept their own company, or that of fellow costers. But Jane Freestone had some news, she was expecting a baby and wanted to celebrate. Thomas and her had been hoping to have a baby, but nothing had happened. Then, Sarah was expecting and Jane felt that, in some strange way, this had helped her by 'taking the curse off their home'. Sarah was a little puzzled by this statement, but she was happy to drink to their good fortune, and it would help to take her mind off of her own problems.

She was taken, by them, to a typical coster beer house; not somewhere that she would naturally frequent herself. As they entered she noticed that the place was full of costers jabbering amongst themselves at great volume. Over in one corner was a thick tobacco haze, below which was a long table full of men playing with cards that were dirty and almost illegible. In the adjacent corner were a couple of shove-halfpenny boards where the players were surrounded by men shouting loudly as each coin was launched. Having got their drinks, Jane and Sarah made for a quiet corner where a few women were chatting to each other; typical of coster ale houses, the women and men kept separate company. Tom joined a gang of rowdy costers at the bar where they were having a heated discussion about the business of that day. The drinks were flowing thick and fast and Sarah was soon feeling their effect. Suddenly, there was a commotion at the bar and Sarah could see two men facing each other off in an aggressive manner. The landlord behind the bar immediately produced two sets of boxing gloves which were quickly donned by the men and a sparring bout began. Sarah watched fascinated as the two men fought with each other to the excited shouts of encouragement from the crowd gathered round them; looking at the bar, she could see that the landlord was taking bets on the outcome. After about fifteen minutes, the bigger of the two contestants landed a heavy punch on the face of the smaller man, whose nose immediately began to bleed. A loud shout went up 'it's a noser!' At which the fight stopped; the man with the bleeding nose being declared the loser.

It was a tipsy, swaying trio that returned to their small room late that evening. The two expectant women, arm in arm, singing at the tops of their voices, it was the happiest Sarah had felt for some time. But, the following day, her uncomfortable time at work continued, made worse by a splitting headache.

It was the 14th June 1840 and it was a bright, hot, sunny day. Jimmy and Sarah were making their way up Mare Street towards the Hackney Parish Church of St John's to attend the baptism of the new baby of one of Sarah's friend's. Jimmy had asked Sarah if she was sure that she could make the journey, as it was quite a long walk from her lodgings. But, she had assured him that she was alright; she had spent much of her life walking long distances. He had decided to accompany her anyway, just to make sure.

Their progress had been slow because of Sarah's condition. But they eventually reached the church and spotted a small group of people waiting outside in the summer sun. Sarah recognised her friend Maria Tagell standing with her mother and sister Jane. Jane was holding Maria's baby which was swaddled in a white shawl. Sarah and Jimmy walked up to the group. Sarah introduced her brother and Maria introduced her mother and sister. Sarah looked at Maria's baby, lying quietly in Jane's arms, and asked her what she was going to call her. To her surprise Maria replied that she was going to call her Sarah, after her mother, who was also called Sarah. Everyone laughed at this, there did seem to be a lot of Sarah's around.

Sarah had met Maria Tagell at the tailor's shop, where she had worked as a seamstress, until she had to leave to have her baby. They had got on very well and chatted often to each other. Sarah knew that Maria was unmarried and that the father of her child had vanished as soon as she told him she was expecting. That had drawn them even closer together.

Maria's mother came over to Sarah and Jimmy and invited them back to her house, after the baptism, and then on to the Woolpack Tavern in Morning Lane, for a small celebration. Maria's mother and sister had been very supportive to her, her father having died some years earlier. The Reverend Ratcliffe came out of the church door and told them that he was ready to proceed, so they all filed in and took their places by the old stone font.

After the ceremony, people were leaving the church and the Reverend Ratcliffe was standing at the door talking amiably with them. Sarah and Jimmy stepped out into the bright sunlight. Sarah had been feeling dizzy during the ceremony, probably brought on by the long walk in the hot sun. Now, standing in the open with the sun high in the sky beating down relentlessly, her head started to spin. She started to sway, then let out a moan and pitched forward onto the ground. Jimmy knelt down beside her and was concerned to see blood oozing from a cut on the side of her head, where she had struck the hard ground. The incumbent and several others came over. The Reverend Ratcliffe knelt down beside Jimmy and was also concerned about Sarah's injury, but he noticed something else too, the trickle of clear liquid running from between Sarah's legs. Her pregnant state was clear for all to see, and he knew that she needed attention fast.

The Reverend stood up and looked around. The gardener was tending some bushes by the side of the church path and he called him over. A few minutes later, Sarah, the Reverend and Jimmy were sitting in the back of the gardener's trap, on top of some leaves and twigs. Jimmy and the Reverend were either side of Sarah supporting her. The gardener was urging his tired old pony into as fast a trot as it could manage. Soon, they were rattling down the High Street, shedding twigs and leaves across the road as they bumped along.

They pulled up at the entrance to the Hackney Union Workhouse. The Reverend Ratcliffe was well known to the Workhouse Master, a Mr. John Sunderland, and Sarah was quickly admitted to the lying-in ward, where she was examined by the Matron.

Jimmy waited in a front receiving room, with the Reverend and the Workhouse Master. The Master took Sarah's details from Jimmy, to complete the formalities of her admission. After about half an hour, the Matron walked in to announce that Sarah was not in any danger, she had merely swooned in the heat. But the prolonged walk had hastened the arrival of her baby, which would not be long in coming.

Having assured himself that Sarah was not in danger, the Reverend left to return to his church. Jimmy was not permitted to see Sarah until the accorded visiting day, which was the following Wednesday. So Jimmy left and made his way back to Whitechapel to let their family and Nell know about Sarah's condition.

The following day was a Monday and Jimmy called in at the tailor's shop, where Sarah worked, to inform the owner that Sarah would not be coming in that day and would probably be absent for a few days; the owner was not best pleased with her absence, coming on top of Freddy still being missing. As Jimmy stepped outside, he was aware of a figure following him out the door. He turned, to face George Linford. "I overheard what you said," George Linford started.

"Yes," said Jimmy, non committal.

"I know that things have not been well between us," George continued, "but I have a high regard for your sister, and am truly concerned for her."

Jimmy looked at him for a moment. Sarah had told them all about George Linford's conversation with her, and her expressed opinion that he was a decent and honest man. "She swooned yesterday and was taken to the Hackney Union Workhouse where she waits for the baby to come," he said.

"I see," said George Linford, "would it be possible for me to visit her?"

Jimmy was taken aback by this question, and took a little time to think about his answer. His initial thought was to tell the man to go to hell, but his son was the father of Sarah's child, and he was not in any way being unpleasant. So, Jimmy simply said, "visiting day is Wednesday. Please yourself," and with that he continued on his way. George Linford returned to the shop with a worried expression on his face.

It was Saturday 20th June 1840, and Sarah had just given birth to a baby boy. The baby was big and healthy. With the Matron's help, Sarah was learning to breast feed the infant. It had been impressed upon her that it would need great care and attention over the next few weeks if it is to survive.

Sarah herself was very weak. The birth of such a large baby had not been an easy one, she was in great pain and lost some blood. There was a fear that she would haemorrhage, but this had now receded. It was painful for her to move and she remained still for most of the day, holding her new baby tightly to her chest.

Sarah was in the institution which would become the Hackney Hospital. Originally, in 1750, the Wardens, Overseers and Trustees of the Parish of St John, Hackney, had ordered that a room be reserved in the Workhouse in Homerton High Street which was 'for the lodging, maintaining and employing of poor persons', so that sick paupers could be treated separately from other inmates. A Matron and one nurse were appointed and the history of Hackney Hospital began. By the following year a larger room was needed and it was extended to include the insane as well as the sick. To cover the extra staffing requirements, the Matron in charge was able to order any of the healthy inmates to help her in treating the unfortunates. Social conditions in Hackney then, as now, were among the worst in London and there was a continual need for the Workhouse and its Infirmary to expand to meet the demands made upon it. In 1840, when Sarah found herself an inmate, it was a very poorly run establishment and chronically overcrowded. The people tending to her were paupers themselves and, although generally well meaning, were completely untrained. Most of what they did was more harmful than beneficial, particularly as most of the nurses never washed and spread infection wherever they went. The fact that Sarah and her son survived childbirth was more by luck than ministration.

The following Wednesday 24th June, Sarah was told that she had a visitor. Picking up her baby, she walked slowly and carefully to the reception room. She found a number of visitors there, but at first, no one she recognized. Then, she spotted her brother Jimmy's smiling face. He walked over to her and put his arms round her and the baby. "How are you Sarah?" he asked, concern showing on his face at her pale appearance.

Sarah grimaced a little. He saw the pain register on her face. "I'm a little sore," she said, "but the Matron says that I will make a good recovery, given a little time."

Jimmy looked down at the chubby baby. "My he's a cute thing isn't he," he said.

"He's not a 'thing'," she said scolding him, "he's a little boy." Then, holding him closer, "aren't you my sweet."

"Sorry," said Jimmy, then, "I called in the tailor's shop and told them you won't be in for a bit." He left out the fact that the owner was most displeased at her absence. Then, "look Sarah, I don't know if I did right, but that George Linford asked about you."

"Oh did he," she replied, "and what did you tell him?"

"Well, I told him the truth. About you being in here and having the baby."

"And, what did he say to that?" she asked.

"He wants to come and visit you." Jimmy stated flatly.

"What!" exclaimed Sarah. "Why does he want to visit me?"

"Well," said Jimmy hesitantly, "I don't rightly know, to be honest, but he seemed genuine enough. I don't think he means you any harm."

Sarah didn't know what to make of it either.

When Jimmy left and she had returned to the lying-in ward, she sat on the end of her bed, cuddling her baby, thinking about what George Linford wanted; if anybody should be visiting her, it should be the baby's father Freddy. But she didn't think that he would want anything to do with a Workhouse baby. Her eyes started to moisten over. She held her baby closer.

On the following Wednesday 1st July, Sarah was told that she had another visitor. Thinking that it was Jimmy again, she walked, holding her baby, to the reception room. She now had much less pain and was better on her feet. Looking around the room, she couldn't see Jimmy. Then her eyes alighted on George Linford.

He walked over to her, a smile on his face. "Hello Sarah," he said, "I hope you don't mind my seeing you?"

She smiled back at him, "No I don't mind at all. Would you like to see the baby?" she asked.

"I would love to," he said.

Sarah softly pulled back the shawl of the sleeping bundle, to reveal his face.

George Linford studied the baby's face for some time; it was a slightly thin face with high cheekbones and very distinctive eyelashes that were almost feminine in the way they arched round his eyes. His lips formed a cute little pout. His hair was somewhat fairer than the

Valentines' usually had. It also had a distinct curl to it. Sarah noticed that George Linford's face wore a strange, almost startled, expression. But his only comment was. "My, what a handsome boy."

Sarah beamed a smile at him. She wondered why it was that George Linford had come, and not Freddy, the baby's father. They talked for a while and George asked her if there was anything she needed. She answered a firm no. She had no wish to be beholding to this family.

On Sunday 12ᵗʰ July, Sarah was up and about, feeling a great deal better. She was still moving about quite slowly, but the pain was nowhere near so bad. One of the Workhouse staff came into the lying-in ward and walked up to her. She told her to go to the Master's office immediately. She asked one of the other mothers if she could keep an eye on her sleeping baby while she was gone. The mother nodded and smiled at her. Sarah followed the woman out the door and down the dark corridor to the Master's office at the front of the building, wondering what was wrong. She knocked on the door and was told to enter.

The Master was sitting behind his desk, writing on a piece of paper. After a few minutes he looked up at her, a stern expression on his face. "Take a seat Sarah", he said.

Sarah took the chair directly opposite his desk. He cleared his throat.

"Under the new legislation that the Government has brought in, it is necessary for the birth of your baby to be registered with the authorities." He looked up at her expectantly. She returned a blank look. He continued, "I have taken the liberty to do this for you at the Civic Offices in Mare Street." With that he handed her a piece of paper, "This is an official copy of the registration."

Sarah took the document and looked at it. It was completely meaningless to her, as she could not read a single word on it.

A few days later, on the Monday 20ᵗʰ July, Sarah had another visitor. This time it was the Reverend Ratcliffe, from St John's Church. He was in the habit of visiting the Workhouses in his local area. He was a conscientious, kindly man and devout in his attempts to bring the Christian faith to all whom were within the ministrations of his

Parish. He particularly devoted some of his time to the young girls who had babies in the Workhouse. He was fully aware that many were unmarried, but was careful not to be too judgmental and did not overtly hold that against them. Instead of chastising them, he preferred to offer them the warmth of the Christian faith.

Sarah showed him her son's birth certificate and asked him what the words meant.

He held the document in his hand and scanned the text. "It records your name, Sarah Valentine, as the mother of this child," he said.

"What does it say of the father?" she questioned.

The Reverend paused for a moment. "It does not mention a father," he said.

"But, it must say something?" she queried.

The Reverend paused again as he considered his reply. "Yes, my dear," he said. "It states that your son is a bastard."

Shocked at this revelation, Sarah took the document from him.

"Where does it say this?" she asked.

The Reverend pointed out the word, in the space marked 'Name of Father'.

She could not read the word, but she saw that it had a thick black line under it which made it stand out on the page. She could see no other words thus marked out. "And why is there no writing in this space?" she asked, pointing to a blank section.

"It is blank because the child has no name," he said.

Sarah stared at the document with horror on her face. Tears formed in her eyes.

"So this wretched paper marks my baby out as a bastard with no father and no name!" she wailed. "Does it say he has a loving mother?" she demanded.

The Reverend Ratcliff put his hand gently on Sarah's shoulder. "Do not distress yourself," he said, "of course it has your name on it as his mother," he pointed out the words to her.

Her tears slowed down a little, but she was still clearly very distressed.

The Reverend Ratcliffe was always ready to offer his services freely to those in need. One service he was keen to offer to the young unmarried mothers was to baptise their children. He saw this as a first step on the path to persuading them to embrace the Christian faith. And it was this service that he offered to Sarah. "Sarah," he said, "we cannot alter this document, but we can correct some of the things it says. For instance, we can give your son a name, recognised in the eyes of God. If you will permit me I can baptise your son."

After only a moments thought, she readily agreed to this and a date was set for the next Sunday.

On the Wednesday, Jimmy came to visit Sarah, at the Workhouse, and she told him of the forthcoming baptism at St John's Church. He said that he would come and meet her at the Workhouse on the Sunday morning, to help her walk with the baby to the church. Sarah put her arms around him and kissed his, ever sooty, cheek. He was always so caring and considerate. She really did not know what she would do without him. He was always there for her.

So, on the morning of Sunday 26th July 1840, Jimmy presented himself at the Hackney Union Workhouse and, with his strong arm supporting Sarah and her baby, they walked the half mile along the High Street to St John's Church. She had recovered excellently from the difficult birth and was almost back to full health. The baby had also done well during the five weeks of its young life, putting on good weight, and looked quite rosy in health.

It was a warm and pleasant summer's day. High in the sky, the bright yellow disc of the sun shone out from an azure sky; they soon reached their destination.

Sarah was in tears when she saw her whole family standing outside the church. They had all made the, nearly three mile, walk from Whitechapel; even her father was present. Jimmy was pleased to see her so happy. It was not without considerable argument and some threats thrown in, that he had succeeded in getting both his parents to attend. Nell and her brood were also there, making a large and very noisy group.

In the church, they gathered round the ancient font. The Reverend Ratcliffe was pleased to see so big an attendance, and immediately wanted to proceeded with the ceremony.

He walked up to Sarah. "And what is the child to be called?" he asked.

Sarah had thought long and hard about this. The bestial and cowardly behaviour of the baby's father meant that she had no intention whatsoever in calling her child after him. She had been tempted to call him Jimmy, as her brother had been so supportive of her. But then, she knew that the child was a Linford and should have an appropriate name, so she had decided to name him after the father's brother Edwin. This was in the hope that he would take after Edwin rather than Freddy. So she had made her decision. "The baby is to be called Edwin," she said simply.

"That means that he will be called Edwin Valentine then," said the Reverend.

"But, his father is called Linford?" said Sarah.

"Yes my dear," said the Reverend kindly, "but, as you are not married, he will take your surname of Valentine."

"Oh, is that so," said Sarah weakly. This confused her. It seemed that the baby's father was getting ever more distant.

The ceremony proceeded, with all the family and friends gathered in a large group round the font. As Sarah handed the baby to the Reverend, she spotted a single figure standing alone at the rear of the church. Looking more carefully, she suddenly realized that it was George Linford. She wondered what he was doing here. Her eyes roved round the back of the church to see if his son Freddy had decided to attend, but he clearly had not seen fit to put in an appearance to see his son baptised. Then, as the Reverend called out the name of the baby, although he was some distance away, she was sure that she saw George Linford's eyes water over.

After the ceremony, her seven-year-old sister Caroline came over to her and asked. "Who was that man at the back?"

"Why is that Caroline?" responded Sarah.

"He was asking me questions," replied Caroline.

"What sort of questions?" asked Sarah a little alarmed.

Seeing the worried expression on Sarah's face, Caroline said, "He was very nice to me. He just wanted to know the names of who was here. That's all."

"He's just a friend from where I work," Sarah answered. But she was still a little confused by his presence.

For the next month, Sarah remained in the Hackney Union Workhouse, but she was troubled. She still had vivid memories of Agnes and the anguish she suffered when her baby sister was taken from her, to be left to die with no one to care for her. She was aware of the vagaries of rigid Workhouse rules. Sooner or later she would be taken from the lying-in ward and placed in a womens' working ward, where she would be set to work and she was very much afraid of baby Edwin being taken from her. Every time she saw Matron, or any other Workhouse employee, she gripped Edwin tightly, fear in her eyes. She knew she must leave soon as she was pretty well recovered, but her prospects on the outside were slim indeed. The more she thought about what she would do, the less she could come up with viable options. Things were now a little better with her family. After the baptism, they had gone for a drink together and many old wounds had been patched over, but she knew that they could not support her. They were barely able to support themselves, let alone adding an unemployed woman plus child to their troubles. She also thought about George Linford. Why had he come to the baptism? What was in his mind? She also badly missed her friend Sarah Murray and her cheerful support.

The Workhouse troubled her so much that, in the end, as September arrived, she upped and left of her own accord. She could no longer stand the uncertainty that she might have her baby taken away from her. She could not bear to lose him and would not risk it, so she applied to leave and, after the formalities had been completed, found herself standing in the Homerton High Street. Baby Edwin was wrapped in her shawl and she held him close to her chest. It was a pleasant Autumnal day, with a light breeze blowing a scattering of leaves across the pavement. She started walking down the High Street. She cut through Morning Lane towards Mare Street.

After forty minutes of steady walking, she found herself at the Mutton Lane triangle. She turned off down Mutton Lane and Sheep Lane and soon found herself walking along the Regent's Canal towpath, towards Haggerstone. After a few minutes she passed under the Hackney footpath bridge and paused for a rest at the Acton Lock where she sat on the grass bordering the towpath. She watched as the massive shire horses pulled the barges along the canal and watched as a heavily laden barge passed through the lock. She was reminded of the times that she had walked down this same path, arm in arm with Freddy Linford. Sober, he had been kind and considerate, but his true colours had come to light when drunk. However, time had marched on, now here she was, sitting on the same towpath alone, holding his son. As if responding to her thoughts, Edwin gurgled and she pulled back the shawl to look at him. She rocked him gently and he closed his eyes; he settled down, comfortable in her arms. She smiled at him and wrapped the shawl closer round him.

After a few minutes rest, she got up and continued walking along the towpath. She left the canal and crossed the Agostone Bridge, by the Imperial Gasworks. As she crossed the bridge, she twitched her nose at the familiar smell and could see the massive gasholders on her right and the tower of St Mary's Church ahead of her. As she turned right into Haggerstone Lane, she recalled the many Sundays that she had walked, in the Workhouse crocodile, to the church. Reaching the Kingsland Road, she crossed over and went down Philips Street; she made her way back to the room she had shared with the Freestones. She did not know what her reception would be as she had been in the Hackney Workhouse for more than two months and had not paid a penny rent in that time. But, it was where she had left her meagre belongings and she could think of nowhere else to go. Reaching the lodging house she walked down the hall to their door and knocked. She stood there, cuddling baby Edwin. She had no money and little prospects of work. She expected to be turned back out onto the street. In the event, after hearing her explanation of what had befallen her, the Freestones were both happy to see her and baby Edwin went down well with them. Jane Freestone was swelling with her own child and doted on young Edwin; the topic of her contribution to the rent was held in abeyance for now.

The following Monday, Sarah set out to walk to the tailor's shop, to see if there were any prospects of regaining her employment. Jane Freestone had agreed to look after her son Edwin.

First she went to the baker to meet with Sarah Murray. But, after some minutes waiting around, her friend had not appeared, so she inquired of the baker only to be told that she had not shown up for the bread for over a week. Apparently, it was now collected by a young boy, who should be in soon, so Sarah waited until he showed up. After he had collected the bread, Sarah accompanied him back to the house where Sarah Murray worked. In response to her questioning, he told her that Sarah Murray had been dismissed and had returned to the Workhouse. Saddened by this news, Sarah continued on her way to the tailor's shop.

When she arrived at the shop, she found the owner quite cold with her. In her absence, he had employed another girl; by all accounts the new girl was a good worker, and *reliable*. He stressed the last point with some force. It also occurred to her that he blamed her for Freddy's vanishing act, he would also have to be replaced; it was quite clear that there would be no prospect of re-employment here.

As she left, she was followed out onto the street by George Linford. He smiled and inquired after her health. She replied that she was now quite recovered. It was clear that there was something else he wanted to say and Sarah waited patiently for him to come to the point. After a short while he suggested that they go over to the Globe Tavern for a few minutes as he wanted a quiet word with her. They entered the Globe to find the bar room empty at this early hour, but John Herbert was behind the counter and was happy to serve them drinks. George Linford bought them a glass of wine each. They sat at a table for some minutes with George Linford seemingly raising the courage to say something. Eventually, it came out. He wanted her to bring her baby round to his house, to show his family. Sarah was not too happy about that, but he was persistent. If she was worried she could bring her brother, indeed, any members of her family she wished. He begged her to please consider it. She agreed that she would think about it. Happy with her response, George Linford drank his wine quickly down and made his excuses as he could not remain long from the shop. Sarah had no wish to rush her drink and remained at the table where she spent some time considering the conversation she had had with George Linford. His request for her to take her son round to his house left her quite troubled. She had no wish to encounter his wife again, but the inescapable fact was that their son was Edwin's father, and the child was their first grandson; under the circumstances, his request was not totally unreasonable; she resolved to discuss it with Jimmy and the rest of her family.

Finishing her drink, she rose and walked to the bar with her empty glass; she noticed that a few early customers had drifted in whilst she had been sitting at her table. Just as she placed her empty glass down on the bar, Martha Herbert strode in from the door at the back. Sarah stood rooted to the spot at her sudden appearance.

Noting Sarah's startled expression, Martha smiled her enigmatic smile. "Don't worry so Sarah," she said, "don't worry about the present, look to the future for I can see that you have many happy and healthy years ahead of you."

Sarah was intrigued by this statement, once again recalling the discussion she had had with Susan Smith about Martha being 'clairvoyant'. "How can you know that?" she asked.

Martha looked into her eyes, "I can see death in people, it is like a dark aura surrounding them. When I see that I know that they have not long in this world." She was staring round the room looking at the dozen, or so, early customers.

Sarah followed her gaze, started to talk, felt a tickle and coughed to clear her throat, "can you tell if any of these people are soon to die?" she whispered.

"Yes, quite clearly," Martha replied.

Sarah drew in a breath, shaken by this simple statement. She found herself asking, "Is anyone in here soon to die?" she held her breath. Then, aware that Martha Herbert had not yet answered her, she turned her gaze back from the bar room to look at Martha. She was struck by the sad expression on her angelic face.

Martha Herbert gave Sarah a weak smile and turned to walk off down the bar. As she moved away, she talked quietly, but Sarah clearly heard her words. "Someone here in this room will die very soon, but it will not be one of the customers out there."

Unsettled by Martha's words, Sarah hastened from the tavern and made her way back to the Freestone's abode.

A few days later, Sarah, carrying baby Edwin, together with Jimmy and her young sister Mary, arrived at No. 9 Caroline Street, off the Hackney Road; they knocked on the door. It was immediately answered by George Linford. He smiled at the little party and directed them into a small, but neatly set out, front parlour. Seated on a chair in one corner was a small pasty faced, sickly looking girl, with a head of thin, fair hair, who was introduced as Mary Ann Adelaide Linford. To Sarah, she seemed such a frail little thing to be carrying round such a big name. Her skin was so white that it was almost transparent. They were followed into the parlour by a teenage girl, who he introduced as his daughter Caroline Amelia. Sarah looked closely at her, she was a mousy looking girl with short cropped fair curly hair and seemed rather downcast and a little melancholy. But when she looked up and stared straight into Sarah's eyes, Sarah was startled to see such open hostility. Then, she remembered George Linford's comments about her, and how she doted on Freddy and begged him not to go away. Sarah rightly surmised that this girl blamed her for Freddy's disappearance. George Linford instructed Caroline to fetch some tea. Meekly, she left the room to do his bidding; Sarah found herself feeling a little sorry for her.

Mary and Jimmy were not used to drinking tea. It was still quite expensive, but far less so than say, 20 years earlier. It was now coming within the reach of the more well off working classes, and was rapidly gaining in popularity with them; Sarah was more used to it from her various domestic positions.

Talk lapsed whilst they awaited the tea. Young Mary was walking round the room transfixed by the ornaments on the window ledge, and a picture on the wall. A few minutes later, Caroline Linford entered the room carrying a tray, on which was arrayed several cups and saucers, together with a china teapot. She busied herself laying out the cups and saucers on a small occasional table set against one wall; she then poured the tea out. It was taken without milk and sugar, as was common at that time. Once prepared, the tea was handed round. As Sarah was holding the baby, her cup was left on the table.

At that point, the door opened and Jane Linford entered the room, a frosty expression on her face. George Linford started to say something to her, but she pointedly ignored him and walked straight up to Sarah. Sarah looked a little apprehensive at her approach and Jimmy tensed, ready to intervene if anyone tried to attack his sister again.

Jane Linford stared into Sarah's face and addressed her sharply. "So this is the baby you claim to be my son's is it?"

Sarah brindled at her words. "Be sure that this baby is your son's!" she replied equally sharply.

Jane Linford's eyes then travelled down to the baby in Sarah's arms, and she looked it straight in the face. Then, a bizarre event occurred. Jane Linford stared down at baby Edwin in silence for a moment and a gradual transformation came over her face: her eyes grew wide, her jaw sagged down. Just then, as if he was aware of the sudden scrutiny, the baby opened its eyes. For a few seconds Jane Linford and the baby locked eyes, staring at one another intently. Then, Jane Linford gasped and took a step back. Clearly, in dire shock, she turned on her heel and rushed from the room. As she passed through the door, she stammered, in a low almost inaudible voice, the one word. "Freddy!"

Languidly, the baby closed his eyes and returned to his peaceful slumber, completely unaware of the commotion he had just caused.

The occupants of the room were in a stunned silence after witnessing this tableau. After a few minutes, George Linford apologised for his wife's bizarre behaviour but, looking closely at his face, Sarah could detect no element of surprise etched there. In fact, for a brief moment, she could have sworn she glimpsed a faint, fleeting smile; then it was gone. Sarah expressed her disappointment that the baby's father had not decided to put in an appearance to see his son. In answer to her query, George Linford said that his son Freddy had 'disappeared' but he did not expand on why, or where to; Sarah was given the distinct impression that he had run off in the face of parenthood. Conversation lapsed. Jane Linford did not reappear. They finished their tea and departed.

As they walked down Caroline Street towards the Hackney Road, Sarah was left wondering why on earth George Linford had been so insistent that this, apparently pointless, meeting should have taken place. She would have been much more enlightened had she been an observer at the scene now taking place in the Linford's home.

After they had gone, George Linford had joined his wife in their little scullery. She was standing in a corner weeping. George looked at her for a moment. He knew exactly why she was weeping. Indeed, it was what he had fully expected to be the outcome of his carefully arranged meeting with the Valentines'. He went over and put his arms round his wife's shoulders.

She turned to him and in a weak voice said. "He looks exactly like our son Freddy did as a baby. Like two peas in a pod!"

"I know my dear," George said simply. Then, "He is surely Freddy's son. There can be no question my dear. Can there?"

"Oh what are we to do?" she said between tears, "he will have no future with that wretched girl!"

George had a grim, fixed expression on his lined face. He knew full well what he wanted to do, but it would take a lot of organizing.

CHAPTER 23

Sad Times & Bad Times

BACK AT THE room Sarah shared with the Freestones, Jane Freestone had given birth to a big bouncing baby boy, which they called Thomas, after his father. Their small, ten foot square room, was now accommodation for five souls, two of whom were non-rent-paying cuckoos. Sarah realized that her days here were numbered. With no earnings, she relied on Jimmy for small hand-outs in order to feed herself and her baby; he could not stretch to paying her rent as well.

Meanwhile at the Linfords' home things had moved on a pace. With the realization that Sarah's son Edwin was, without doubt, their grandson and that Sarah was not a scheming charlatan. Jane Linford's thoughts now turned to the baby and, of more concern, its future prospects. She found it difficult to forgive her husband for arguing with their son Freddy and causing him to run off. But, in his absence, she was determined that his baby would have a good upbringing. The trouble was, how would that happen in the company of a worthless, penniless, Workhouse tramp? She discussed the options at great length with her husband. A decision was arrived at. It was her husband's task to implement it.

It was a bright sunny Sunday in September, Sarah, baby Edwin and Jimmy were sitting in a small tavern, in the Kingsland Road, supping ale. Edwin, now nearly six-weeks-old was taking more interest in the world. He was sitting on uncle Jimmy's lap watching the people in the tavern.

Their conversation was the usual. What was to become of Sarah and Edwin? She had told Jimmy that the Freestones had been incredibly patient with her, but she had not told him that they said she must leave by the following week. She had rejected Jimmy's suggestion that she move in with him; there was no room in his sparse accommodation in Pidgeon Court, for her and a baby. She would not go back to her father's house, even if he asked her (which he had not). Nell was already sharing her house with two other families and an old woman. She really had nowhere to go. If she returned to the Workhouse, Edwin would certainly be taken from her and she would probably never see him again. This she would not contemplate. She would live on the streets first; which, at that moment was looking to be her only option.

Despite many hours of deliberation, no answer was forthcoming. They parted, Sarah walking north, with baby Edwin in her arms, Jimmy south, each to their own lodgings.

The next day was a Monday, and evening was drawing in. The sky was filled with large drops of rain from an autumn shower. The rain drops settled on the top of George Linford's hat; he was standing on a street corner, contemplating his next move. He had observed Jimmy Valentine in the Hackney Road several times over the last few days. He knew that Jimmy was a sweep and lately he had taken a little time off to follow him. He was waiting, leaning against a wall, just opposite the big house, with many chimneys, that Jimmy was working in. He was waiting for him to finish his day's work. He stamped his feet to clear the water from his shoes; he felt a sudden wind on his cheek. Then, Jimmy appeared. As he left the house, he pulled his collar up against the rain and walked out into the street, shouting goodbyes to his workmates.

As Jimmy crossed over and started to walk up the Hackney Road, George Linford pushed himself off the wall, hastened along and fell into stride beside him. "Hello Jimmy," he said in a friendly voice, "how goes it with you?"

Jimmy was a little startled by George Linford's sudden presence at his side, but was in a genial mood. "I'm fine George," he said, "and you?"

"Look Jimmy," said George earnestly, "would you permit me to talk with you?"

"Well, talk doesn't cost anything," said Jimmy, "what's on your mind?"

George pointed out a nearby tavern. "How about if I buy us both a drink?" he asked.

"Fine by me," responded Jimmy.

A short while later, they were both seated at a quiet corner table; Jimmy had a glass of ale in front of him and George a glass of red wine. There was silence for a few minutes. Jimmy could see that George was settling in his mind exactly what to say. Jimmy waited patiently, not sure what to expect.

"It's about your sister Sarah, and baby Edwin," George started.

"Ah! Ha!" said Jimmy, "I thought as much!"

"Please!" said George, "hear me out."

"Carry on," said Jimmy taking a big swig from his ale. As far as he was concerned, George Linford had bought the ale and so he was prepared to hear his tale.

"I'll be straight with you," George said, "mine and my wife Jane's concern, is for baby Edwin, our grandson."

"Yes," said Jimmy, "I can understand that."

"Jane and I have discussed it at great length. And I mean no offence in what I say. But the baby has little prospects with your sister. Eventually, it is inevitable that she will end up back in the Workhouse and then Edwin will be taken from her; he will have a doubtful future at best." He paused. "And likely as not, a short one at worst." He finished with emphasis.

His words were not lost on Jimmy; young babies did not usually last long in the Workhouse. "Yes," said Jimmy, "Sarah and I have also discussed this topic at great length, but what is to be done?"

George Linford hesitated. Jimmy waited. Eventually, George blurted it out. "The child could live with Jane and me."

Jimmy was quite taken aback. It was not what he had expected. "But, your wife..." he started.

George Linford held up his hand to stay Jimmy's words, "Jane was concerned that the child was not fathered by our son. But, be assured that she is now fully aware that this child is our grandson. That single fact has completely changed everything for her." He paused for a moment before continuing, "When Freddy was a baby, she doted on him and despite our other children, she always favoured him. His son Edwin is the spitting image of Freddy as a baby and she wants only the best for him. She will love him every bit as much as she did Freddy. You can be assured of that. He will want for nothing."

A silence descended between them. Jimmy's mind was racing. George Linford sensed Jimmy's confusion and gave him time for thought; he took a sip of wine. Jimmy was no fool. He immediately grasped the significance of the Linfords' offer; it was not to be dismissed lightly. Baby Edwin would be brought up in a good, stable, working class, family. He would certainly not suffer. "It is an offer worthy of consideration," Jimmy finally said, taking another sip of his ale.

"Yes," said George, "he will have a good upbringing. He will be educated to read and write. I will apprentice him, as I did with my sons Freddy and Edwin. He will become a journeyman tailor. First class."

This last statement was not lost on Jimmy. He knew that a good profession was worth its weight in gold. It ensured employment, kept you off the streets and out of the Workhouse. They chatted about it for a while longer. Jimmy promised to talk it over with Sarah. They parted company.

Jimmy had much to think about as he made his way back to Shoreditch.

It was Sunday evening, Sarah, baby Edwin and Jimmy were sitting in the same small tavern, in the Kingsland Road, supping ale. Sarah had still not told Jimmy that she and Edwin would have to leave the Freestones' lodgings on the following day and that they had nowhere to go, she did not want him to worry about her.

Jimmy had related his conversation with George Linford and repeated their offer to bring up baby Edwin. At first Sarah was violently against it. Looking at her baby, sitting happily on Jimmy's knee, she felt she could not bear to be parted from him. But, at the same time, she knew that she had a heavy responsibility for him. What could she offer him? A life on the streets, or alone in a Workhouse. Then a thought. "What role will his father take in this?" she asked.

"None," said Jimmy, "George was quite adamant that the child will be brought up by himself and his wife." He repeated George's assurance that he would be taught to read and write and given an honourable profession to secure his future.

It was then that Sarah realized with a terrible jolt that she would have no hope of doing any of those things for her son and that she could not deny him this opportunity; to do so would be selfish and cruel. Suddenly she burst into tears, jumped up and ran from the tavern. Startled, Jimmy watched her go, unsure what to do; baby Edwin, sitting on his knee, watched his mother run out the door.

Outside, the cold evening breeze jolted her mind into focus. She lent against the wall of the tavern. Slowly, she pulled herself together, her mind racing.

A filthy old man, dressed in rags, walked up to her. "Come with me dearie. I'll show you a good time," he said.

Pushing herself away from the wall, she brushed past him and walked back into the tavern. Wiping her eyes with her sleeve, she went back over and sat down at the table with Jimmy. They sat in silence, only broken by baby Edwin, cooing at the other drinkers.

Sarah leant forward, her elbows on the table and her head in her hands; she was staring at her baby. Tears started to stream down her face. Jimmy felt his eyes watering at the distress in his sister's heart rending sobs. "I really have no choice, do I?" she muttered into her hands.

"No, not really," said Jimmy sorrowfully, leaning forward to run his hand through her hair.

The next day, it was a sad looking threesome that made their way down the Hackney Road on the Monday evening and turned into Caroline Street. A young man and a young woman, carrying a baby boy, wrapped snugly in a clean, but worn, shawl, against the early evening wind. They paused for a moment outside No. 9. They seemed reluctant to walk up to the door; but they were expected, and they had been seen. The door was opened. George Linford stood on the doorstep, an encouraging smile on his face. They followed him in and gathered once again in the front parlour. No tea was offered this time. It was to be only a brief visit.

A few moments later and a dour, grim faced, twosome left. The young baby was no longer with them. The twosome exited the top of Caroline Street, crossed the Hackney Road and entered the tavern on the corner of Weymouth Terrace, where they proceeded to get thoroughly drunk. The young woman seemed unable to stop weeping.

It was very late when Sarah and Jimmy left the tavern; his money had run out. It was raining and there was a cool wind. Jimmy offered to see Sarah home. She refused and said she wanted to be alone. After a few minutes of fruitless remonstrating with her, Jimmy reluctantly left her and made his way home, down the Kingsland Road. Sarah stood for a while letting the rain wash over her. She had nowhere to go; she had left the Freestones' earlier that day as she had no way of paying the rent. She had no money, but did not care; she walked aimlessly up the Kingsland Road. She had drunk too much and her progress followed a meandering path. She passed the Shoreditch Workhouse on her left, but did not even notice it.

The loss of her son Edwin played heavily on her mind; he had only been with her for a short time, but she had come to love him dearly. Giving him up had shattered her heart. She could not bear to contemplate an existence without him. She kept trying to convince herself that she had done the right thing, but she desperately wanted him back. She reached the bridge over the Regents Canal. Stopping in the middle, she leaned over the stone wall at the side of the bridge and stared down at the dark murky water below; the rain had eased off and It was as still as a millpond. She could see her face reflected in the water in the light of a full moon. Tears started to stream down her face and she let out a pitiful wail. She felt utterly useless; of no use to her own son, or anyone else for that matter. What was the point of her worthless life. She climbed unsteadily on to the stone wall and sat looking down into the water. She waggled her feet and saw her shoes fall off and splash into the water. Her head spinning, she watched the ripples as they spread out to the banks of the canal. She put her hands to her head and let out another wail.

The old bargeman had been sitting on the bank of the canal, close to his tied up barge, smoking his old clay pipe, his hat pulled down over his head to screen his weather-beaten face against the recent rain. With the rain easing off he was feeling quite content staring up at the full moon, when his eye caught sight of a young girl leaning over the canal bridge. She was bonnetless, her wet hair plastered to her face; she seemed to be crying. Then she let out a pitiful wail. It was such a painful sound that his heart went out to her; what on earth had befallen her to be so distressed? Then, he saw her get up unsteadily on to the bridge wall. Alarmed, he climbed to his feet, unconsciously knocking out his pipe on the side of his barge. The next minute she let out another wail and he watched her pitch forward headfirst into the canal waters. Shouting for the night-watchman at the nearby warehouses, he grabbed his grappling hook from the barge and ran down the towpath to the bridge. When he reached her, she was face down in the water seemingly out cold. He hooked the back of her dress and pulled her into the side. He was joined by the night-watchman, alerted by his shouts. They pulled her out of the water and lay her on the towpath. She was not moving and water was streaming from her nose and mouth. After a few moments of discussion, they decided to take her to the Shoreditch Workhouse, just down the road, which they knew had an Infirmary and medical facilities. The night-watchman collected a wheel-barrow from the warehouse and they gently placed Sarah in and wheeled her off down the Kingsland Road.

When they reached the Workhouse, they knocked up the gatekeeper, who was none too pleased to be disturbed. However, as soon as he saw the girl, he immediately recognised Sarah as the one he had been paid to turn a blind eye to when she was taken from the Workhouse by Freddy Linford. Worried, he summoned Eliza Ribnell, the nurse who had also been paid off. Eliza looked closely at Sarah and found that although soaking wet and unconscious, she seemed to be still alive. So, they decided to put her back in the sick ward and keep quiet about her leaving. Eliza told the bargeman and night-watchman that they would take care of the girl and they departed. Sarah was carried to the sick ward where Eliza removed her wet clothes, replacing them with the Workhouse gown, then she was put in a bed in the sick ward where she had originally been. Eliza rolled Sarah's dress up and tucked it under the folds of her own dress to dispose of later.

Over the next couple of days Sarah's health returned, though her sorrow at the loss of her son would not diminish; she had been surprised to wake up in the Workhouse sick ward, but cared little of what happened to her. Eliza Ribnell had explained to her that she should keep quiet about her absence from the Workhouse, or they would all be in trouble. There were hundreds of people in the Workhouse and the sick ward was jammed full. No one had noticed her departure, or her reappearance.

After a few days, Sarah having recovered physically, Eliza arranged for her to be transferred to a womens' working ward, claiming that she was now well enough to work. She was placed in ward 16, but would not have cared if she had been placed in ward 14 with all the lunatics, such was her state of mind. She was put to work in the kitchen and hardly registered the mountains of washing up, all she could think of, as she automatically carried out her work, was the loss of her son. Of an evening she talked with no one, just climbing into bed and staring up at the ceiling. Sleep was always difficult in coming and when she did drift off she dreamed of holding Edwin in her arms, he was always staring up at her, eyes wide open with a disappointed look on his little face, she was always sobbing. She woke frequently in the night and found herself reaching out for him. But, of course, he wasn't there and the tears would start again.

As the days passed, she started to take a little more notice of her surroundings. Her pain over the loss of her son did not go away, but she found herself more able to push it to the back of her mind. The first thing that she noticed was that there had been a number of changes since she was last in the Workhouse. The first was that, although the thin woman was still there, the vixen had gone; she was quite happy to see the back of her. The next was that the slop shop had gone. It seemed that trying to get the Workhouse inmates to make acceptable garments had proved a dismal failure and the initiative had been discontinued. She was also quite happy about that, as the likelihood of meeting up with Freddy, in the Workhouse, had now gone away.

Now that she was out of the sick ward and in a working ward, she was considered able bodied and suitable for outside employment. It was just under a month later when, one morning, she was summoned to the Master's office. She had been found a position, albeit a temporary one, as a Maid of All Work for a gentleman and his brother. They lived in the Hackney Road and were planning to emigrate to America. They had need of a temporary servant whilst they made their preparations. It would be for a period of 6 weeks only. She would not be paid but would have a roof over her head and be fed; as much as a Workhouse girl could expect.

Her original dress, that she had arrived in after running away from Freddy, was returned to her. Examining it, she saw that it was torn and bloody. She was surprised to see his poesy ring still in the pocket, then remembered that she had taken it off and placed it there when she ran off from Freddy's attack on her; she took it out, unsure what to do with it. The dress was clearly not wearable and she had lost her shoes when she ran off. So a worn, but serviceable, garment was found for her, together with a mis-matched pair of battered shoes, three sizes too big, that required paper stuffed in them to remain on her feet. She put Freddy's ring in the pocket of her replacement dress.

So, on the 28th October 1840, she left the Shoreditch Workhouse to take up her temporary position. The house she was to report to was towards the end of the Hackney Road not far from the tailor's shop, so she decided to call in the shop to see if there was any news of Freddy and to find out how her son Edwin was getting on, living in the Linford home. She was still a little wary of Jane Linford, having been attacked in the street by her and was anxious to ensure that her son was being looked after properly by her.

Reaching the shop she peered in the doorway and spotted George Linford talking with the shop owner. Not wishing to enter the shop with the owner present she waited outside. George Linford looked up and saw her standing there. Whilst the owner was preoccupied with some material on the counter top, he pointed towards the Globe Tavern over the road. Interpreting this as an indication he wished to see her in the tavern, she crossed over and entered the Globe. John Herbert was standing behind the bar arranging clean glasses; Sarah walked over to him and, as he looked up at her, suddenly realised that she had no money with which to purchase a drink. Unsure what to do, she asked after his wife Martha, to bide time until George Linford turned up.

It was as if she had slapped him round the face! He dropped the glass he had been holding in his hand, which smashed in pieces on the stone floor, then turned and glared at her. Sarah took a step back at his fierce expression. Seeing her surprise, his face softened. "You don't know then?" he said quietly.

"I'm sorry," stammered Sarah, "know what?"

His eyes misted over, he was clearly overcome with strong emotion. Sarah immediately regretted her inquiry. An uneasy silence descended between them.

"I'm sorry," Sarah repeated and made to leave.

"Wait!" John Herbert said, "Martha was always concerned for you."

This last comment caused Sarah to halt. She turned and faced the publican.

After a few moments, he wiped his eyes with his hand and began to talk quietly, "it was a Saturday evening, the 19th September last it was, Martha said goodbye to me and our children, smiled at us and went up to lay on her bed. She closed her eyes and never opened them again."

Sarah's mouth fell open, her knees went weak and she put her hand on the bar for support.

John Herbert was continuing, "the doctor came and found that her heart had stopped beating, but he could find nothing wrong with her to explain why. She was still smiling, but we couldn't rouse her."

"Was she ill?" said Sarah.

"Never a day's illness in her short life," he replied, then continued, "the doctor was completely mystified over why she died. It was so impossible to explain that the District Coroner wrote on her death certificate that she died 'by the visitation of God'. The undertaker's over the road arranged her burial at St Leonard's Church Yard. They were in awe of her. Edmund and Charles Roper attended her and said it was impossible to believe that it was a dead body. It was as if she was sleeping and about to wake up at any minute." He paused to wipe his eyes, then carried on, "There was a strange incident that night; when I spoke to the children, they said that their mother had told them to be strong and her last words to them were, 'I must go, the angels are calling'."

Seeing the grief on John Herbert's face, Sarah mumbled her condolences. She was shocked to the core. She recalled the strange conversation she had had with Martha Herbert the last time she had spoken with her in the Globe. She had said that someone was about to die but, 'it would not be one of the customer's out there'. They had had that conversation on the Monday and she had died 5 days later! Had she known of her own impending death?

Further conversation was halted by the sudden arrival of George Linford. He strode up to the bar, clearly flustered. He asked Sarah what she wanted; he seemed a little abrupt. When she said she was inquiring about Freddy and her son Edwin, He stated that Freddy had gone and her son was fine. She was about to ask him if she could visit her son when he turned on his heel and left the tavern saying that he had much to do and could not dally. Having no money, Sarah had little option but to follow him out. She stood outside the Globe and watched him stride back to the tailor's shop. As she walked on to her new place of work, her mind was in a turmoil, she found herself worrying about George Linford's strange behaviour and wondering about Martha Herbert's unlikely death; both seemed equally inexplicable.

When she arrived at her new employer's residence she was met by the cook, a rotund, substantially built woman with a fat, florid face and unkempt thick black hair bulging out from under her dirty, presumably once white, hat. Her bare arms were covered in a further mass of black hair and Sarah was startled to notice that she sported a fine black moustache that any city gent would have been proud of. It soon became clear that Sarah's appointment was at the insistence of the cook who had been expected to include the household chores in her duties. Sarah was pleasantly surprised when she was shown to a small, but neatly appointed, bedroom with a small bed with elaborate wooden headboard and comfortable looking flock mattress. A small dressing table sat against a wall under a small window with lace curtains. A candle sat in a shiny holder on the dresser and a coloured print of some saint hung on the wall. She could see no beetles or rodents. It was quite the nicest bedroom she had ever seen and she was astonished when the cook informed her that, for the duration of her stay, it was to be hers alone.

Over the next few days she settled into her new station. Her duties were the usual: making beds, cleaning grates, filling scuttles and generally keeping the place neat and tidy. The cook fed her scraps and leftovers, keeping the best for herself, but she was generous with the tea and seemed happy to share a pot with her. Of her Master, the gentleman, and his brother, she saw very little. They were absent all day, making their preparations for emigration; the cook served them at the evening meal and they were early to bed, making an early start to the morning. She was not allowed outside, the cook being worried that she might abscond, leaving her to do the household chores again, but by far the best part for Sarah, was the bedroom. She delighted in sitting at the dressing table, which featured a vanity mirror. She found a comb in one of the drawers and combed her hair, preening herself in the mirror. The bed was the most comfortable she had ever known and she snuggled under the covers against the chill winter air. The only down side was her sorrow over her son Edwin. He was growing up without her; she bitterly wanted to see him and hold him in her arms.

All too soon her six weeks was up and she gathered her belongings and said farewell to the cook; she was very sad to leave her bedroom. Outside, in the street, the snow was falling and a cart stood, drawn up to the kerb. Men were loading two large wooden trunks and several leather cases; presumably the brother's possessions to be shipped to America. Sarah had no idea where America was, neither did the cook. Sarah stood for a moment and contemplated where she would go now she no longer had either a job or a roof over her head.

The snow was falling heavily and a cold wind blew a blizzard of white flakes into her face as she trudged down the Kingsland Road.

She only had on the worn dress, donated by the Workhouse, not even a shawl to put round her shoulders. But, still bitterly depressed by the loss of her son Edwin, she was oblivious to the cold. A horse and cart clattered past in the road. Mud and freezing slush was thrown up splashing Sarah's legs and soaking through the paper stuffed in her battered shoes. She seemed not to notice. The street was full of people rushing about. More than once she was barged and jostled. Again, she seemed not to notice the intrusions. Finally, she arrived at her destination.

Having been dismissed from her temporary employment, with no immediate prospects of work, nowhere to live and a freezing winter upon the land, Sarah Valentine's choices were limited. So she had ended up at the Court House in Worship Street. Three hours later she was standing at the door to Shoreditch Relieving Officer John Coste's office with a summons from Magistrate Benett clutched in her hand. A further two hours later and Sarah was walking through the Shoreditch Workhouse door with a ticket from the Relieving Officer in her hand.

So, on Tuesday the 8th December 1840, she was admitted, by the Master, for the fifth time in her short life. He remembered her from her previous admission and fixing her with a dark glare, stated forcefully that he firmly believed in able bodied inmates being given work in the community, rather than living in the Workhouse at the Parish's expense. She would not be expected to stay long as work would be found for her. She nodded her acceptance.

She went through the usual admission ritual and when they took her possessions, she realised that she still had Freddy's poesy ring in her dress pocket. It brought back sad memories and, for the second time, she was tempted to throw it away, but in the end she replaced it in the pocket and handed over her dress in exchange for the drab Workhouse garb.

She had a pleasant surprise when she was admitted to the female working ward 15. In the next bed was her old friend Sarah Murray. She rushed over and embraced her, but looking into her eyes, she was dismayed. In place of the bright fun loving light usually there, she saw fear. Her face looked swollen, much wider somehow, her cheeks red and blotchy, and on examining her more closely, she could see that she had lost considerable weight; she was no more than skin and bones. As she was examining her, Sarah Murray burst into a fit of violent coughing; it was clear that every cough racked her with pain. She held her chest tightly with both arms and rolled over onto the bed. Sarah waited until the coughing fit subsided and lent over to put her arms round her dear friend. As she did so, she was alarmed to see flecks of blood on the top of the bed where her friend's face had been. Although she had no knowledge of medicine, Sarah knew that her friend was in desperate trouble.

Over the next few days Sarah nursed her friend as best she could. She had no idea what to do to help her, but knew instinctively that to bring her poor condition to the attention of the Workhouse staff would undoubtedly result in her being taken away to the terrible sick ward where she would lie in the desolate hands of strangers unconcerned whether she would live or die. She well remembered her own experiences of that terrible ward and her thoughts kept drifting to the fate of poor Agnes's sister. She would not allow that to happen to her best friend. Quietly, without drawing unnecessary attention, she would lay with her to comfort her in her fits of coughing. As she lay there she noticed that her friend's hair was wet and matted, as though she was gripped with a fever. On looking into her eyes she was startled to see that they sparkled with a feverish brilliancy, but their gaze was fixed and showed no interest in the world around her. She spoke soothing words to her, but for long periods she received no acknowledgement of her presence. At meal times she tried desperately to get her to eat, but she stubbornly refused; she was getting weaker with each day that passed.

Slowly, between coughing fits, during periods of awareness, Sarah got the story of what had happened to her friend. Apparently, part of her work at the house, in the Hackney Road where they used to meet, had been to look after three young children. At first everything was fine then, one of the children started coughing. After a few days it became incessant and the other children also started to cough. All manner of sweets and honey had failed to remedy the coughs. After a time, she noticed blood on their bed sheets and then, a few weeks later, the youngest had died. The other two followed within the space of a few days and she had been dismissed and sent back to the Workhouse. Shortly after her admission, she had started to cough, and was now also coughing up blood. She was very frightened of what might happen to her. Sarah consoled her as best she could, but could offer no respite. She held her tightly as her friend alternately coughed and sobbed uncontrollably.

They both worked in the kitchen and it was clear that Sarah Murray was not up to heavy physical work. Sarah tried her best to cover up her friend's weakness, by taking on the more strenuous tasks, leaving her the more simple jobs. She found herself doing more and more and by the time the day's work was finished, she was dog tired and hardly able to stand up. Even so, she frequently had to support her friend on their walk back to the ward.

She was beside herself as, over the days, Sarah Murray slowly faded away. She stayed in her bed with her most nights, holding her close to comfort her. As time went on, she became aware that her friend's breathing was becoming very short and irregular and she was subject to night sweats which would force Sarah to back away from her. But, despite Sarah's devout attentions, there was little she could do to stop the deterioration. Each day that went by she seemed a little weaker.

On the morning of Thursday 31st December, Sarah had been sleeping in her friend's bed, cuddling her to sooth her violent coughing, which had been disturbing the other women in the ward. She awoke to the feeling of a warm wetness on her arms. She sat up and was horrified to see that her arms were covered in blood, she screamed and leaped out of the bed. She stood there, blood covering her front and dripping from her arms. A younger woman in the bed opposite let out a loud screech at the terrible sight of her. Just then, the ward door was unlocked and the thin woman strode in. She was about to shout something, when she spotted Sarah. Her mouth fell open when she saw the blood and she rushed out of the ward. She returned a few minutes later, accompanied by the Matron, Louisa Slee and a nurse, called Mary Collis. They soon established that the blood was from Sarah Murray, who was taken from the ward. Sarah Valentine was escorted to the washrooms to clean up.

The rest of the day Sarah Valentine spent in a virtual coma. She worked in the kitchen, more by the instinct of ritualistic familiarity, than any conscious will. She was desperately worried about her friend.

Just before night bell, the nurse Mary Collis was visiting the ward to tend to a wound one of the women had sustained during the day. Sarah ran over to her anxious for news about Sarah Murray.

The nurse started to say something, then wheezed and started to cough. After a few minutes, the coughing died down and she said. "Yer mean the girl coughing up blood?"

"Yes," said Sarah, "she's my best friend and I'm very worried for her."

The nurse looked at her for a moment, a hand clutched to her chest as she started wheezing again. Sarah waited for news. The second fit of wheezing and coughing died down. "She died soon as we got 'er to the sick ward," the nurse finally said, "consumption [Tuberculosis] they all die of that," she added.

But Sarah was not listening to her. She was in shock. Sarah Murray was so full of life. Happy, always laughing. How could she be dead? Stunned, she walked back across the ward and collapsed on her bed. She cried her heart out. All she could think of was the clumsy tousle haired girl with the bubbling, effusive character who brought light and fun wherever she was. Her light had been extinguished. She would laugh no more.

CHAPTER 24

The Faux Pas, 1841

IN THE NEW Year of 1841, the death of her best friend had hit Sarah hard. When she had let her baby Edwin go, she had felt part of her life go with him. Now, it was happening again, and so soon after. The double blow was too much for her to bear and for the next month she was inconsolable. Most evenings she spent weeping in her bed unable to cast out the dreadful thoughts. Eventually, she would drift, exhausted, into a fitful sleep. The morning bell would drag her from unconsciousness with a painful jolt. The days were spent in a dull cloud, blindly following the Workhouse routine. She was now more automaton than ever.

It was during one of her occasional spells in the laundry room, that she talked to Mary Durrand, the laundress, about her friend Sarah Murray and the nurse Mary Collis's verdict on her death. At this Mary Durrand burst into a peal of laughter. "Nurse!" she exclaimed, "you call that Mary Collis a nurse!" She was overcome in a paroxysm of laughter punctuated with fits of coughing. "She's no more a nurse than I am the Queen of England!"

"But, she took her to the sick ward to look after her," said Sarah.

"Look after her," said the laundress, "kill 'er more like. She's a pauper, just like you and me. She don't know how to nurse anyone."

SARAH VALENTINE. NO GREAT EXPECTATIONS

Sarah was quiet for a while, trying to come to terms with what she had been told. It made her even sadder to think that her friend might have died through lack of care.

As the days rolled on, Sarah endured the Workhouse routine, maintaining a constant sad, distant and melancholy air. Most evenings she cried herself to sleep. It seemed to her that life just wasn't worth living. She barely noticed the days passing by. She felt at her lowest ebb.

At the end of January 1841, came a visit from the Church Wardens. Their objective was to get as many of the able bodied inmates into work as possible. Sarah was taken before them and they questioned her about what work she had done before. She told them that it had mostly been as a servant girl.

After 56 days in the Workhouse, on Tuesday 2nd February 1841 Sarah was collected from the kitchen by the thin woman. "We 'ave some very fine people arriving this morning," she said, "they are looking for a domestic servant girl and I am to take yer to them. These people are very posh. They usually have a living in Maid of all Work, but she was indiscrete so they got rid of her. Their usual agency can't get a permanent for them for some time, so they 'ave come here to see what we can offer. And very particular they are!" she added with feeling. "So be on yer best behaviour!"

She was taken to a side room and told to wait. The thin woman returned with Sarah's dress and shoes. She was told to change out of the Workhouse uniform, put her own clothes on and tidy herself up as best she could, to put in a good appearance. This she did, but when the thin woman returned, she stared horrified at Sarah who was standing there in the badly worn dress and large mis-matched scruffy shoes that had been donated to her. Pursing her lips, the thin woman disappeared, shortly to return with a slightly better dress and a pair of black Workhouse shoes that, although worn, did at least have the merit of being a matched pair. As she removed her old dress she felt Freddy's poesy ring in the pocket. She was tempted to leave it there as it awakened bad memories, but in the end she transferred it to the pocket of her new dress. Thus attired, Sarah presented a slightly better sight. She was told to sit down and wait.

About an hour later, the thin woman appeared at the door and she was taken to the Master's office. The thin woman knocked on the door and she heard the Master shout. "Come!"

The thin woman opened the door and pushed Sarah in, closing it behind her. Sarah walked up to the Master's desk and tried a clumsy curtsy. The Master grunted and turned away from her. Following the direction of his gaze, Sarah saw two chairs, side by side. Sitting on the chairs were a large woman in a huge expanse of a dress, holding a pair of glasses on a stick and a younger girl, of similar look, probably her daughter, sitting on the chair next to her. "This is the girl I told you about, I believe that she does have some experience of domestic service."

With a loud "Hurrumph!" Of disbelief, the woman in the voluminous dress looked Sarah up and down, a sour expression on her face, whilst her daughter glared malevolently at her. The woman rose from her seat, walked up to Sarah and looked closely at her hair with her glasses pressed to her face. She turned to the Master. "Is this girl clean?" she asked, then added, "I have never availed myself of a Workhouse girl before, but one must do one's bit for the paupers."

"She is perfectly clean," said the Master, "we take particular care with nits and the like."

"She looks quite shabby to me!" the daughter said in a high pitched voice.

Sarah was feeling quite degraded as these people passed disparaging remarks about her. They treated her as if she did not exist.

Eventually, it was agreed that this woman would take Sarah into service. That settled, the two women rose and swept out the door. Sarah was unsure what to do next until the Master shouted. "Move along girl! Get away with you!"

She followed the women down the hall and out of the Workhouse main door. Just outside, she saw a gleaming black horse drawn coach. The two women walked up to the parked coach. The driver immediately dismounted, from his high seat, lowered some steps at the side of the coach and assisted them inside. Their voluminous dresses filled the inside completely and Sarah stood on the pavement not knowing what was expected of her. "Get up with the driver girl!" shouted the daughter.

The driver mounted his seat and pulled Sarah up beside him. He looked about the same age as her father, perhaps a bit older, with a heavily lined parchment like face, which had clearly weathered many winters out in the elements. He was dressed in a black frock coat with a tall black leather hat. He smiled at Sarah, revealing a few remaining black teeth. He released the brake and urged the horse forward. Soon they were rattling north, up the Kingsland Road. They clattered across the Kingsland Road Bridge over the Regent's Canal, where Sarah had fallen in. Soon she found herself travelling through a new and unknown countryside, well beyond the limits of where she had been before.

This was the first time that Sarah had been on any form of transport. With little money, her only method of getting anywhere was to walk, no matter how far the distance. From her perch, high above the road, she felt like a queen; it was with an effort that she prevented herself from waving at the people on the pavement. She dearly hoped that she would pass someone she knew. She would have taken great delight in being seen transported in such a grand manner. Unfortunately, she was not so lucky. After a while, they passed a little green on their left. Sarah asked the driver where they were. He said the green was called Kingsland Green and they veered left round the green, taking the left hand fork, still driving northwards away from London. She found out from the driver that they were heading for Newington Green. After a while they turned suddenly to their left and passed a church.

Sarah was carefully noting the way, anxious to know where she was bound, she was also conscious of a change in the landscape, it was getting more countrified, with more green spaces. She was also very aware of the change in aroma as they moved further away from town, it smelt altogether more pleasant. The early part of her life had been spent in the slums of Whitechapel, where the predominant smell was that of raw sewage. Shoreditch and Bethnal Green smelled mainly of the many animals kept by the residents: cows, pigs, chickens and ducks. Now her nose was greeted by the more pleasant, fresh country air; an entirely new experience for her.

Soon she saw that they were entering a lovely little village, with a handsome square, surrounded by grand houses and neat rows of tall trees. She could see squirrels running along the branches; birds flitted from tree to tree. It was the most wonderful sight she had ever seen in her life. She found herself wondering what it must be like to live in such a splendid place.

They pulled up outside a large house, fronting the road. It had a wide gleaming black door bounded on either side by tall stone pillars. Four wide, deep stone steps led up to the door. Sarah eyed the wide expanse of steps carefully; something told her that, likely as not, she would end up having to scrub them clean at some point in the not too distant future.

Suddenly, the door swung open and a short, plump woman in a maid's uniform emerged. The driver jumped down and opened the carriage door. He lowered the steps and, with some difficulty, the two ladies extricated themselves and walked into the house, without a backward glance.

The maid walked up to the coach and looked at Sarah. "You're the new Maid of all Work then?" she asked.

"Er yes," answered Sarah, completely out of her depth.

"Come with me then!" said the maid sharply.

Sarah clambered down from her seat and followed the maid indoors. The hall was wide and high, with a large curved wooden staircase at one end. Of the two ladies, there was no sign. She followed the maid down the hall and through a door round the back of the staircase. Just inside the door, the maid stopped and turned to face Sarah. "Under no circumstances are you to enter the hall or mount the staircase unless specifically instructed!" she said sternly.

Sarah nodded.

"Today you will assist cook in the kitchen," the maid said, "follow me."

Sarah followed the maid through two further doors and down some worn stone steps. Kitchen smells assailed her nostrils, and soon she found herself in a small, but quite well appointed, kitchen. The maid led her up to a very large woman wearing a heavily stained apron, of indeterminate colour.

"The new Maid of all Work," she said simply. Then turned on her heel and left the kitchen at a smart walk, as if her continued presence there would be beneath her dignity.

The cook ignored her and stared at Sarah. Sarah looked up into a large florid face, covered in a patchwork of red veins.

"About time!" the cook snarled, "I can't be expected to do everything round 'ere!"

She grabbed Sarah by the arm and dragged her to a sink overflowing with a mountain of cutlery. "Get to work cleanin' that lot!" she said, "and when yer finished there's them ter do," she added pointing to an even bigger pile of pots, pans and crockery.

Sarah sighed, at least this was familiar territory. She rolled up her sleeves and set to work.

It was immediately clear to Sarah that the cook was very lazy. The kitchen was a mess. Even the Workhouse kitchen, though much bigger, was a palace compared to this place. She spent the whole day cleaning; it was a never ending task. Each meal of the day added to the mess and she was finding it difficult to keep up as she was also expected to assist the cook in the preparation of the meals. By the end of the day she was absolutely exhausted and ready to collapse. She had also not eaten and was starving hungry. She saw that the cook was taking off her apron, indicating the end of her day. She walked up to her. "Cook, ma'am," she started weekly, "what am I to do. I'm hungry?"

The cook looked at her. "You've not bin in service long have yer?" she said.

"No ma'am," Sarah said.

"You can eat the bread, and whatever food is left at the end of the day. You can take water from the well out back. Take anything else and I'll thrash yer!" she added with a snarl.

"Where do I sleep?" said Sarah.

The cook took her over to a cupboard in the corner of the kitchen and opened the door. Inside was a small space, no more than three feet high and four feet deep. A straw mattress lay on the floor. "You sleep in there!" said the cook. And with that turned and strode from the kitchen.

Sarah stared with dismay at the dark cubby hole that had now become her bedroom; it was barely large enough for a dog. Memory flooded back of the lovely bedroom she had enjoyed at her last employment; there was no comparison. But she was very tired from her day's toil and clambered awkwardly in and lay curled up on the mattress; she was soon fast asleep.

Early the next morning, she was rudely awakened by the door to her cubby hole bedroom being wrenched open. The cook's large fleshy red face glared in at her. "Get up!" she shouted, "there's work ter do!"

Rubbing the sleep from her eyes, Sarah squeezed out of the cupboard and tried to stand up straight. She yelped as a stabbing pain shot up her back; she had been forced to curl up in order to fit in the cupboard and her body was now complaining at being straightened up. After moving around for a while, her aching muscles eased a little.

Over the next few days Sarah got used to the ritual of work. The cook drove her mercilessly and she seldom had a single moment to herself. It also became clear that the cook had a nasty temperament and was not averse to hitting Sarah if her work was felt to be not up to the Master's exacting standards. At the end of the day, it was frequently the case that Sarah would not just be tired, but also battered and bruised where she had been viciously beaten with the cook's favourite heavy wooden spoon. It reached the stage where her little cubby hole became a welcome haven.

When Sunday arrived, she found out that it was a general cleaning day. The Master and his family went to the local church and then to the grand estate of Peter De Beauvior, Lord of Balmes; they would not return until late. During their absence, the whole house was given a clean up.

It did not surprise Sarah to find herself, bucket and brush in hand, scrubbing the massive stone steps that she had observed on her arrival. This was followed by a remorseless array of many and varied cleaning tasks. The workforce carrying out all of this work appeared to consist of herself and a young lad, about her own age. From him, Sarah learned that the cook, the maid and a male servant usually took the opportunity of the Master's absence to spend a little time at the nearby Golden Lion Tavern.

The cook put in an appearance later in the day to inspect Sarah's work. Her even ruddier face and worse temper indicated the amount of beverage she had supped at the Golden Lion. She laid into Sarah with her wooden spoon and made her scrub the front steps again, saying. "The Master's particular about the front step. Says it tells the whole neighbourhood of the important standing of the family. He's very particular about keeping up appearances."

It was late in the day before Sarah finished her tasks. No meals had been cooked as the household had been out all the day so there was no left-over food for her to eat. She had found a little discarded stale bread, but nothing substantial. She was thoroughly exhausted, dead on her feet, starving hungry and hurting from the cooks beating's. She crawled into her small cubby hole and, despite her pain, was soon deep asleep.

Over the next few weeks the merciless, unending labour continued. Then, one morning, she was, once again, dragged from her slumbers by the cook. But today was to be different, for it was the household washday. The cook led Sarah to a basement room off the kitchen where she was presented with a massive pile of laundry, which had been deposited there by the maid. A short while later, she found herself up to her elbows in soapy water, washing various items of clothing and bed linen. She sighed to herself, she had expected better. She had arrived by grand coach, to work for people of a higher class than she had ever encountered before, but here she was, back to scrubbing clothes. Moreover, she had been used to doing this for more modest tradesmen, with far fewer items to wash than the mountain before her.

After several hours, she had a pile of wet laundry to dry. There was no one about to ask what to do with it, so she decided to act on her own initiative and do what she usually did at the Workhouse, namely hang it out to dry. Finding a large wicker basket, she loaded washing into it and lugged it out through the kitchen into the garden; it was a large and beautiful garden, with trees and bushes of all types. But, though she looked long and hard, she could see no sign of a washing line on which to hang the wet laundry. There was still no sign of anyone to ask of, so she figured that they probably put the line away somewhere when not in use. She spotted a wooden shed in one corner of the garden. Walking over to it, she opened the door and looked around inside. After a few minutes searching around, she found a length of rope, coiled neatly in a corner. Ah, she thought, this must be the line. Picking it up she walked back out into the garden; now where to put it out? There was nowhere obvious. Then she spotted a fence, bordering the neighbour's garden. She could use one of the fence posts for one end of the line, but what about the other? Then she saw the tree, one of its branches hung down and would make a fine tether for the other end. A few minutes later and Sarah was proudly standing back and admiring her handiwork; it may not be where they usually put the line, but it would do the job admirably.

Half an hour later and she had put nearly all the washing out on her makeshift line; it made a pretty sight, flapping and fluttering in the breeze. Suddenly, a face appeared over the fence; it was that of a middle aged woman, wearing a pretty bonnet. However, her face was far from pretty. She wore an astonished expression, and at the sight of all the washing fluttering in the breeze let out a screech, followed by a howl of pain as she fell off whatever it was she had been standing on to gain the height to see over the fence. Sarah was puzzled as to what had so upset the woman. She initially thought that her choice of the fence post to anchor her washing line had upset her, but that seemed preposterous.

She was still puzzling over the woman's strange actions, when she heard a bellow of rage from behind her. She turned around and an even more strange sight greeted her. Her employer, the large lady in the voluminous dress, was running across the garden towards her. She was followed by her daughter, the plump little maid, and the cook in her dirty uniform, complete with white hat. As Sarah watched, the large woman took a tumble, her bonnet flew off and she rolled, head over heels, crinoline flying in all directions. To Sarah's astonishment, the woman completely ignored the fall and staggered to her feet to continue her run across the grass. The pack of runners reached Sarah and, completely ignoring her, they ran past towards the washing line. On reaching it they set about ripping the wet laundry off the line like wild dogs. Sarah had to pinch herself to make sure that she was not dreaming. The sight of these elegant ladies grabbing handfuls of wet laundry made her wonder if she had not ventured into some mad house.

Within seconds all the laundry had been removed from the line and lay on the ground.

Sarah was still standing, rooted to the spot, when the daughter of her employer walked up to her. On reaching her, she slapped Sarah hard across the face; Sarah took a pace back, startled by the sting of the blow. "How dare you shame us this way!" screamed the daughter, rage making her face red.

Sarah took another pace back; it was clear that this girl was more than prepared to strike her again. But instead, the daughter burst into a flood of tears and ran into the house. The rest of the pack of runners followed her back to the house; all pointedly ignored Sarah, save the maid. She walked up to her and, after a moment catching her breath, said. "Pick up that washing. Take it back to the laundry room and wash it again! And, *take that line down!*" Then, after giving Sarah a withering look, she followed the others back to the house.

Completely baffled by what had just taken place, Sarah meekly picked up the wicker basket and started to gather up the laundry, which had been scattered in all directions across the lawn.

Sarah was completely unaware of the sheer magnitude of her faux pas. At this time, the populous was rigidly divided into three broad classes: The upper class, represented by the nobility. The middle class, represented by a wide range of businessmen and artisans. And finally, the working class, which covered labourers and working people usually earning less than £100 per year. There was a sub-class, below the working class, into which Workhouse inmates, street paupers and beggars fitted.

The classes were rigidly defined by certain measures, but the boundaries were sometimes blurred. For instance, the upper class was defined by rank. However, the third or fourth son of a minor Lord might have to survive on, say a few hundred pounds per year, or less; his elder siblings inheriting the land and such wealth as there was. Whereas, the upper middle class, rich industrialists, generated huge wealth gained through exploitation of the rapidly developing technologies of nineteenth century England. They built massive country mansions and great town houses which far eclipsed those of the lower nobility.

The lower middle class was very readily categorized by appearance, behaviour and job (if any), but not specifically by income. Indeed, a labouring man may well earn more than a lowly clerk in the city. But the clerk would insist that he firmly sat in the middle class, by virtue of his 'elevated' profession and the manual labourer would sit firmly in the labouring, or working, class. Attempts to move out of the working class were usually treated with derision and generally regarded as impossible. You were born into your class and there you remained, for life.

Of them all, the middle class was the most wide-ranging and complicated to categorise. Most of the media segregated the 'layers' of the middle classes by annual income. The vast majority of the middle class were the humble clerks and city workers, many of whom walked vast distances into central London, from the 'suburbs', and earned less than £100 per year. Other 'layers' were established, up to the upper realms of the middle class, where annual income was £1000 or more. All the classes had rigid codes of conduct, befitting their status, and woe betide any who stepped outside those codes.

Residents in the upper middle class area where Sarah's employers lived had their specific codes of conduct, befitting their status. These codes of conduct were cast in stone and daily reinforced by the writings of many eminent journalists of the time. One of the things that was *never*, under any circumstances, done in upper middle class neighbourhoods, was to hang one's washing on a line in the garden, to be openly viewed by one's neighbours. To do so would be to describe the offending householder as low and vulgar. They would *immediately* be shunned by all civilised society. They would be vilified, by their peers, for dragging down the whole area; in reality, the only options thereafter, for the householder, would be emigration, or suicide.

Sarah was summoned to the front parlour. The Master of the house stood rigid in the middle of the room, his face set in stone, a mask of fury. His wife and daughter stood by the front window weeping into their handkerchiefs; they were mortified over their shaming by Sarah. The Master of the house's vilification of her was brief, cutting and merciless. Under his instructions, Sarah was taken away to the laundry room, where the cook took a horse whip to her. She was thrashed across the back until her dress was in tatters and blood splattered the walls. She was then sent sobbing from the house.

For a while she wandered aimlessly through the streets. She had no bonnet or shawl and her torn dress and bloodied back attracted many curious stares and remarks from passers by; she took no notice of them, merely staring fixedly ahead of her.

In the evening, the weather turned cold and a drizzle of rain fell. She continued to walk aimlessly. Her hair was matted and plastered to her face with the rainwater, her dress was sodden, clinging to her skin; she presented a pitiful figure. Without thinking, almost by instinct, she had been retracing the route the coach had taken and she ended up at the end of the Hackney Road where, too tired to walk any further, she sat down in the doorway of St Leonard's Church. Completely exhausted, she fell into a slumber; she dozed fitfully, assailed by dreadful dreams of pain and torture.

The following morning, Tuesday 2nd March 1841, the incumbent of St Leonard's Church, the Reverend John Williams found her lying there propped against his church door, like an abandoned doll.

Seeing the whipping injuries to her back he was appalled and took her inside. One of the church workers was summoned and she bathed Sarah's wounds and an old shawl was found to cover her shredded dress. She was taken to the Shoreditch Workhouse and admitted to the sick ward. It had not changed since the last time Sarah was there, after falling in the Regents Canal. It was still jammed full of sick and feverish women, coughing and moaning in pain. The intense smell was the same, a mixture of sweaty bodies, urine and excreta. She could barely breathe the air; she felt an urge to vomit.

The nurse Eliza Ribnell immediately recognised Sarah and was appalled when she saw the whip marks on Sarah's back. Although she had had no formal medical training and was an inmate of the Workhouse herself, she did her best to tend to Sarah's injuries; she found herself feeling sorry for her obvious suffering and made a point of talking to her to help raise her spirits.

It was during one of these conversations that Sarah heard Eliza's sad story. She had lost her husband and was left with a young daughter to look after. Unable to find work, she had found herself destitute, walking the streets. The Workhouse was the only option left to her. It was then that Sarah discovered that Eliza's second name was Ribnell; the name Ribnell rang a bell. Then she remembered Beth Ribnell, the young girl in ward 12 who had occupied the bed next to her missing sister Charlotte. She remembered one of the girls telling her that Beth's mother was a nurse in the Workhouse womens' sick ward. With sudden hope in her heart, she asked nurse Eliza Ribnell if she remembered Charlotte Valentine. She replied that she had a vague recollection of a young girl brought into the sick ward some five or six years ago by the Reverend Scott, the Curate of Christ Church Spitalfields. She remembered that the girl had been half frozen to death and had injuries that looked as if she had been severely beaten, but she had not stayed in the sick ward; there was no room at that time, she felt that she might have gone to the girls' room, but had no knowledge of what had happened to her after that. Sarah was horrified at this news and that evening lay in her bed with a heavy heart full of concern for what had happened to her little sister; for the moment, her own sad state had been banished to the back of her mind.

Over the next few days, responding to Eliza's caring attentions, Sarah slowly started to regain some of her old sparkle. The painful memories would be with her for the rest of her life, but she was increasingly able to push them to the back of her mind and get on with the business of living, such as it was.

After 5 terrible days in the sick ward, she was placed in the womens' working ward 16. In the working ward, she was placed in a bed next to a dark skinned girl, about her own age. Sarah observed her closely, she had short black hair and deep black eyes surrounded by deep black bushy eyelashes. She was quite slight in build, not unlike Sarah herself, but she carried herself in a regal upright manner, almost as if she was descended from royalty. Overcome with curiosity Sarah spoke to her. "Hello," she said, in her most engaging manner, "my name's Sarah Valentine."

For a few moments it seemed as if the girl had not heard her. Sarah was just about to repeat herself, when the girl turned to face her directly.

Sarah found the stare from her deep black eyes somewhat unnerving. "I am Jane Navarri," she said simply, in a curious accent.

With nothing further apparently forthcoming, Sarah tried to probe a little more. "You're not from these parts are you?"

There was another momentary silence, as if Jane Navarri was considering her answer. Finally she said. "I have lived more than half my life in your country, but I was born far away from here."

Now Sarah was completely intrigued. She pushed for further information. "Where was that?" she asked.

"India," replied Jane.

Sarah considered this answer. She had no idea where India was. In fact, she knew of few locations beyond Whitechapel and East London.

Further discourse was prevented by the shout from a girl on the other side of the ward, who had been observing them closely. She glared at Sarah. "Whatcha talkin' to 'er for?" she shouted, "she's a blackie, can't yer see!"

Sarah realised that this girl was expressing an all too familiar reaction to foreigners on London's streets. Early Victorian London was becoming ever more popular a place for people from all over to seek work. This meant less work for the indigenous population; a fact that they resented wholeheartedly. The Irish, Germans and other Europeans did not stand out so much. But dark skinned people like Jane Navarri did, and usually bore the brunt of the resentment. Sarah decided that the best course of action was to ignore her. She turned away and quietly addressed Jane. "I think I've seen her before, who is she?"

"That's Maggie Orme," said Jane, a worried expression on her face, "she and a horrible girl called Liz Weston ganged up on me when I was admitted a couple of weeks ago."

Sarah sat up, alarmed at the mention of the dreaded Liz Weston, "she's not in here is she?" she whispered.

"No," said Jane, "She was sent to the House of Correction for beating an old woman up very badly."

"Thank God for that!" said Sarah, mightily relieved that she was not here.

It was as Sarah was glancing at Maggie Orme that she saw a girl she did not want to see again. It was Sophia Crafts and she was walking across the ward directly towards Sarah! She stopped at the foot of Sarah's bed and stood there with her hands on her hips. Sarah was acutely aware of how big she was; with her big face, fleshy lips and dark matted lank hair she looked more like a man than a girl. She bent down and pushed her face into Sarah's. Alarmed, Sarah stared into her pig like eyes and held her breath. "We don't talk to shit like 'er!" she bellowed, pointing at Jane Navarri. With a warning glare she turned and moved off.

Sarah realised that she was still holding her breath and gasped, sucking air in. She gave a frightened look at Jane.

CHAPTER 25

Sarah The Benefactor, 1841

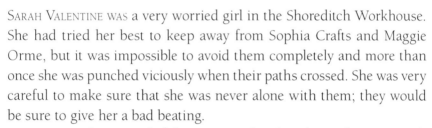

SARAH VALENTINE WAS a very worried girl in the Shoreditch Workhouse. She had tried her best to keep away from Sophia Crafts and Maggie Orme, but it was impossible to avoid them completely and more than once she was punched viciously when their paths crossed. She was very careful to make sure that she was never alone with them; they would be sure to give her a bad beating.

It was with some relief that, on Tuesday the 9th March 1841, Sarah was told that she had been found a position as a servant, to an elderly couple. When she was preparing to leave, the dress that she had worn, when she was admitted, was given back to her, she found it to be too torn and bloodstained from her whipping to be serviceable. As she was examining it, she felt a lump on one side, which transpired to be Freddy's poesy ring, still in her pocket. She was given a well worn faded cotton dress and an old patched shawl for her to wear and she put the ring in the pocket of her replacement dress.

Her new employers were not particularly rich and maintained a run down house just off the Bethnal Green Road. It was not a live-in position, so she was forced to seek accommodation and found herself in Edward Street seeking out the Freestones once again. She knocked on the door and it was answered by Jane Freestone. Jane was pleased to see Sarah and invited her in. They spent some time talking about what had happened to them since they last met. Inevitably, the subject of Sarah's baby Edwin came up and she tearfully told Jane what had transpired. Jane was sympathetic and assured Sarah that she had done the best thing for her child. However, that did nothing to appease Sarah's sense of loss. When the topic of Sarah's accommodation came up, she discovered that Jane now found herself spending most of her time looking after baby Thomas, who was six-months-old. This meant that she was no longer able to help her costermonger husband, who was struggling to earn enough money to support them all.

It transpired that they were happy to take her in, particularly as she had a job and could pay her share of the rent. So, Sarah placed her small bundle of belongings on the floor and took up her old position in the corner.

She did not need to start her new job until the next day, so she set out to visit the tailor's shop and get some news of her son Edwin from George Linford. When she arrived at the tailor's, she looked in the front window and saw that George Linford was alone in the shop. She pushed the door open and looked in; he was surprised to see her, but walked over and stepped outside to talk with her. They stood in Goldsmiths Place for a moment, looking at each other. Sarah was conscious of how shabby she looked in her old well worn clothing and was about to say something about her appearance when she noticed the sad expression on George Linford's face. "Is there something wrong?" she asked, getting suddenly worried that something might have happened to Edwin, "is Edwin alright?"

He gave a weak smile, "yes, Edwin is doing fine."

"What is it then?"

He didn't speak for a moment then, his eyes watering over, he told Sarah that their little girl, Mary Ann Adelaide Linford had died last week and they had just buried her at St Mary's Haggerstone. Sarah felt sorry for him, she remembered the frail little girl, sitting in the corner of their parlour. Silence fell between them again.

It was Sarah who broke it. "Can I see my son?" she asked.

George Linford's face hardened, "I'm afraid that won't be possible just yet. Not until he gets a bit older."

"But why?" Sarah exclaimed; shock on her face.

George Linford was clearly uncomfortable with this conversation and kept shuffling his feet. "Well," he finally said, "Jane is insistent that he not be confused at his young age by having two mothers. She wants you to stay away until he is old enough to understand the situation."

Sarah put her hand to her mouth in horror, "no! you can't stop me from seeing my own son!"

He had a sorrowful expression on his face as he replied, "I'm sorry, but she will not permit you in the house. She is adamant on that point."

Sarah was struck dumb. She turned away from George Linford and walked slowly back down the Hackney Road with tears streaming down her face. He watched her for a few moments then, with a slight shake of his head, he opened the door and entered the shop.

The next morning, a resigned and tired looking Sarah set out for her new employer's house, which was quite a reasonable walk being about half way down the Bethnal Green Road. When she arrived, she found that the only other servant was an elderly cook, who had been with them so long that she was more family than servant.

Her Master and Mistress were kindly but demanding. Their age was such that they could do little for themselves and Sarah found that her work was quite extensive. It was very clear from the outset that, as she was by far the youngest member of the household, she would be expected to bear the brunt of the work.

It was early in March and the evenings were still a little cold for the elderly inhabitants and Sarah's first job of the day would be to clean out five fireplaces. This would involve clearing out the ashes and cinders from the night before, cleaning the fireplace surround and polishing the cast iron grate with black lead. This was a dirty job and usually resulted in getting the thick oily black lead all over her. The fireplaces were then laid with paper, wood and coal, ready to be lit. She would also need to fill the coal scuttles with fresh coal, gathered from the coal cellar. As three of the fireplaces were upstairs, this meant hauling the scuttles up and down the extensive staircase. She would then be expected to clean the dining room, hall, study and, of course, the all important front steps.

It was also her responsibility to polish the furniture, polish the brass, clean the windows, brush the curtains and carpets and see to the beds.

She was also expected to help out in the kitchen, where the lazy old cook was always complaining of her joints which, 'ached something terrible'. This usually meant that Sarah would have to clean all the cutlery. The knives were a particular problem as they were old silver and discoloured readily with each use, requiring extensive rubbing with emery powder. This was a tedious and dirty job that the cook was doubtless very happy to pass to Sarah. Sarah also had to do all the food preparation, peeling potatoes, cleaning greens, trimming meat, plucking chickens. All under the strict supervision of the cook, who would be sitting down, resting her joints and drinking tea. Although the added labour was very draining, the one good thing to come out of this chore was that Sarah started to get a good education in cooking. In particular, the cook was very canny in stretching the household budget as far as possible. From her, Sarah learned that the cheapest butcher's meat was cow's cheek, sheep's head, liver and ox heart. The cheapest cuts of meat were from the thick flank and round, but you had to be sure not to pay more than seven pence a pound or you'd be lining your butcher's pockets. These cuts would need long slow cooking to make the best of them.

Once a month, on a Saturday morning, the Master and Mistress would take a bath in their bedrooms. This was a particularly onerous task for Sarah. The Master and Mistress had separate bedrooms and each had to have a separate tub of water. This entailed hauling the bath tubs up the stairs from the washroom, at the back of the kitchen, where they were kept. Then filling them up with hot water, which had to be boiled and tediously carried up the stairs, bucketful by bucketful. After their baths, the dirty water had to be carried back down again and the empty baths returned to the washroom. Sarah had to accomplish this entirely by herself as there was no other help available.

The only concession to her was on the monthly washday, when the Master condescendingly employed a Saturday Girl to help Sarah wash all the garments, cloths and bed linen. One Saturday washday, Sarah got a pleasant surprise when she opened the front door to admit the

Saturday Girl, only to find out it was Sarah Chamberlain, her old friend from the Workhouse. For once the washday went by quite quickly as the two girls nattered away about their experiences since they had last met, some four years ago, at the old lady's 'employment bureau' on the Kingsland Road.

Whilst Sarah and her friend from the Workhouse were pounding away at the tubs of washing, the Shoreditch Relieving Officer, John Coste and his friend the Beadle were enjoying their customary beverage in the Cock and Magpie Tavern on the corner of Worship Street and Wilson Street.

The Beadle was looking closely at his friend who wore a worried frown. "What's the matter John?" he asked, "You've been quite maudlin for days now."

John Coste looked up from his ale. "It's those damnable girls, I'm at my whit's end with them."

The Beadle couldn't resist a wry smile. "Yes," he said, "I've got two of 'em locked up in the Station House cells. That Eliza Waghorn and Elizabeth Prior."

"Yes," agreed John Coste, "Those two are pretty bad and are where they belong, but that awful Elizabeth Weston beat up a woman in the House so badly that we put her before a Magistrate and she was sent to the House of Correction. And I despair of that Sophia Crafts. Do you know that she attacked two male orderlies who were trying to stop her beating up a coloured girl called Jane Navarri. Damn near took the eyes out of one of them. We managed to get the coloured girl a position in service, but that Sophia Crafts continued to cause so much trouble that we sent her to the Magistrates and now she is in the House of Correction as well.

"Well at least that's one more of 'em off the streets," remarked the Beadle.

"Huh!" said the Relieving Officer, "Their just the tip of the iceberg, there are plenty more; take Mary Murphy she's the daughter of an unmarried prostitute, been in and out of the Workhouse, real troublemaker, and there's Magdalene Orme, stirs up trouble, Caroline Copeland, another troublemaker, I could go on." He broke off in despair.

"I think we need another drink," said the Beadle getting up and walking to the bar.

Sarah received two shillings and six pence a week for her labours, one shilling and three pence of which she gave to the Freestones for her share of the rent. This left her with one shilling and three pence a week. This was not a great sum, but she was so tired after a gruelling day's labour that she staggered home and fell asleep immediately. In the morning, she forced herself awake and rushed straight off to her work. There was so much work to do that she could not even take a Sunday afternoon off. The result of this was that she had little time to spend her meagre earnings. The cook allowed her the leftover scraps from the meals to eat and she was allowed tea to drink, so she did not need to buy food. She had dropped by Petticoat Lane one evening and got herself a better dress, shawl and bonnet, but by September, after six months of heavy work, she had amassed a veritable fortune of twenty one shillings; one whole guinea. It was so much money that she had spent a penny on an old second hand purse to keep it all in, together with Freddy's poesy ring. She dare not leave it anywhere and kept it tucked deep in her dress pocket. Carrying it around with her seemed more trouble than it was worth, but having led such a frugal existence all her life she had no idea what she might spend it on.

It was November 1841, and starting to get quite cold. Sarah had not seen her family for months and had pleaded with the cook to allow her some time off. She was told that she could take the Sunday afternoon off whilst the rest of the household went to church, but she would have to be back in the evening to help the cook to prepare the evening meal.

So, that Sunday, she set off down the Bethnal Green Road and turned left down Brick Lane towards Whitechapel. Reaching Wentworth Street she turned right and started to walk down it. After a few minutes she was approaching the Stak Tavern on her left. There was a group of noisy louts hanging about outside, jostling each other and blocking the pavement. She decided to cross over to the other side to get past them. As she drew level with the front of the tavern, they started shouting and whistling at her.

"How much dearie?" And "I've got a ha'penny, you can turn a trick for that!"

She ignored them and quickened her pace. After a while, they lost interest in her and went back to jostling each other. She crossed back over the road and soon reached the narrow alleyway that led to the top end of Essex Street. As she dodged around the piles of rubbish, the familiar rancid smell of raw sewage assaulted her nostrils. Passing the Throwstik's Tavern she turned into the narrow low entrance to Martins Court. As she passed by Nell's house, she stepped round a dead cat being ripped apart by a mixture of rodents and birds. Then she spotted Nell's daughter Beth standing just inside the doorway. Sarah shouted a greeting and Beth walked over; the two of them chatted, catching up on local news. There were several scruffy children, some almost naked, running round the court. A slightly older girl, with dark tangled hair hanging lankly over a filthy face and dirty scarred bare feet, detached herself from the group of children and ran over to join Sarah and Beth. Sarah stared at the girl's filthy black face and tattered dress with some distain. Then, with a sudden shock, she realised that it was her younger sister Caroline! She could not believe the wretched state that her sister was in.

After saying goodbye to Beth, Sarah walked with her sister to No. 5, the door was standing open and she looked in. She was appalled at the state of the place. There were no chairs and no table. All they had to sit on was their two straw mattresses. The grate was empty, save for a handful of coal dust. She looked in horror at her family assembled in the small room. Her mother, sister Mary and baby Henry were all in rags, just as bad as Caroline's; Sarah was stunned at the state of them all. After intense questioning, Sarah finally discovered that the table and chairs had fallen apart and been used for a fire. Money was particularly tight, as Jimmy was not living with them and her father didn't bring much home. After the rent had been paid and some food purchased, there was little left for furniture and clothes. Sarah rather suspected that the reason for this latter fact was that he spent too much time and money drinking with his mates, but she did not pursue the issue. She was incensed at the terrible state of her family.

Then, sudden realisation dawned on her, she had the means to change their situation; it seemed a good thing to do. So, her resolve settled, she stormed out the door and went round to Nell's room. She begged her to look after Baby Henry and Mary for a while and asked if she could 'borrow' Beth, who was a big sturdy girl. Then, she marched her mother, Beth and Caroline down to the pawnbrokers at the bottom of Essex Street, number 105 on the corner of the High Street. Rummaging around the 'stock', she found a serviceable table, some chairs and a pretty crochet table cloth, to which she added a couple of candlesticks and a picture of a country scene which rather took her fancy. Then, she noticed a couple of china flower vases; she recalled her mother's sadness at the loss of her grandmother's vases, so added them to her pile of goods. After heavy negotiations with the proprietor, a price was agreed. Much to her mother's surprise, Sarah took the money out of her purse and paid for it all. They then gathered up the items and, helped by the pawnbroker's son, lugged them back up Essex Street to Martins Court, where the table and chairs were set down in her mother's room. Sarah set the white crochet cloth on the table and arranged the candlesticks, whilst the pawnbroker's son mounted the picture on the wall and Sarah's mother set the vases on the window ledge.

Sarah gave the pawnbroker's son two halfpennys for his trouble, thanked Beth for her help and ushered her mother and Caroline out once more. This time they walked to the top of Essex Street and turned left down Wentworth Street. Reaching Petticoat Lane, Sarah marched them down to the second hand clothing stalls; every form of clothing imaginable was on display. Dozens of dresses were hanging on a myriad of hangers stacked up high in the air. After half an hour of raking around they selected second hand dresses for the girls and Sarah's mother and some items of clothing for Henry. Sarah also selected some worn, but serviceable, shoes for them all; looking at Caroline's matted hair, she added a sturdy comb to the bundle. Raking round the stalls, she also added some candles, Lucifer matches and a bunch of colourful flowers, After paying for all the goods, Sarah marched them all back again. Once back at the house, she ushered Caroline and Mary to the pump in the court and supervised their ablutions, assisting with the removal of the more stubborn, ground-in dirt. She spent some time with her two sisters' hair. Amid much howling and screeching she finally managed to produce two neatly combed heads. She then watched over them whilst they changed into their new outfits. When Sarah walked back into the room her mother had already put on the dress Sarah had bought for her and changed Henry as well. Sarah watched her as she arranged the flowers in the new vases and set them on the window ledge where they caught the rays of the sun. She could see tears running down her mother's face and felt her own eyes watering. Wiping her eyes on the sleeve of her dress, she put candles in the candlesticks and set the Lucifer matches down on the table beside them, ready for the evening. She stepped back and looked round the room, the transformation was incredible. It was no longer an empty hovel, it was a splendid room.

She then ushered them all outside and lined them up in the court where she carefully inspected them. Satisfied that her family could now show their faces to the world, she gathered Nell and her kids, and they all went round to the Throwstik's on the corner for a celebratory drink.

As Sarah bought the drinks, she noticed that the publican, Jane Dyke, was not behind the bar, instead there were a younger couple serving. When she collected her change, she surveyed the few coins remaining from her one guinea. She shrugged her shoulders and handed them to her mother to buy a few coals with. To her mind the money had been put to good use; it had only been burning a hole in her purse anyway.

When they sat down, Sarah asked Nell where Jane Dyke was.

Nell's head immediately shot up and she stared at Sarah for a few moments, then said. "Of course! You don't know do you?"

"Know what?" said Sarah, now quite curious.

Nell then told her the tragic story. Jane had burned herself quite badly and an infection had set in which caused gangrene. She became bedridden and her daughter Ann, with husband Ambrose Everard, had moved in to help with running the tavern. They were evidently the young couple who had served Sarah. Sadly Jane Dyke had died a few months back, in June, and been buried next to her deceased husband in St Mary's. Sarah was saddened by this news as she had fond memories of Jane.

When the drinks were finished, Sarah said her goodbyes and made her way back to her employer's house. But, as she walked, she was harbouring dark thoughts about her father. How could he go out drinking, leaving his family in such a poor state? Then a thin smile crept onto her face as she realised that he would not thank her when he came home and saw the transformed room and his now respectably clothed family and found out that she had been the one to step in and show him up for shirking his responsibilities. Serve him right!

Whilst Sarah, family and friends, were enjoying their drinks in the Throwstik's, the subject of her thoughts, namely her father Jim, was with his mates Tiny, Tom and Tom's son, standing on the bank of the River Thames at Rotherhithe. It was a cold and blustery day. There was a mist in the air and a drizzle of rain was falling. The only reason that they were braving the elements was because of an article in a local paper that the avid reader Tom had noticed. It announced that a rash American, by the name of Samuel Scott, was going to perform daring feats. There was an immense concourse of spectators all jostling for a view of the anticipated proceedings. They were looking up at the topgallant yard of a coal brig moored just off shore.

Suddenly a figure appeared on the yard arm, high above the deck of the brig. Despite the fact that it was blowing a veritable gale, he ran up and down the yard, with no safety rope. After a few minutes of this he positioned himself in the middle of the yard, and placing his head down on the wood, proceeded to stand on his head, with arms and legs above him, flailing in the wind. On several occasions, as gusts of wind swirled round, he seemed in danger of being blown from his perch to almost certain death. However, he survived and, running to the far end of the yard arm, seized upon a rope which he secured to the centre of the yard. He then tied a noose around his neck. This completed, he jumped from the yard, to amazed gasps from the crowd.

"The mad bugger's 'anged hisself!" A man to Jim's right shouted.

The American remained suspended, by his chin, for a few minutes, swinging to and fro in the wind. Then, with great dexterity he pulled himself hand, over hand, back up onto the yard. He stood there, waving his arms high, to intense applause. Then he shouted out to his audience. "Come back tomorrow and you will see me hang myself again."

Some twenty minutes later, now back in the Red Cow Tavern, Jim and his friends were chatting at great length about the events performed by the American. They all regarded him as being completely mad, but they would be back tomorrow to see him perform again.

It was the beginning of December 1841 and Sarah was at the sink, elbow deep in water, busy washing the cutlery. She was so tired that she was almost asleep on her feet. The lazy cook was sitting on a chair at the table, drinking tea, watching her work. Suddenly, the door to the kitchen opened and the Mistress of the house walked in. The cook immediately jumped up and walked over to the sink to make it appear that she was helping Sarah with the washing up; Sarah glared at her. However, the Mistress ignored the cook and asked Sarah to follow her. Her arms dripping water, she followed the Mistress into the front parlour, where the Master of the house was standing in front of the fireplace with an erect posture and arms stiff by his sides. Sarah stood in front of him, dripping on the carpet, wondering what this was all about.

The Master of the house explained to her that they could no longer afford to employ two servants and had decided to dispense with her services. The cook would remain and they would make do with a Saturday Girl to carry out Sarah's duties. At that statement Sarah only just stopped herself from bursting out laughing. 'God help the Saturday Girl' she thought.

She walked back to the kitchen where she saw that the cook had resumed her position sitting at the table still drinking her tea. Looking at the sink, it was abundantly clear that she had done absolutely nothing with the washing up, merely waiting for Sarah to return and resume the chore. She felt the cook's eyes boring into her as she dried her wet arms on a towel and went over and collected her shawl and bonnet from the corner where she had left them. She threw the shawl round her shoulders and was making for the back door, fastening her bonnet, when the cook bellowed out. "Where do yer think your goin'? There's still work to do 'ere!"

Sarah stopped and looked at her. For some strange reason, she actually felt a little sorry for the old woman. So, she just said. "Well you'd better get on with it then. I've been dismissed!"

She would remember that look of absolute horror on the cook's face for a long time to come.

Sarah spent the next few weeks unsuccessfully searching for employment. Her money then ran out and she was unable to continue to pay her share of the rent. With a resigned shrug of her shoulders, she gathered together her few belongings and said a sad farewell to the Freestones'. She found herself out on the street with no money and no prospects of getting any. The weather was freezing cold and she pulled her shawl closely round her shoulders as she walked down Philips Street to the end where she turned right into the Kingsland Road. As she walked down the Kingsland Road, she could hear the sound of the St Leonard's Church bells ringing in the distance. It was Christmas and the pavement was full of people striding purposefully on their way. They all seemed to have places to go, things to do. Occasionally, she was jostled as she meandered aimlessly on her way, uncertain of her purpose. She felt cold to her bones, and very alone. It was not long before she was standing outside the Court House in Worship Street, once again. She paused for a few minutes, undecided what to do, but a sudden flurry of snow blew across her face and made her mind up for her. It would at least be dry in the Workhouse and she was very hungry. So, she made her way to the door and entered the Court House. Some hours later, she had her summons from Magistrate Benett and made her way to the Parish Offices. On entering she beheld the usual scene of bedlam, with all manner of paupers milling around. She made her way to the Office Keeper's desk. There was a girl talking with him and a family standing in line behind her, Sarah fell in behind the family. While she was waiting, she looked at the family in front of her. There was a woman, she took to be the mother, holding a small baby, with three young girls desperately clutching the hem of her dress; the youngest, no more than two-years-old, was crying. Sarah found herself feeling sorry for them and wondering if they had a father; perhaps he had died and that was why they were here. Then the girl who had been talking with the Office Keeper turned round and walked away from his desk. The mother, in front of Sarah, ushered her brood forward and started an animated discourse with the Office Keeper, but Sarah was still looking at the girl walking away, she knew that face from somewhere.

Then, as memory returned, she called out. "Beth! Beth Ribnell, is that you?"

The girl turned round, then recognised Sarah and walked over. "Hello, it's Sarah Valentine isn't it? Did you ever find that sister of yours, Charlotte wasn't it?"

"No," said Sarah, suddenly a little saddened at the memory of Charlotte, "we have no idea what became of her."

They stood and chatted together for a while, until it was Sarah's turn to talk with the Office Keeper. She stepped forward and handed in her summons, then was told to wait.

Two hours later and a little band was walking up Kingsland Road to the Shoreditch Workhouse, chatting amongst themselves. Sarah discovered that the family from the Parish Office were the Driscolls: mother Mary and four little daughters. She talked to Beth Ribnell about her mother, the nurse, who had helped her. At the Workhouse, Beth and the young Driscoll girls went to ward 12 and their mother Mary, with the baby, to a lying-in ward. As she was led away, Mary seemed unhappy at the way the family had been split up.

Sarah was the last of the group to stand in front of the Master, she had been ten months on the street, but he still recognised her as one of his ins-and-outs. It was Wednesday 22nd December 1841 and he was not pleased to see her again. At Christmas time the Workhouse was usually full and this year it was bursting at the seams. The weather had been exceedingly cold and many old and infirm people had descended on the House for shelter and food. There was no room for her in any of the wards and she was given a straw mattress in one of the cold, windy corridors. After only two days she was found a temporary position as a slavey, to help out in a house over the Christmas period. It offered no pay, just food and a roof over her head. The Workhouse Master made it clear to her that she must accept this position, or go out onto the street; there was really no choice in the matter.

At her new employer's house, she was given a lumpy mattress in a corner of the kitchen to sleep on, which meant that she could not retire until all the work had been done and the kitchen was empty. She was back to familiar territory, washing and cleaning an endless supply of pans, dishes and cutlery. She soon discovered that she had been placed here, in one of the Parish Councillor's houses, as a favour to the Workhouse Master, to relieve the strain on the Workhouse accommodation. It was made very clear to her that this Parish Councillor regarded Workhouse inmates as worthless scroungers who prostituted themselves on the good auspices of rate-payer's such as himself. In his esteemed opinion, she should be grateful for some food and a roof over her head. So much for the Christmas spirit.

The year of 1841 ended in a freezing spell of ice and snow; but at least the kitchen was warm.

It was Tuesday 11ᵗʰ January 1842, and Sarah's father Jim, together with Tiny, Tom and Tom's son, were standing on the north bank of the river Thames, looking out at Waterloo Bridge. They were looking at a temporary scaffold structure, some ten feet high, erected above the second arch of the bridge. They were there to see the latest stunt of the mad American Samuel Scott. Like many Londoners of the day, they had been avid followers of his daredevil antics. His notoriety had grown to the extent that there were many thousands of people lining the banks, crowded onto the bridge and in numerous small boats on the river. Jim could not recall so many people out in one place to witness a show. He stamped his freezing feet to ward off the cold winter air.

Suddenly, a figure appeared on the scaffold, to tumultuous applause from the waiting crowd. The figure acknowledged the crowd, waving his arms high in the air. An expectant hush descended. He commenced his routine by repeating his previous daredevil dancing on air acts. He dangled by his feet, from a rope, upside down, swinging, back and forth, across the river. Then, returning to the scaffold platform, he placed a noose around his neck and jumped forward into the air arms spread wide. At the end of the rope's travel, he was brought up short and, after a few seconds swinging back and forth, high over the river, he started to twist and turn, his legs jerking from side to side. To all of the rapt observers he gave a good impression of a man being hanged. The thousands of onlookers shouted with admiration at this realistic performance. Then, one of Samuel Scott's team realised something was terribly wrong. The noose had become tightened round his neck; he really was being hanged!

By the time he was cut down, it was too late, he was dead. Even as he was being carried away, the audience was applauding, thinking it was all part of the act.

Meanwhile Sarah was still working in the Parish Councillor's house. She had been there for three weeks, during which time she was worked ruthlessly and given no time off. She was up at dawn and toiled until late in the night. Her hands were red raw and ragged, with her skin peeling off. By bedtime, she was barely conscious. Sometimes she would collapse where she stood, unable to make it to her mattress. She would fall into a deep sleep on the hard stone floor, unmoving in slumber as if she were in the warmest feather bed. That was until dawn, when the cook arrived to kick her into wakefulness. It was then that she would realise that she had been lying on cold stone all night; her body would be frozen solid, her joints would not move. She would struggle to gain her feet, her circulation grudgingly running the cold stiff blood through her body. All the time the cook would be kicking, pushing and berating her to get on with her chores.

This was the harshest treatment she could ever remember receiving and when, on Saturday 15th January 1842, she was told that she was no longer needed and was sent back to the Workhouse, she almost cried with relief.

Now back in the Shoreditch Workhouse, Sarah was told to share a bed with an older woman called Ann Pontin in the womens' working ward 16. Ann Pontin was a small slightly built woman with thin mousy hair and very pale skin, she had grey watery eyes and a permanent racking cough. She was pleasant enough, but Sarah was not too happy about sharing a bed with her, she seemed very sickly.

On her first evening back in the Workhouse, just before the night bell, they were both sitting on their bed and Sarah was looking round the ward to see if she recognised any of the other inmates. With some alarm, she immediately recognised a girl a few beds down as Maggie Orme, who she was startled to see was glaring malevolently back at her, she quickly looked away. Then, looking across the ward, she spotted an old acquaintance from her previous spell in the Workhouse. It was the dark girl Jane Navarri from, where was it? Yes India, wherever that was. She got up off her bed and walked over to talk to her. She found out, from her, a bit more about Maggie Orme. Apparently, she was the daughter of a costermonger, her parents threw her out because of her bad behaviour and she was generally regarded as trouble for all who came near her. Sarah was alarmed to hear that she had only recently returned to the Workhouse from a spell in the House of Correction for her bad behaviour. Sarah decided to keep her distance, at least as much as she could. As she walked across the ward back to her bed, she became aware of a girl she did not recognise, sitting on a bed under a high window, staring at her with a malignant glare. The girl had short dark hair and was heavily built with a plump. ruddy face which, despite her young age, was already ravaged with prominent veins; a sure sign of excessive consumption of rough spirit. Puzzled by the attention she was getting from this girl, she did her best to ignore it and turned her face away. Then, in horror, she spotted Sophia Crafts, sitting on a bed at the far end of the ward and not far down from her was Kate Copeland, the girl Sarah Murray had warned her about, before she died. Sarah was now quite worried, it seemed like all the rotten apples were now grouped in the same ward with her, it could only spell bad trouble.

Over the next week the atmosphere in the ward grew tense. There was bad feeling hanging in the air. It was so palpable that one could almost touch it. Sophia Crafts seemed to be the ring leader; she was by far the biggest and enjoyed throwing her weight about. Maggie Orme and Kate Copeland needed little encouragement to follow her lead. The evenings, after supper, before the night bell, were the worst as the trio roamed the ward causing trouble with everyone. But it was another girl who was to inflict the first injury on Sarah.

It happened in the kitchen, she was carrying a pan of hot water across the floor to fill one of the sinks, when suddenly a foot came out and tripped her up. She stumbled and fell to the floor on her knees. Hot water spilled out on to her hands, scalding her and her knees were grazed. She looked round to see who had tripped her and saw the same dark haired girl who had glared at her in the ward, on her first arrival. One of the cooks came over and shouted at Sarah for being so clumsy and she was made to clean up the floor.

That evening, still nursing her red swollen hands and scraped knees, Sarah discussed the incident with Jane Navarri and pointed out the girl who had tripped her up. She was sitting on her bed staring at them. Jane told her that the girl was called Mary Murphy. She was generally regarded, by most, as an unpleasant piece of work, she was in and out of the Workhouse and frequently found herself in the Tramps Register. Her usual practice was to leave the Workhouse in the morning, get drunk during the day, earning her drinks by whatever dubious means she could muster, and turning up in the evening, much the worse for drink, to secure a bed for the night. She had already made herself very unpopular with both staff and inmates.

As Sarah walked past Mary Murphy's bed on her way back to her own, she heard her say. "If I was you, I'd be careful who I talked ter."

Sarah stopped and looked at her. Mary Murphy glared back at her. Sarah decided to ignore it and continued on to her own bed and sat down next to Ann Pontin who, she noticed, was looking very pale.

As the days wore on, It became clear to Sarah that the trouble centred around the coloured girl Jane Navarri. Sarah had not concerned herself with any form of hatred for foreigners, but she was well aware of seeing that feeling in others. She resolved that it would not stop her from talking to whomsoever she wished. But, despite her resolve, she had trouble getting to sleep most nights.

Sophia Crafts and her two cohorts, Maggie Orme and Kate Copeland, were quite forward in their aggression, frequently punching and kicking Sarah and Jane. One dinner time, Sarah and Jane were sitting together, at the table, with Ann Pontin, when Sophia Crafts walked past and deliberately pushed their plates into their laps. They were forced to retrieve as much food as they could from their Workhouse uniforms.

By contrast, Mary Murphy was much more sly, she would taunt Jane Navarri and frequently tripped her and Sarah up.

Sarah was aware that these activities were having a bad effect on Ann Pontin, who was looking more ill as each day passed. At night her incessant coughing was keeping Sarah awake, but she did not want to admonish the poor woman as she clearly could not help it.

Sarah was angered by what was happening, but dare not remonstrate with Sophia Crafts; she had watched Sophia Crafts hold her own against two male orderlies and knew that she would stand no chance against her, so she tried to keep her distance from them. On the other hand, Jane Navarri seemed to take it all in her stride. At all times she resolutely maintained her aloof air. However, this only served to rankle her tormentors further. On one occasion, working in the kitchen, scalding water was 'accidentally' spilled over her feet by Mary Murphy. The painful burns had to be treated by the nurse Eliza Ribnell. But her treatment, which consisted of smearing the burns with lard, had little effect and they remained quite painful for several days.

Sarah also had to be particularly careful in the kitchen. All of the troublemakers worked in the kitchen and she was always conscious of the fact that, with scalding water and sharp knives around, accidents could very easily be made to happen to her as well.

On the 9th February Sarah got a shock. During the night she had noticed that Ann Pontin had stopped coughing. At first she was relieved by this, but when the morning bell sounded and she rose, she was more worried when she saw the still woman lying beside her. Gingerly she tried to shake her to rouse her, as her hand touched her, she immediately realised that she was stiff as a board. Looking into her wide open eyes, she could see no sign of life; clearly she had departed this world.

Sarah was badly shaken by Ann Pontin's sudden death; waking up to a dead body lying beside you is not something easily dismissed.

Sophia Crafts, observing Sarah's distress, walked over and looked down on Ann Pontin's body. She cackled and muttered "good riddance," as she walked off down the ward.

CHAPTER 26

More Trouble In The Workhouse, 1842

Then finally, the day after Ann Pontin's sudden death, on Thursday 10th February 1842, it all came to a head in the kitchen. Sophia Crafts had been taunting Sarah and started pushing her. Sarah was cleaning some crockery in one of the sinks and tried to ignore her. Meanwhile, Jane Navarri was taking a pan of hot water off the stove when Mary Murphy deliberately barged into her. Jane Navarri dropped the hot pan back onto the stove, but not before hot water had splashed down her front, causing her to howl in pain. Taking advantage of the distraction Sophia Crafts seized Sarah's head and thrust it into the sink water. Sarah struggled to pull her head out of the water, but Sophia Crafts was a very big, strong girl and held her firmly under. Sarah started to panic, she couldn't breath, she was drowning, Sophia Crafts seemed intent on killing her.

Meanwhile, with her hands on fire from the scolding water, Jane Navarri's resolve snapped. It was the final straw, she had had enough, she whirled round and went for Mary Murphy. Jane was only of slight build, but she was fuelled by pent up anger, and Mary Murphy was caught unawares; she had not expected Jane to fight back. But, fight back she did. She locked her hands in Mary Murphy's hair and pulled with all her might. The two of them crashed around the kitchen, knocking pots and pans to the floor in their struggles. Mary Murphy was screaming with pain as Jane ripped handfuls of hair from her head.

While Jane and Mary Murphy were fighting, Sarah was choking on dirty dishwater as she tried to take a breath, in desperation she kicked back her heel into Sophia Crafts's shin. Sophia Crafts let out a howl of pain and stepped back, releasing her hold on Sarah's head. Sarah pulled her head out of the sink, coughing and gasping out dishwater. One of the cooks had seen Sophia Crafts try to drown Sarah and grabbed hold of her. This proved to be a big mistake, as Sophia Crafts, enraged by Sarah's kick, turned round and punched the cook full in the face. Blood spurting from her crushed nose, the cook fell back onto the floor. Sarah meanwhile was regaining her wits and had grabbed the nearest weapon, which turned out to be a large pan. Raising it above her head, she brought it down as hard as she could on Sophia Crafts's head. Sophia Crafts's eyes glazed over and she fell to the floor alongside the cook.

Seeing her nemesis lying on the kitchen floor, Sarah smiled grimly, then turned to see what was happening around her. Jane Navarri still had hold of Mary Murphy's hair and they were both still staggering about, but Maggie Orme and Kate Copeland were descending on her. Kate Copeland had a knife in her hand and was waiting for an opportunity to stab Jane Navarri with it. Sarah threw the pan she was holding at Kate Copeland and was happy to see it strike her in the eye. With a yelp, she dropped the knife and clutched at her face.

Then, Sarah saw Maggie Orme seize hold of a large ladle and step up behind Jane ready to strike her with it. She shouted. "Don't you dare!" And grabbed the back of her hair to pull her back. Maggie Orme screamed and dropped the ladle. Falling back under Sarah's assault her arms swung about wildly as she tried to keep her balance. She fell to one side knocking a large pile of plates onto the stone floor. Broken crockery scattered everywhere. Pandemonium broke loose. The cooks were shouting at the tops of their voices trying to restore order.

Meanwhile, one of the cooks had run to the Master's office to report the trouble. The Master, accompanied by three large men, stormed into the kitchen. The men waded into the fracas; Sarah found her arms gripped in two strong hands and she was forced to the floor. Maggie

Orme started to kick her as she lay there, but was also grabbed and restrained. The men quickly broke up the fighting.

A few minutes later, they were all gathered in the Workhouse Master's office. In front of his desk were the six girls: Jane Navarri, Mary Murphy, Maggie Orme, Kate Copeland, holding her face, Sophia Crafts, looking dazed and Sarah, with wet bedraggled hair; they did not present a pretty sight. Just behind them were the two senior cooks, one with a bloody nose. The Workhouse Master was seated at his desk, the three men standing behind him; they all wore fierce expressions. The Master asked the cooks to explain what had happened. They reported that the fight had started between Jane Navarri and Mary Murphy and that Sophia Crafts had tried to drown Sarah and punched a cook. They also stated that Sarah had grabbed Magdalene Orme's hair and that Kate Copeland had been involved but, lucky for her, no one had spotted the knife she had dropped.

It seemed clear to the Master that Jane Navarri, Mary Murphy and Sophia Crafts were the root cause of the fight but, despite his intense questioning, none of the three girls seemed anxious to say anything. With an angry grimace, he turned his attention to Maggie Orme, Kate Copeland and Sarah, but they had also decided to say nothing. The Workhouse Master dismissed Maggie Orme, Kate Copeland and Sarah and told them that their fate would be considered later. However, he had decided that the main miscreants were to be severely punished as an example to others. So Jane Navarri, Mary Murphy and Sophia Crafts were dispatched to the Magistrates who sent them to the House of Correction.

Two days later, Sarah, Maggie Orme and Kate Copeland were summoned to the Master's office. He explained to them that they were to be punished for fighting in the kitchen. They were sent to the Robert Street Station House. On arrival at the Station House, they were questioned by the Beadle, who decided that, because of their fight in the kitchen, they should be placed in separate cells.

Sarah was taken down some worn stone steps and along a dark corridor by a uniformed Police Officer, who held her tightly by the elbow. He stopped at a cell formed of iron bars running from floor to ceiling and, producing a large bunch of keys, opened the door and pushed her roughly inside. Sarah looked around her; the cell, in which she found herself, was very dark and smelled of damp and urine. it was already occupied by three rough looking women who, roused by the door being opened, started to shout abuse at the officer, demanding to be let out. He shouted back at them, calling them strumpets and stating that they would be going before the Magistrate soon enough. The discourse made it clear to Sarah that she would be sharing the cell with three local prostitutes. This left her with an uneasy feeling. The cell door was slammed shut and the key turned in the lock; Sarah was locked in!

The prostitutes were clinging to the bars yelling their heads off and Sarah looked at them with some misgiving but, for the moment, they seemed more concerned with yelling at the officer and hardly aware of anything else. Initially, Sarah could see very little of her surroundings, but as her eyes grew a little more accustomed to the dim light, objects came into view; she could see no bed, although she did see a pot in the corner. The cell was barely eight feet square and there was a metal locker, standing about two feet above the ground, that ran the length of the wall at the back. She walked over and sat on that, looking with some trepidation at the prostitutes clinging to the bars of the cell, still ranting and raving. The officer walked up the stone steps and vanished. With the object of their anger gone, they gave up their abuse and turned away from the bars; six malevolent eyes fixed on Sarah. She felt her blood freeze in her veins; she was aware that she presented a distinctive sight, still in her striped Workhouse uniform. The women advanced to the locker where Sarah was sitting. One of the women stood directly in front of Sarah, her hands on her hips in a confrontational stance.

"That's my place, geroff you Workhouse tramp!" she snarled.

Sarah was aware of the other two women glaring at her. She got up and walked carefully around the woman standing directly in front of her, careful not to touch her, she went over to the furthest corner of the cell and leaned against the bars, staring out into the dark corridor wishing for all the world that she was somewhere else. After a few minutes she stole a sly glance at the three women. They were sitting on the low locker top complaining to each other. Thankfully, they were taking no notice of Sarah. Then one of the women raised her voice.

"It's your damn fault the watch was called and we ended up here!" she shouted at one of the other women.

Next minute both women were on their feet facing each other off. Sarah's heart skipped a beat as she watched the two women squaring up to each other; it occurred to her that it was a very small space for a fight to break out. But the potentially explosive situation was defused by the third woman who shouted at them to 'sit down and shut up!' An uneasy silence descended on the cell. From her position at the bars, Sarah could hear noises coming from the other cells, they did not sound friendly; it occurred to her that this place was a powder keg waiting to explode. With her heart still pounding, Sarah dropped down to the cold stone floor, leaned back against the cell bars and contemplated the sorry position in which she now found herself.

Later that day they were all brought bread and cold tea, after which, the three prostitutes lay down on the locker and fell asleep, snoring noisily. Sarah lay on the floor. It was cold and hard and they were not provided with any covering; sleep was difficult, she could not stop shivering.

After three days, during which Sarah spent a harrowing time trying her best to stay out of the way of her three cellmates, the prostitutes were finally taken out by an officer, to be set before the Magistrate and Sarah never saw them again. She was kept locked up for a week in the freezing cell, fed on stale bread and cold tea, after which she was returned to the Workhouse and put back to work in the kitchen.

A week later, Maggie Orme and Kate Copeland were returned to the Workhouse, from the Robert Street Station House. Maggie Orme was placed in a different ward, but Kate Copeland was placed in ward 16 with Sarah. Arriving back from supper that evening, Sarah noticed her sitting on a bed in a corner. It was with some satisfaction that Sarah noticed that she was sporting a large black and blue bruise round her left eye as a result of Sarah throwing the pan at her when she was trying to stab Jane Navarri. Seeing Sarah looking at her, Kate Copeland glared daggers back at Sarah, who tried her best to ignore her. Sarah spent a sleepless night wondering what Kate Copeland would do. It occurred to Sarah that she would want to get her own back so she decided to keep a very close watch on her. To her chagrin, Sarah found that Kate Copeland had been assigned to work in the kitchen which meant that they would be working close together once again.

Then, four days later, on the 2nd March everything changed for the worse. Mary Murphy, Sophia Crafts and Jane Navarri had finished their sentences in the Middlesex House of Correction and were all returned to ward 16. Sarah was pleased to see her old friend Jane Navarri, but was seriously worried about the arrival of the others. When Sarah walked over to her friend's bed, she immediately noticed that Jane looked unusually haggard after her period in prison; it had certainly knocked some of the poise out of her. She had harrowing tales to tell of her time spent there. One of the worst aspects was the Oakum picking that she and most of the women were compelled to do. Old rope was piled high in huge mountains and the women were supposed to pick it apart with their hands into loose fibres, called Oakum. This was used to fill the spaces between the wooden planks of sailing ships. The trouble was that the old rope was hard and often covered in caked tar. Pulling it apart ripped nails and tore the skin from fingers. Jane's previously slim and elegant fingers were now a painful swollen mess.

Sophia Crafts made her intentions clear from the start. She was angry at Sarah for flooring her with the pan and soon let her know that she was going to get her back for it. She had hoped to be set to work in the kitchen with Sarah, where there would be plenty of opportunities to hurt her, but it was not to be. After her previous actions in the kitchen, she was set to work elsewhere. However, Mary Murphy and Kate Copeland were to work in the kitchen, with Sarah and Jane Navarri; they both realised that they would have to keep their wits about them if they were to avoid serious injury.

It did not take long for the trouble to start. It was only 2 days later, on the 4th March, in the kitchen. Sarah and Jane Navarri were at one of the sinks washing some dishes. Kate Copeland and Mary Murphy kept walking past, behind them, and each time they passed, they kicked or punched Sarah and Jane; it wasn't long before they were both quite battered and bruised. But Kate Copeland was not satisfied with that, she wanted revenge badly. Looking round the kitchen, she noticed that the cooks were not around, so she grabbed a metal skillet and walked over to Sarah. Following her lead, Mary Murphy picked up a large ladle and moved in behind Jane Navarri. They both moved together, Kate Copeland struck Sarah on the side of the head with the skillet and Mary Murphy proceeded to batter Jane Navarri round the head with the ladle. Sarah yelled in pain and surprise as the skillet struck her and she fell to the floor, blood poring from the side of her head. Meanwhile Jane Navarri was beaten to the ground with a stream of blows from Mary Murphy's ladle. Half dazed, Sarah looked up and saw Kate Copeland standing above her with the skillet raised in the air to strike her again and an evil grin on her face. Sarah was too dazed to move, she was convinced this was the end; Kate Copeland had murder in her eyes. Sarah, completely helpless, watched in horror as the skillet started to descend, Kate Copeland let out a yell of triumph. Then, suddenly, thick arms wrapped themselves round Kate Copeland and pulled her away, the skillet falling from her hand, crashing to the floor, inches from Sarah's head.

The senior cook with the broken nose, courtesy of Sophia Crafts fist, well remembered the girls from the fracas in the kitchen and had been observing them from a distance. She had seen Kate Copeland and Mary Murphy kicking and punching Sarah and Jane Navarri. Anticipating trouble she had left the kitchen and went to get two of the male attendants. On her return she saw the attack and watched Sarah and Jane Navarri fall to the floor. The two male attendants rushed forward and grabbed Kate Copeland and Mary Murphy. A struggle broke out as the two girls tried to fight off the men; more male attendants arrived and Kate Copeland and Mary Murphy were dragged away cursing and shouting. Sarah and Jane Navarri were taken to Matron who dressed their wounds. They were then returned to the ward, where Sarah collapsed on her bed and lay there with a dizzy head.

Kate Copeland and Mary Murphy were sent before the Magistrate who put them in the Middlesex House of Correction for 14 days.

Meanwhile, at the Robert Street Station House, a meeting was taking place; four men were sitting round a table engaged in an earnest discussion about the Shoreditch Workhouse troublesome girls. The meeting had been called by Edwin Chadwick, who was most concerned about incidents which had been brought to his attention concerning the antics of some of these girls. The other three men were: John Coste, the Shoreditch Relieving Officer, the Beadle and the Master of the Shoreditch Workhouse.

Edwin Chadwick was reading from a sheet of paper in front of him. "This Elizabeth Weston has badly assaulted Police Officers and Workhouse Attendants on several occasions, she has been locked up here and in the House of Correction a number of times, as has this Sophia Crafts. Similarly, a Mary Murphy, Caroline Copeland and a," he paused to look more closely at the piece of paper, "Magdalen Orme, is that her name? Have disported themselves in a similar manner. That Mary Murphy had only been out of the House of Correction for two days when she was sent back in for her bad behaviour. All are from the Workhouse," he glared across at John Coste and the Workhouse Master, "What do you propose to do about these girls?"

"With all due respect Mr Chadwick, there is little we can do, they are a law unto themselves. Short of putting them in irons, which I am not permitted to do, my hands are tied," said the Workhouse Master.

"Hurrumph" said John Coste as he cleared his throat, "We have no choice but to put them in the House, I get handfuls of summonses from Magistrate Benett every day, we can do little else with them."

"Yes," said Edwin Chadwick, "they have rights, even as paupers, but can you not keep them apart?"

"If we had an infinite number of wards and dining rooms, perhaps we could. But we do not." Replied the Workhouse Master somewhat testily."

"Might I make a suggestion," said the Beadle, "we know well who these troublesome girls are, why not keep them under observation. Then when they are observed starting trouble an early intervention might be undertaken to stop it quickly."

"I like that idea," said Mr Chadwick, "you should take good account of that."

"I am not sure if I have enough men to accomplish such an activity," said the Workhouse Master.

"Well do the best you can," said Mr Chadwick, "It sounds an excellent recourse to me!"

Back at the Shoreditch Workhouse, following the incident in the kitchen, Kate Copeland and Mary Murphy had been removed to the House of Correction and Sarah was now more worried about Sophia Crafts as she was far bigger and stronger than all the others and clearly presented the biggest threat. Sophia Crafts herself was itching to pay Sarah back and watched her carefully at every opportunity. Following the meeting with Mr Chadwick, the Workhouse Master had decided to move Sophia Crafts to another ward and had instructed his attendants to keep a close watch on her. Since she did not work in the kitchen and was no longer in the same ward, there were few opportunities for her to attack Sarah. She did try to hit her once, at dinner, but was immediately restrained by two male attendants. After that she started to look around her and noticed that she was always being shadowed by Workhouse staff. It was clear that they were keeping an eye on her. This was going to make it more difficult, but she was determined to get Sarah and bided her time awaiting a good opportunity. After some thought, she realised that a good time might be during the Sunday visit to St Mary's Church, when there would be a large number of people to hide among. She made her plans for the next Sunday; she stole a knife and hid it in her uniform.

On Sunday 13 March, the Workhouse inmates were making their usual way to St Mary's Church, Sarah was walking along with the other inmates, unconcernedly glancing at the houses they passed, unaware that she was being carefully watched. Sophia Crafts had hunched down low and concealed herself in the mass of people. Keeping Sarah in her sights she was slowly closing the distance between them. At the same time she was carefully noting the positions of the attendants accompanying the group. She saw that some of them were chatting among themselves, clearly not expecting trouble on the Sunday trip to church. She was now right behind Sarah. Her plan was to ram the knife into Sarah's back and then sidle away and lose herself in the mass of Workhouse inmates. She grinned as she withdrew the knife from her Workhouse uniform and prepared to ram it hard into Sarah's back.

Jane Navarri had been following just a little behind Sarah and to one side. She became aware of a large hunched figure coming up alongside her. She was unconcerned, until she caught sight of a glint of light in the corner of her eye; looking across she saw that the hunched figure now had a knife blade in her hand and, with sudden recognition, realised that it was Sophia Crafts about to stab Sarah. She let out a yell of warning and pushed Sophia Crafts hard in the side. The push deflected the knife thrust slightly so that instead of the intended deadly thrust into the back, the knife struck Sarah in the arm. Sarah screamed in pain as the knife penetrated her arm and jerked to one side in agony. Sophia Crafts pulled the knife from Sarah's arm and made to strike her again, but Jane Navarri, still yelling at the top of her voice, pushed her a second time. Angered by the push, Sophia Crafts turned on Jane Navarri and made to strike her with the knife; Jane Navarri backed rapidly away from her. The Workhouse inmates that had been screening Sophia Crafts heard Sarah's scream and, seeing the bloody knife in Sophia Crafts hand, had also rapidly moved away, and she now found herself standing on her own.

Alerted by the cries, the male attendants looked round and saw Sophia Crafts, now out in the open, with a knife in her hand; they moved quickly towards her. She looked round and saw the attendants descending on her; Sarah meanwhile had staggered away. This was not how she had planned it. With a blood curdling scream of rage she leapt at the nearest attendant, he put his arm up to protect himself and was stabbed in the hand. With his free hand he grabbed her wrist and valiantly held on, grunting in pain, whilst she was pushed to the ground by the rest of the attendants and eventually subdued.

Sophia Crafts was dragged back to the Workhouse and locked in the dark room, yelling and cursing all the way. Sarah was helped back and she and the injured attendant were treated by Matron who put a strap round Sarah's injured arm; she had lost a lot of blood and returned to the ward where she lay down and fell into a fitful sleep.

The following day, Monday 14th March, Police Officers were summoned to the Workhouse and Sophia Crafts was taken to the Robert Street Station House. From there, she went before the Magistrate and was sentenced to 18 months in the Middlesex House of Correction.

Following this incident, life in ward 16 calmed down somewhat. On the 18th March, Kate Copeland and Mary Murphy returned to the Workhouse from the House of Correction. They were placed in ward 15 and did not get assigned to work in the kitchen. Over the next few weeks, Sarah made a good recovery and she and Jane Navarri made the best of putting the episode behind them.

Two months passed without incident, then, on the Tuesday 10th May, Sarah was summoned to work in the laundry with Mary Durrand, once again. When she entered, Mary came over to her. "You remember that so called nurse, Mary Collis?" she asked

"The one that took my best friend Sarah Murray away?" Sarah replied.

"Yes 'er," Mary Durrand responded. "Well, they found 'er dead this morning."

"Did they?" said Sarah startled, "How d'yer know?" she asked.

"One of the other nurses, Eliza Ribnell told me."

"Oh I know Eliza," said Sarah.

"Well," continued Mary, "according to Eliza, Mary Collis hadn't turned up for her work in the sick ward, so she went to get her. Found 'er, stiff as a board, still lying in 'er bed."

"Oh," said Sarah. She didn't like Mary Collis much. She was sure she did nothing to help her friend, but she was shocked to hear of her sudden death; it seemed to her that the Workhouse was not a very safe place to be in.

It was just over a week later, when Jane Navarri was released into service and on Thursday 19th May 1842, Sarah was also released into service. They were both sent to the same household. They were given live-in positions in a large, slightly run down house in Bethnal Green. It was situated just to the eastern side of the green itself and was owned by a Jewish trader. Some of these large houses were falling into disrepair as the area was on a rapid downhill slide. It was already categorised, by a Government report, as the second worst, most deprived area in London. In a few years time it would be the worst.

Her new Master was of Jewish Ashkenasim faith and could trace his ancestry back to Eastern European origins. However, he and his family had been in East London for many years and had been in the clothing industry for many generations. He was a sober man and drink was strictly banned from the house. He was a caring member of the community and served on the local Parish Council. He helped his fellow Jews, but also gave generously to the whole local community. He was particularly concerned about the Workhouse; he would never see one of his fellow Jews reduced to entering it. It was an institution he despised and was one of the reasons he made a point of employing one or two Workhouse inmates as lower level servants in his household.

Sarah was employed as a slavey and part time childminder, Jane was a Maid of all Work. Both girls had to sleep in a basement kitchen on a smelly old straw mattress with a grubby straw filled cover. The covering material was so worn that the straw continually fell out and they were always having to stuff it back in. At night, the basement kitchen was damp, dirty and crawling with black beetles. It made them both feel very wretched.

The Master was strict, but the Mistress was not unkind. The cook was a large jolly woman who was allowed the used tea leaves. She was able to re-use them several times and was always to be found drinking tea. She was quite happy to share some with Sarah and Jane; Sarah was now gaining quite a liking for tea. The cook was often seen lacing her tea with some spirit from a small bottle she kept secreted on her ample person, which may have accounted for her jolly, red faced appearance.

Both girls were expected to wear a working gown. With typical Jewish frugality, they were made to pay 6 pence each for them, which was deducted from their pitifully small wages. The work was hard, but manageable. Jane had five fireplaces to do. Each morning, she had to clear the ashes out from the previous evening and clean the grates. The fireplace surrounds and cast iron grate had to be polished with oily black lead; it was a filthy job and Jane detested it. She then filled all the scuttles with coal ready for the evening fires to be laid.

Sarah remembered doing the fireplaces in one of her previous employments and, although she was sympathetic to Jane, she was heartily thankful that it was not one of her jobs. Her duties included helping the full time childminder, who was responsible for looking after five children and a new-born baby. Sarah would carry the water up the stairs for their morning wash, whilst the childminder got them out of bed. Once washed and dressed, the older ones would be got ready for school. When they were ready they would be marched down to breakfast.

The three older children attended a Jewish school and it was Sarah's job to escort them there, whilst the childminder looked after the younger ones. The Jewish school and chapel were a very short walk from the green and she soon returned to the house.

She was also expected to help Jane with some of the household chores and once a week, on the childminder's afternoon off, Sarah would take the baby out in the pram with the other toddler in tow. She quite enjoyed this time in the open air.

Between them, Sarah and Jane also helped in the kitchen. Sometimes Sarah would be sent on little errands, by the cook. Usually, these would involve visits to local traders to instruct them on their deliveries of food. The cook would give her one or two pence for her trouble. It seemed to Sarah that the cook always had some money on her. The food deliveries would usually arrive at the back door to the kitchen and Sarah would help with their unloading and storage. Sarah also noticed that they had other, more discrete, visitors to the back door. Sarah would usually be sent out of the kitchen when they turned up.

One day, curious as to what was transpiring Sarah, having being ordered from the kitchen by the cook, stopped outside the door. Leaving it open a jar, she peered through the crack. She saw the cook take some items from the pantry, one of which she could see was a tub of dripping that they collected from the cooked joints of meat. The cook put them into a large bag held open by the man at the back door. Closing the bag, he handed the cook some coins then, raising his hat to her, bid her farewell and scampered off. So, thought Sarah, this is where the cook gets her money from!

Sarah was never short of work. Among her many tasks was cleaning all the household's shoes, washing all the floors and, of course, cleaning the massive steps that led up to the huge front door. Of an evening, Sarah would collect the older children from school and help the childminder to prepare them for supper. They would then be taken downstairs and presented to their father in the drawing room. Their father would inspect them carefully and woe betide any dirty faces or scuffed shoes. Any imperfections would draw severe criticism and would need to be corrected immediately, usually by Sarah. After supper, she would take them upstairs and assist the childminder to put them to bed. Meanwhile, Jane would have made up the grates and lit the fires.

The oldest child was an eleven-year-old girl and, whilst the younger ones generally demanded more attention, the older girl was quite capable of getting herself to bed. So, whilst the childminder concentrated on the younger ones Sarah usually attended to her. She was very intelligent and diligent at school and Sarah usually sat on the side of her bed and chatted with her for a while. Sarah was particularly interested in what the young girl had done at school. Sarah herself had not had any formal schooling. She could handle certain numbers as a result of the necessity to count money. She knew the denominations of the coins she handled and that there were twelve pence in a shilling and four farthings in one penny. As a result of her experiences in the Workhouse, she could also read some signs. But, she could not decipher the written word, nor sign her own name. In keeping with the beliefs of the time, most of the young Jewish girl's schooling was directed at womanly pursuits: sewing, embroidery and music were constant topics. She was also given some instruction in history and geography; Sarah found these topics fascinating and was always quizzing her, in depth, about them.

It was one evening and Sarah had just tucked her into bed, when the young girl started to talk about Valentine's Day. "You should know about this day," she said, "it's your name, isn't it?"

"Yes," laughed Sarah, "my name is Valentine. What do you know about it?"

"Well," she said, "we have lessons about the celebrations of other religions, and today we were told about Saint Valentine."

"You must tell me all about it!" said Sarah eagerly.

"Well," she said again, in a girly story telling voice, "Valentine was a priest who lived in ancient Rome many, many years ago. He was a devout Christian who secretly practiced his faith. But, like the Jews, he was not allowed to preach and so was taken and imprisoned. When he refused to denounce his faith, he was sentenced to death. While he was in jail, the jailer's daughter befriended him and visited him often. But, he was put to death on February 14th and he left a farewell note for the jailer's daughter. He signed it 'from your Valentine'. Ever since then it has been a day when boys and girls express their love for each other by presenting them with gifts, like flowers or confections."

Sarah was quite taken by this story and mused over it. In fact, it would stay with her and influence her later in life.

But, meanwhile, the young girl was still talking. "I wish I had someone to send a Valentine to," she said with a distant look on her face."

"Well, that's enough of that young lady!" Sarah said, "I think it's time you went to sleep."

But the girl was in a mischievous mood. "Do you know how to find out how many children you will have?" she asked.

Curious, Sarah replied, "No."

"Well," said the girl in her sing song voice, "You must pick a dandelion that has gone to seed. Take a deep breath and blow the seeds into the wind, just the once. Count the seeds that remain on the stem. That is the number of children you will have."

Sarah laughed, "Have you tried it?" she asked.

"Yes," said the girl, "and I will have fourteen children."

"Well," said Sarah still laughing, "If your going to have that many children, you had better get a good night's sleep to keep your strength up." With that she covered the girl up and blew out the candle. On her way downstairs, her smile faded as she remembered her own child, who she had not seen since the day she had handed him over to the Linfords.

The eldest girl influenced Sarah quite strongly during this period. She was impressed by the youngster's intelligence. She knew many wonderful things and Sarah was in awe. She started to teach Sarah to count and to write and understand numbers. Sarah proved to be a willing pupil, but the written word was still well beyond her.

The young girl also spoke very well, as did all the members of the household. Jane was also quite well spoken, though with an accent. The childminder in particular, was always correcting Sarah, particularly with regard to her use of East London slang, 'don't talk like that in front of the children' she would say. During this period, under this influence, Sarah's speech and manner were significantly improved.

One morning, Sarah and Jane were told to put up bunting and decorations for a celebration. It was the young boy's fourth birthday. Sarah and Jane quite enjoyed themselves helping the cook and the Mistress's Chamber Maid to put up the decorations. Several children were brought round from the surrounding houses. There were games and music and the young boy opened many presents.

Sarah was enthralled by the celebrations and was watching the young boy with his presents when Jane asked her when her birthday was and how old she was. This was not an easy question for her to answer as neither she, nor anyone in her family, had ever celebrated their birthday, and no particular date came to mind. As for the years, she was well aware of the day of the week, on a day to day basis; this was frequently necessary for her work. But to know what the year was, was irrelevant to her and, over time, the precise number of years that had passed was forgotten. The only time her age had been mentioned, was when she was admitted to the Workhouse, as the Master had to enter the figure in the admissions register. However, most times, as she was such a frequent entrant, he would merely repeat the age at her last entry. The result of this was that her age had tended to drift over the years and now bore little relationship with the date of her birth. She did remember that, on her last admission, the Workhouse Master had stated her age as nineteen, but she was not very sure how correct that was. As for her birthday, she felt it was somewhere around the turn of the year but was not sure of the actual date. The only date that came to her mind was Valentine's Day. So, that was what she told Jane. And, from that date on, Sarah made a point of celebrating Valentine's Day as her birthday.

Although the work was hard Sarah was not unhappy and she was allowed the odd Sunday afternoon off. She usually visited her family in Whitechapel on those days; if he had the time off work, her brother Jimmy would also visit. Things were still a little strained between her and her father, particularly as a result of her providing clothes for her family and furniture for their home. She took great delight in noting that the room was still looking good; the vases on the window ledge sported bright flowers and the picture was still adorning the wall. She had to smile when her mother told her that her father had been astonished when he had finally made it home that evening and beheld the transformed room and his family attired in good clothes with shoes on their feet. When he had been told that it was Sarah who had paid for it all, he had stared at her in disbelief, shame written indelibly on his face. An interesting by-product of this incident had been him getting home a little earlier in the evenings and providing her with a bit more money.

It was a fine summer and during her visits to her family Sarah usually went out for a walk with her brother Jimmy and sisters Caroline and Mary, leaving her mother looking after young Henry. Sarah was struck by how quickly her sister Caroline was growing up. She was lively and bubbly and Sarah found her enchanting.

There was a curious incident one Sunday afternoon. Sarah and Caroline were walking round the edge of Spitalfields market, chatting away to each other. Their brother Jimmy was some distance away amusing Mary, who was running about squealing with joy. It was not a market day and few people were about. Sarah and Caroline stopped and watched as two dogs scuffled over some rotting fruit left by some market trader.

Caroline turned to Sarah. "Sarah," she said.

"Yes," replied Sarah

"Do you wonder if you will ever get married and have lots of children?"

A little taken aback by this question, Sarah murmured, "well, sometimes, yes. What about you?"

"Oh, I think about it all the time," said Caroline, "I would love to know how many children I will have. I want lots and lots"

Sarah considered her reply. Then she remembered her little chats with the precocious daughter of the Jewish trader that she was working for. "Well Caroline," Sarah said, with a mischievous gleam in her eye, "I think I can answer that question for you."

Caroline looked up at her with a quizzical look on her face, "how?" she said.

Looking round her, Sarah spotted a white fluffy dandelion, gone to seed. Pulling it out of the ground she handed it to Caroline. "You must blow hard on that dandelion, just the once. The number of seeds left will tell you how many children you will have."

Laughing at her, Caroline blew on the dandelion. To the dismay of both of them, all the seeds blew away and Caroline was left with a bare stalk. Neither girl said anything for a while. Caroline had a sad expression on her face. Sarah was upset that her little game had turned so sour; it cast a bit of a shadow on the day and both girls walked back home to Whitechapel in silence, whilst Jimmy and Mary laughed and played together, ignorant of the downcast expressions on their two sisters' faces.

One bright Monday morning on the 13th June 1842, Sarah Valentine was walking down the Hackney Road towards Shoreditch, on an errand for her Master. She had strict instructions to hand-deliver an important package to the Curate at St Leonard's Church. Her Master and the Curate were both on the Parish Council and it was important that the Curate got this package before the next Council meeting. Her Master had impressed upon her the importance of this task and she gripped the parcel tightly to her chest.

She felt a slight twinge as she walked past the top of Caroline Street; her baby Edwin would be two-years-old soon. She knew it would be pointless trying to visit him. Jane Linford had made it quite plain that she was not welcome. Her husband George Linford had warned her off trying to see her son and when, in frustration, she had decided to call on them, Jane had said, 'we must not confuse the child, you must go away immediately. It is for his sake and, it is better if you do *not* call again'. This last point was made quite firmly. Casting the sad thoughts from her mind, she continued on her way.

She soon reached the end of the Hackney Road and, as she walked along the iron railings alongside the church, she saw ahead of her the junction with the Kingsland Road, at the top end of Shoreditch. As ever it was bustling with activity. She could see several horse drawn carriages clustered outside the Kings Arms Tavern almost completely blocking the junction and causing much consternation among traffic and pedestrians alike. As she drew level with the front of the church, she glanced through the railings and saw that a wedding had just finished and the bride and groom were walking out. She paused for a moment to watch. She found herself wondering whether she would ever be married. Her thoughts drifted and her eyes alighted on a well dressed young man, standing to one side of the bride and groom. The bride kissed him lightly on the cheek and with a smile she walked up the church path to the street, arm in arm with her new husband. They looked a nice young and happy couple, embarking on a new life together. Sarah wondered about the young man the bride had kissed; old friend, brother perhaps? He was certainly very handsome, well set out and with shiny polished shoes. As she looked at him, her heart fluttered and she felt a strange attraction.

But, she had work to do. She turned away and walked briskly on, turning the corner and walking along the railings to the front entrance to the church. She watched as the new bride and groom crossed the junction towards the Kings Arms Tavern. Walking through the entrance into the Church Yard, she looked about her and spotted a gardener. She walked up to him and paused while he pulled out a stubborn root; he looked up at her and smiled.

"Can I 'elp yer my love?" he asked.

"Yes," replied Sarah, "I have an important package to deliver to the Curate."

The gardener looked over at the church. "There he is," he said, indicating a tall man in church regalia, standing just inside the church doorway, "Your in luck, he's just finished that wedding. You should be able to catch him before the next one."

Sarah looked at where he was pointing and saw the man turn and walk back into the church. Anxious to catch him and complete her mission she hurried off towards the church door. As she rushed down the path, she brushed against the well dressed young man she had been observing earlier who was standing admiring the impressive building. She turned, looked up and muttered an apology. He looked at her and smiled. She was struck by his intense deep blue eyes and, for a second, it looked as if he was about to say something. Then, to her great embarrassment, she felt her face suddenly redden; she quickly looked away and dashed into the church.

What Sarah did not know, at that time, was that she had just brushed against her future husband, Mr Edward Sturman Mason. In fact, this was exactly as predicted by Martha Herbert, the clairvoyant, from the Globe Tavern in Goldsmiths Row. She had told Sarah that, regarding her future husband, she would, 'set eyes on him soon, but his name will not yet be known to you.'

He had, in fact, been attending, and was a witness to, his sister, Frances Mason's, wedding to Alfred Robinson. That couple, were destined to be witnesses at her own wedding, which would take place on Valentine's Day. But that was still some years in her future.

Her errand now completed, Sarah left the church to make her way back to her Master's house. She glanced round as she left the Church Yard; it was empty, the smart young man had gone.

It was nearly a month later, on the 2nd July, when Jane Navarri came up to her with a grim expression on her face.

"What's the matter?" said Sarah.

"I'm to go back to the Workhouse," she said.

"Why?" exclaimed Sarah.

"The Mistress told me that they need to reduce the number of servants, so I am to go."

She looked very sad. There was nothing that Sarah could say to comfort her. She watched with some dismay as Jane gathered her few belongings together and left the house.

Sarah worked on with some trepidation. It was clear that something was wrong. Furniture was being moved out and she frequently found the Mistress of the house with tears in her eyes. It was Monday 1st August and Sarah was cleaning the grate. She had been trying to do Jane's work as well as her own and was quite tired. She heard shouting from the parlour. The Master and Mistress were arguing. Their voices were getting louder and louder. Soon, it was clear to Sarah that they were in trouble. From the words that Sarah could hear, it was clear that their clothing shop was losing money and they were having to cut back on expenses, much to the Mistress's chagrin. That night, Sarah found it difficult to get to sleep. She felt sure that trouble was imminent.

She was not wrong, the next morning she was summoned to the parlour. She knocked on the door and was told to enter. Inside was her Mistress who was talking to two distressed maids. There were also two male servants, one in livery, standing solemnly to one side. On seeing Sarah enter, the Mistress waved her over and told her to stand beside the two maids. Looking round, she saw the Master of the house, standing in front of the ornate fireplace, looking very stern.

The Master cleared his throat. "Hurrumph! I have some unfortunate news for you all. It is no longer possible for us to employ such a large number of servants. I am afraid that you will all have to leave forthwith."

The two maids next to Sarah wailed in unison.

"Shh!" said the Mistress.

"Hurrumph!" The Master cleared his throat again, "I appreciate that some of you have been with this household for some time now." He looked at the maids and his gaze drifted over to the two male servants. They stared back at him with blank expressions on their faces; he did not look in Sarah's direction.

"I have chosen to explain to you that it is *not* the case that you have been in any way lax in performing your duties. Indeed, I shall provide each of you with an excellent written 'Character', which should enable you to secure a good position in another household." He paused, seeming to consider what to say next. "I believe that you deserve some reason for your demise. It is the case that times are becoming very hard for all of us." He paused again. "Business in this area is declining. Indeed, the whole area is declining in status. We seem to be replacing good people with vagabonds and fine houses with slums. Poor tenements are growing around us with a depressing pace. In addition, this is not helped by the Government heaping more pain on the populace by re-introducing that reviled Income Tax. It was introduced to pay for the war against France, and most believed that to be a good enough cause. It was duly abolished in 1816 when that emergency was over. But this new fellow Peel has now chosen to reinstate it. This will take away another seven pence from every pound that we honest citizens earn. For me, and many others in this area, it is one straw too many!"

At this point his voice petered out. It seemed that he had suddenly realised that he was addressing a group of, mostly illiterate, servants. Sarah, for her part, had no idea what he was on about. All she understood was that, once again, she was out of work and would get no further earnings. The Master's address now obviously at an end, the servants filed out of the room. Sarah left the maids remonstrating with a very harassed looking Mistress of the house, and went to collect her belongings. She had enjoyed her time working at the house on the green. It was certainly one of her better experiences and she recalled her many chats with the eldest daughter of the house. It had given her much to think about

Feeling quite sad, Sarah decided to get back into the Shoreditch Workhouse and made her way to Worship Street. She was now quite familiar with the ritual and was soon making her way up the Kingsland Road with a ticket in her hand from the Relieving Officer.

So, on Tuesday 2nd August 1842, she presented herself to the Workhouse Master. He recognised her and, entering her details in the admissions register, noted that she was 19 on her previous admission and entered 19 again. She was placed in the womens' working ward 16 and set to work in the kitchen.

It was when she returned to the ward after supper that she got her first shock. She had just sat on her bed and was looking round the ward when she saw two girls she did not want to see again. Kate Copeland and Maggie Orme were glaring at her from their beds. Kate Copeland's face was set in such a fierce mask of hate that Sarah's blood ran cold.

Over the next few weeks Sarah tried her best to steer clear of them. Fortunately, they were not working in the kitchen with her, so the only opportunities to get at her were at meal times and in the ward. Both places were full of witnesses, so the pair contented themselves with sly punches and kicks when they felt no one was looking.

They finally got the opportunity they were waiting for on Tuesday, 30 August, on the way to breakfast. Sarah usually made sure that she was in the company of lots of other women, but this day she had been lax, thinking of her son Edwin, she was one of the last to leave the ward. Kate Copeland and Maggie Orme had noticed this and dallied on the stairs until Sarah arrived. With no one else in sight, they grabbed her from behind and, whilst Maggie Orme held on to her, pinning her arms to her sides, Kate Copeland proceeded to punch her, cackling gleefully. Sarah screamed as she struggled to get free, but Maggie Orme was a big strong girl and she was held tightly. She was punched relentlessly; blood was poring from her nose and mouth, they seemed intent on finishing her off. They might have succeeded except that the Workhouse Master was still arranging for an eye to be kept on known troublesome girls. Two male orderlies had been waiting to see the girls into breakfast and had noticed that Maggie Orme and Kate Copeland had not turned up; they were walking back towards the ward to see where they had got to. They heard Sarah's screams and dashed to the stairs. They immediately seized Kate Copeland and Maggie Orme, pulling them away from Sarah, who collapsed on the floor, sobbing. After a short struggle, Kate Copeland and Maggie Orme were dragged to the Master's office. He promptly dispatched them to the Robert Street Station House as punishment.

Meanwhile Sarah was taken to the Matron, who was, once again, patching up her injuries. "My!" she said, "you are in the wars these day arn't yer!"

When the Matron had finished with her she was returned to the ward. She lay down on her bed in the empty ward; all the other women were at their work. She was covered in bruises, her whole body ached; she put her hand to her face and cried out in pain. She lay on her bed until dinner time when the door was opened and she was allowed to go to the meal room. She looked a frightful mess: her left eye was closed and the whole of the left side of her face was one purple bruise. She was aware of the women staring at her as she walked slowly to a bench and sat down. Her mouth was cut and sore where Kate Copeland had repeatedly punched her in the face; eating was a very painful experience, chewing almost impossible. She swallowed what she could whole.

Supper was not much better and when she laid down after night bell she found sleeping difficult.

The next day, the 31ˢᵗ August, she felt a little better and was able to eat some breakfast. She was set to work in the kitchen. At the end of the day, after supper, she returned to ward 16. As she walked into the ward she was holding her mouth; it was still sore, but not bleeding. However, the sight that met her eyes made her instantly forget her injuries, for there, sitting on a bed directly in front of her, was Mary Murphy, who must have been admitted that day. As soon as Sarah saw her she knew that there would be more trouble. She had not seen Mary Murphy since the fight in the kitchen back in June when both she and Kate Copland were sent to the House of Correction.

Sarah tried her best to avoid Mary Murphy, but once the girl spotted her, she did not let her out of her sight. Indeed, Mary Murphy made it quite plain that she was out to get Sarah. She obviously blamed her for her spell in prison and was intent on making her pay.

The first evening after Mary Murphy arrived, Sarah walked over to her bed to lie down. She was tired after a hard day's work. She pulled the top cloth cover back to find a mass of excrement in the middle of the bed. She looked up to see Mary Murphy laughing her head off. It took her some time to clear the mess up and that evening, lying in her bed, all she could smell was shit.

During the following weeks, Mary Murphy made Sarah's life hell. They both worked in the kitchen and Mary Murphy made a point of doing everything she could to injure Sarah. She tripped her up at every opportunity, and once, when she left her sink to gather more crockery,

Mary put a sharp carving knife in the water; Sarah cut her hand on the blade before she realised it was there.

Most evenings Mary would either shit or pee in Sarah's bed. It got to the extent that one of the Workhouse employees reprimanded Sarah for messing her bed. The smell made the bed impossible to sleep in, and she took to sleeping on the cold hard floor, beside it.

Sarah had pretty well recovered from her beating at the hands of Maggie Orme and Kate Copeland but the trouble she was having with Mary Murphy was getting her down, it seemed that things could not get any worse. Then on 11th October, they did just that, with the admission of Maggie Orme to the ward. After her spell in the Robert Street Station House cells, she was furious and her anger was directed firmly at Sarah, who now had two people trying to hurt her.

She tried her best to avoid them and, following the previous incident on the stairs, she did her best to ensure that she was never alone. But the sly kicks and punches were a constant reminder that they were out to get her. Sarah realised that this harassment was not going to stop and that sooner or later she was going to be seriously injured, either by one of Mary Murphy's stunts, or Maggie Orme's fists. So, with few options open to her, she applied to the Workhouse Master to leave and on Monday the 17th October 1842 she walked out, not sure where she would go and with no immediate prospects of gainful employment.

CHAPTER 27

Commercial Street, 1842

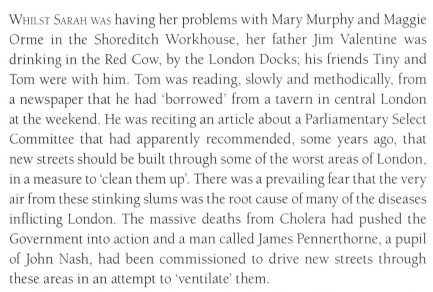

WHILST SARAH WAS having her problems with Mary Murphy and Maggie Orme in the Shoreditch Workhouse, her father Jim Valentine was drinking in the Red Cow, by the London Docks; his friends Tiny and Tom were with him. Tom was reading, slowly and methodically, from a newspaper that he had 'borrowed' from a tavern in central London at the weekend. He was reciting an article about a Parliamentary Select Committee that had apparently recommended, some years ago, that new streets should be built through some of the worst areas of London, in a measure to 'clean them up'. There was a prevailing fear that the very air from these stinking slums was the root cause of many of the diseases inflicting London. The massive deaths from Cholera had pushed the Government into action and a man called James Pennerthorne, a pupil of John Nash, had been commissioned to drive new streets through these areas in an attempt to 'ventilate' them.

Jim was only half listening, supping his ale, until Tom came to the punch line. One of the schemes to be embarked upon was the complete demolition of Essex Street and Rose Lane to make way for a new street, to be called, Spital Street.

At this statement, Jim gagged on his ale, spluttering it across the bar. "What was that you said?" Jim gasped.

Tom repeated his words and the group became silent.

"They can't just knock all our houses down!" Jim exclaimed, then a quieter, "can they?"

"Well," said Tom, peering at the paper, "it says 'ere that a Board of Works has been set up by the Office of Woods and Forests to oversee the purchase of properties required under the….." here he paused whilst he tried to understand the words, "….act of third and forth, something or other, for the….." he paused again, "…..formation of the new street, to be called Spital Street, from the London Docks to Shoreditch."

"What does all that claptrap mean?" asked Jim angrily.

Tom looked at him, "I think it means they are serious about this and are buying up the properties."

Jim looked dumbstruck, but Tom had not finished. "It also says 'ere that properties along the line of the new street, in Essex Street and associated courts have already been purchased and bids are being considered for their removal." Tom looked meaningfully at Jim.

Jim stared into his ale, a worried expression on his face. It seemed to him that it was unthinkable to destroy the homes of such a large mass of people. After all, where would they all go?

At that time Essex Street was roughly 200 yards long, running south to north from the north side of the Whitechapel High Street to the south side of Wentworth Street. From the north side of Wentworth Street Rose Lane continued northwards for about 180 yards, ending at Spitalfields Parish Church. This was the proposed line of the new road.

Along the length of Essex Street there were a number of courts, branching off either side; these were short alleys running at right angles to the street, they had difficult narrow accesses often under low gateways. On the west side, coming from the High Street were; Rose and Crown Court (where Sarah Valentine was born), Martins Court (where Jim and his family currently lived), Moors Court, Essex Court, Elgar Place and Elgar Square, On the east side were; Sugar Loaf Court, Catherine Wheel Court, Reas Yard, Cobley Court, Chapel Court and Greggs Court.

With the exception of Rose and Crown Court, which was uninhabitable, all these courts were packed with the lowest description of houses, built back to back with no rear access and no real facilities;

most of them merely had a pump and a communal privy at the end of the court. They had been thrown together by unscrupulous landlords on the rear gardens of the houses fronting Essex Street to take advantage of the masses of people flooding into the London suburbs and were jammed to bursting point with the poorest populace in the whole of London.

Martins Court, where Nell and the Valentines' lived, was actually two narrow courts running parallel to each other, but with only the one narrow entrance. The northerly court contained a row of houses which were built back to back onto those in the next court, Moors Court. These houses (Nos. 1 to 6) faced Nos. 7 to 12 across a narrow rubbish strewn alleyway, Nos. 7 to 12 were built back to back with another row of houses (Nos. 13 to 18). These faced a further row of houses forming Martins Back Court. Martins Court was one of the worse in the area in that it warranted a special report from the Medical Officer of the Whitechapel Union concerning its 'deplorable condition'.

Essex Street itself contained older, somewhat larger buildings; although most dated back to the fire of London and were in very poor condition. The west side of the street was the most built up and contained the three taverns: the Catherine Wheel at No. 3, nearest the High Street, the Rose and Crown at No. 9 and the Throwstik's Arms at No. 16 which was on the corner of the entrance to Martins Court. There were a few run down shops on the west side: a shoemaker, a fishmonger, a butcher and, incongruously, a hairdresser at No. 8, next door to the Rose and Crown. In view of the state of the local populous, one can only assume that it attracted the occasional drunk who entered mistaking it for the tavern and had their hair cut and money extracted before they realised their mistake! The remaining houses on the west side were the worst kind of lodging houses where, typically, a dozen people would be crammed into one small room. The east side was less built up and apart from a number of lodging houses contained: a stable, some warehouses, a shed used for cork burning and the Crofts Brewery in Reas Yard. It seemed that all of this was to be wiped out.

That night, whilst their children were playing in the court, Jim told his wife what Tom had told him; it greatly disturbed them both.

Meanwhile, Sarah, having left the Workhouse, and with no particular place to go, had decided to walk down Philips Street, to Edward Street and knocked on the door of the Freestones', who she had lodged with before.

Jane Freestone answered the door with a brightly flushed face. Sarah could hear the sounds of childish laughter from within. "Sarah!" she exclaimed, "your just in time. Come in!"

Somewhat bemused, Sarah followed Jane inside. Within the small room, were gathered some six children of varying ages all laughing, shouting and generally running about. She recognised their son Thomas sitting in the middle of the room.

"It's Thomas's second birthday," Jane explained, "and he's just about to open his presents."

Sarah smiled. Attending birthday parties was becoming something of a habit for her. She joined in the fun and watched young Thomas giggling with joy as he opened his presents.

A little later, when Jane's husband Tom had returned home from his coster round, Sarah explained what had happened to her and that she had no work and nowhere to stay. Her face still bore some of the marks and bruises from her beating by Kate Copeland and Sophia Crafts. But, although sympathetic, Tom Freestone was a little grim faced at Sarah's story and it was clear to her that he was not about to offer free board and lodging. However, his wife pushed him away and said that Sarah could stay until the end of the week, on condition that she looked for work and paid towards the rent when she was receiving wages. Happy to have a roof over her head, Sarah readily agreed.

It was Tom Freestone who actually found Sarah a job, with one of his fellow costermongers who needed a childminder. His wife had just died, giving birth to their fourth child, who had also died, leaving him with three young children to bring up. He was an itinerant coster with a long arduous round weaving through densely populated areas through which he could not drag small children. He couldn't afford much, but Sarah was in no position to bargain and agreed to look after them during the day whilst he was at work.

So, Sarah settled into a new work routine. She rose early in the morning and went to collect her three charges. It was a short march back to Edward Street, where she would meet up with Jane and her son Thomas. The two women and four children would then spend their day together. Mostly they would just walk the streets. Occasionally, they would walk down the tow-path of the Regents Canal, where the children would squeal with delight at the sight of the huge horses pulling the barges along the canal. The women had to keep their wits about them to ensure that none of their charges fell into the canal or got trampled underfoot by the massive horses.

Sarah enjoyed her work, she loved being with children, but it was a joy tinged with sadness as she remembered her own son Edwin who she was not permitted to see. However, she was able to push her sadness to the back of her mind as she concentrated on her charges. They seemed so innocent and unaware of the troubles in the big wide world; somehow their playful nature helped her to forget her own troubles as she briefly touched their, much simpler, world. Of course the pay was poor but, in her life, she had learned, the hard way, to be frugal with money and to ignore a rumbling belly. However, one big advantage was that it did leave her evenings and Sundays free. On Sundays, she usually visited her family, taking a casual stroll down the Kingsland Road to Whitechapel. Of a Sunday afternoon, the roads were less crowded as many people took advantage of the holy day to lounge around, relax and do very little. Not many in the East End ventured to church and most of these fine establishments were half empty, much to the chagrin of the ministers.

She greatly enjoyed her time with her brothers and sisters. Her sister Caroline was now a very precocious nine-year-old, more woman than child. Living in the Essex Street, Rose Lane rookery slum had ensured that she grew up quickly. She was worldly wise beyond her years, but alert and highly intelligent. She had far more drive than Sarah and it was obvious that she would soon be fledging the nest and would be certain to do well for herself in the big wide world. As she grew older, Sarah had grown closer to her and they were always engaged in animated conversation. Caroline was always asking questions, her quest for knowledge was unceasing. Sarah found it increasingly more difficult to answer some of her more complicated questions and it was very clear that Caroline was rapidly becoming by far the most knowledgeable member of the whole family; Sarah adored her.

Her younger sister Mary was quite different from Caroline. She was only six-years-old but she was already displaying a caring and kindly disposition. She was much more like Sarah in her lack of driving ambition. She seemed content to accept her situation and whatever the world might throw at her.

Her young brother Henry was only four-years-old, but was already displaying an interest in the world around him and especially what his big brother Jimmy was doing. If Jimmy had a local chimney to sweep, he would sometimes take Henry with him. Henry was alert and interested, and it was soon apparent that he was a quick learner. He was proving to be a fine apprentice to Jimmy, who had high hopes that he might become his working partner when he grew a little older. They would set up a fine sweeps business together.

Sarah had started to look forward to these Sundays and life seemed to take on a better and more appealing aspect to her. She had been quite depressed after giving up her son Edwin to the Linfords'. But now she was enjoying her growing relationship with her siblings and the world looked a much rosier place. However, there was one sour note in that, of late, her parents seemed to be preoccupied by something. They were unnaturally gloomy and reserved. She felt reluctant to bring up her concerns with them and resolved to bring it up with her brother Jimmy.

Her brother Jimmy was working mostly in the Hackney Road, which was well populated with shops and houses, all with a multitude of chimneys, which kept him in full gainful employment. It was Jimmy's habit, after work, to call into the Nags Head Tavern, on the Hackney Road, for an evening ale before making his way back home to Pidgeon Court in Shoreditch. When she had been paid and settled her share of the rent, Sarah sometimes walked to the tavern to meet with Jimmy and have a sup of ale and a chin-wag with him.

It was one such evening and Sarah asked him how his work was going.

"We're doin' alright at the moment," he said, "mainly as a benefit from Liz's Queryin', we've even taken on a new Chummy."

Sarah put her drink down and looked at Jimmy, "fer God's sake Jimmy, will you speak in English! What on earth's Queryin'? And what's a Chummy?"

Cracking his face into a small smile, Jimmy replied, "A Chummy is….. well It's like I used to be, a climbing boy; we're all getting' a bit big for the smaller chimneys now."

"Oh," said Sarah, "and what's a….. what was it, Queerin' or summat?"

Jimmy laughed, "It's sweeps talk," he said, "Queryin' is goin' from door to door at houses with chimneys and asking if they need the services of a Journeyman sweep. A lot of other sweeps don't like us doin' it, but Liz is very good at it and usually gets us work."

Sarah was surprised at this as every time she had set eyes on Liz Ricketts she was quite fearsome looking; face as black as the ace of spades and hair so matted with soot that it was impossible to determine what it's real colour was. She said as much to Jimmy. He looked quite taken aback by her remarks about Liz.

"I'll have you know," he said pompously, "that she polishes up a treat after a few minutes under the pump."

Sarah could not restrain herself, she laughed out loud, ale dribbling from her mouth, "you make her sound like an old piece of furniture!" Then seeing Jimmy's hurt look, she decided that she had better change the subject. Then she remembered what had been on her mind. "I'm worried about mum and dad, they seem to be maudlin' lately, their not unwell are they?" Jimmy's face took on a dark look. Sarah started to get even more worried. "What's up Jimmy, is mum alright?"

"Oh yer, there's nothin' wrong with 'er," then he paused, "it's just that dad reckons their gonna pull down the whole of Essex Street and Rose Lane to make way for a posh new road called Spital Street."

Sarah stared in disbelief at him, "No! That can't be so."

"Well," continued Jimmy, "dad's mate Tom, read in a paper that the Government had set up a Board of Works, or summat, to buy up the property so they can knock it down." He paused to take a sip of his drink. "I don't think it will happen though. They can't throw all of those people out on the streets…..can they?"

Sarah was quite worried when she left the Nags Head and she was troubled by thoughts about the possible demise of Essex Street and Rose Lane as she walked back to her lodgings. Sleep was long in coming that night as she lay behind her curtain, mind racing, listening to the snores of the Freestones.

Sarah's father Jim was also very worried about what Tom had told him and had decided to try and find out if there was any truth in it. So, after work, he visited the Throwstik's and brought the subject up with Ambrose Everard. Since the old publican, Jane Dyke, had died, Ambrose and Jane's daughter Ann had been running the tavern. Ambrose told him that he had had several communications on the topic and had been told that the Licence to sell alcohol would not be renewed again. Other than that, he had no further information of relevance, but he did suggest that Jim talk to the other landlords in the street. So, he decided to walk down to the Rose and Crown. When he got there, Jim opened the door and walked in. He noticed that the publican, Tom Gould, was behind the bar, together with his wife Caroline who was serving a group of dock labourers. Jim nodded at the labourers, some of whom he vaguely knew from the London Docks and walked past them to where Tom Gould was standing alone at the end of the bar. "Hi there Tom," he said, "pull us an ale could yer."

"Sure," said Tom, "how yer doin'?"

"Well to tell yer the truth, I'm a little worried about this rumour that their gonna pull this lot down on us."

Tom handed Jim his drink and looked him straight in the eye, a serious expression on his face, "It ain't no rumour," he said.

Jim had started to lift his drink to his mouth, but Tom's words caused him to put it back down on the bar untouched. "What do yer mean?"

For the next half an hour Tom explained what he knew of the developments so far. Apparently the purchase of the properties had gone much further than Jim had realised. They were not only going to take down the three taverns in Essex Street, but also the Black Swan and the Stak in Wentworth Street, and the Dover Castle, King Harry and Duke of Cumberland's Head in Rose Lane. Jim was horrified, but worse was to come: according to Tom's sources at the brewery, The Government had purchased all the freehold and leasehold interests in most of the houses in all the courts in Essex Street and many of the houses fronting both Essex Street and Rose Lane.

"So," said Jim, "you tellin' me that The Government can pull our houses down when they like?"

"Yes, they could do," Tom replied. Then, putting his index finger on the side of his nose, he leaned conspiratorially across towards Jim. "But they want to make some money out of it, and not get their 'ands dirty, kickin' people out and knockin' their 'ouses down."

"What they gonna do then?" asked Jim.

Talking quietly so as not to be overheard Tom described the Government's plans. They were offering the material of the houses for sale by tender to local builders, who would then have the responsibility to remove the tenants, pull the houses down and remove the materials.

It was a very concerned Jim who finished his drink and made his way back home to Martins Court. That evening he and his wife discussed what Jim had learned. They would have to move, but where to? The whole area was already too crowded and there would be hundreds of people all looking for new homes as well. They decided that, rather than jump the gun, they might as well stay where they were until they were forced to leave.

The next Friday, Sarah had finished her child minding task for the day. She had been paid her wages and given Tom Freestone her portion of the rent. It was a crisp, but clear, November evening and Sarah had a little money left over, so she decided to walk to the Hackney Road and see if Jimmy was having his habitual drink in his favourite tavern.

She walked down the Hackney Road to the top of Birdcage Walk and was soon standing outside the Nag's Head. She opened the door and went in. The place was heaving with the Friday evening revellers. She pushed her way through the throng of people and made her way towards the bar. There was a group of young costermongers between her and the bar, jabbering away at the tops of their voices about the sales they had made and the ones they had missed. As she pushed her way through them, she felt a sharp pain in her backside which caused her to yelp out loud. Whirling round in anger, she confronted a curly haired, ruddy faced young man in a tweed cloth cap that had seen better days. She gave him a piece of ripe London slang for having the audacity to pinch her bum. He burst out laughing at her anger and raised his cap to her. She snatched the cap out of his hand and rammed it into his ale. At this sight, all his mates roared with laughter. Sarah left him with a surprised expression on his face, trying to extract his cap from his glass, and pushed her way through the crowd to reach the bar. Reaching the bar, she soon spotted Jimmy, in his customary corner. She elbowed her way across to him.

Jimmy called over to the landlord's son Billy Standen, who was serving behind the bar. He bought her over a glass of ale and refilled Jimmy's glass. They were soon chatting away about what they had been up to in their respective week's activities. Then, Jimmy started joking with her, as he frequently did lately, about her posh sounding voice. Her face coloured, she was thinking of the language she had reverted to with the young costermonger who had pinched her bum. To cover her embarrassment, she laughed and told him it was about time he smartened himself up. Especially if he wanted to attract a good wife.

They fell silent for a while, and inevitably their conversation turned to the proposed destruction of Essex Street and Rose Lane to make way for a new road. "They can't just knock their home down Jimmy. I'm sure it will be alright."

"I'm not so sure about that," he replied, "not after what dad heard at the Rose and Crown."

Now very alarmed Sarah asked him what he had heard. He explained what Tom Gould had told their father. That night as she lay down to sleep, her thoughts went to her family once again. What would they do if their house was pulled down?

As Christmas drew near, the atmosphere in Essex Street was far from celebratory as it was becoming clear, to all the inhabitants, that its destruction was now inevitable; it was just a matter of time. People were vacating houses in their droves. Strangers were appearing in the street and boarding up the vacant properties. In Martins Court some people had already started to move out and some of the properties were lying empty. But some, like the Valentines' at No. 5, had decided to stick it out until they were thrown out. Nell and her family, at No. 1, were also staying put, but she told Sarah's mother that she was looking for alternative accommodation and her extensive array of relations scattered throughout the area were looking on her behalf as well. Next door to Nell, the Sullivan's at No. 2, were also determined to stick it out.

The remaining residents contemplated blocking the narrow entrance to Martins Court to prevent intruders from gaining entry to destroy their houses. Jim was somewhat sceptical of this as all they would achieve was to trap themselves in. They could not stay indoors indefinitely.

The New Year of 1843 arrived with a cold snap. Freezing cold weather with driving snow covering the streets of London. The result of this was that Sarah's childminding was often confined to indoor activities during January and February.

Valentine's Day arrived. It was cold and blustery. But, determined to celebrate it, she wrapped her young charges up in as many warm clothes as she could find and made her way back to Edward Street. Picking up Jane Freestone and young Thomas, they all made their way to the Victory Tavern at the end of Philips Street, on the Kingsland Road. Sarah had been religiously putting some pennies away in her purse for this day and bought them all drinks until the money ran out. Laughing, Sarah turned her purse upside down to show it was empty, but Freddy's poesy ring fell out onto the table; she had forgotten it was in there. It rolled across the table towards Jane Freestone who picked it up. She looked closely at it. "That's a very nice ring," she said, "why don't you wear it?"

Sarah explained the origin of the ring and that she had wanted to give it back to Freddy, but he had gone.

"That's no excuse for not wearing it. Put it on your right hand. It's too nice to stay in a purse."

Sarah considered what Jane had said and realised that it was quite true, it *was* a nice ring and it was hers, since Freddy had run off. Her incident with Freddy was more than three years ago now and she had pretty well got over it. As far as she knew, he had not reappeared, so why not wear it? Her mind now made up, she put it on her right hand

and placed it flat on the table. Yes, they both agreed that the ring looked very nice indeed.

It was a tipsy pair of ladies, leading a rowdy group of children that left the tavern that afternoon. But Sarah managed to get her young charges safely back home, in time for their father's arrival back from work. He did give her an odd look when she left, banging her head on the door as she opened it, and tottering her way out onto the street; he thought that she might be coming down with something.

Meanwhile, Sarah's father Jim had taken to calling in the Rose and Crown most evenings on his way home from work, to keep abreast of developments in Essex Street. He had cultivated Tom Gould and pumped him for any shred of news. Tom had heard rumours of funny goings on from his contacts at the brewery. Apparently, a ruthless local builder by the name of John Edmunds, who lived in Gun Street by the Old Artillery Ground, had been doing some sly dealing with the Board of Works set up to administer the acquiring of the properties. Tom had it on good authority that this John Edmunds, had organised the Board to accept his offer of £5 per house for 4 houses in Martins Court, 10 in Essex Court, 12 in Elgar Square, 4 in Elgar Place and 10 in Rose and Crown Court, despite the fact that his sealed bid was not the highest; it smacked of underhand dealing. This was further reinforced when it was discovered that he had bought the remaining 18 houses in Martins Court for only £2 per house! He had also bought all the houses in the neighbouring Moors Court.

On his next visit Tom told him that this John Edmunds had been instructed to send his men in to evict all the tenants of Moors Court, as it would be the first to come down. By all accounts, they had done this sort of thing before and were none too gentle in the manner of its execution. Moreover, all complaints about his men's brutal activities had fallen on deaf ears; he clearly had friends in high places and felt he could do as he pleased. In truth, The Government badly wanted this whole area cleared and were not particularly interested in how it was done, so long as it was done expediently.

It was a Monday morning in March 1843, and Sarah's father was walking out of the southern end of Essex Street, where it meets the Whitechapel High Street. He was on his way to the docks to start his day's work. There was a thick yellow smog in the air. Over the last few years the morning smog had got worse and worse. At times it was literally impossible to see more than two or three feet in front of you. Suddenly, he stopped in his tracks. He was startled to see that several large horse drawn carts were parked in the High Street, just outside the entrance to Essex Street and gangs of labourers were milling about on the pavement. Others were collecting barrows, hammers, picks and shovels from the backs of the carts. He wondered what they were up to, but he could not dally, he was due at the docks.

That evening, returning home from work, Jim emerged from the top of Red Lion Street into the Whitechapel High Street, He looked left and right down the High Street, checking for traffic before crossing the road to enter the bottom end of Essex Street. He stepped into the road, and stopped dead in his tracks. Over the other side of the road, directly ahead of him, the entrance to Essex Street was obscured by several horse drawn carts much as it had been when he had left for the docks in the morning. Only now each of them was full with bricks, tiles, wood and the remains of window frames. A cloud of dust surrounded them. Reaching the north side of the High Street he had to walk some 50 feet along the roadway before he could get on to the pavement round the carts. Then, he had to walk back along the pavement to the entrance to Essex Street. At first he was unable to gain access as several burly men were pushing heavily loaded barrows out of the narrow entranceway and he had to step to one side as they exited Essex Street and proceeded to empty their barrow loads into the waiting carts. Eventually, Jim was able to get past and make his way up Essex Street. Just as he reached the entrance to Martins Court he stopped in his tracks once again. Just outside the Throwstik's was a huge mountain of rubble: bricks, slates and planks of wood. Jim could not believe his eyes. He could see people sitting on the rubble, clutching their meagre possessions. Children were crying and women weeping; men were standing around with bemused expressions on their faces. Suddenly he heard an angry shout. "Get out of the road you fool!"

Looking round he saw a group of rough looking men pushing empty barrows up the street and bearing down on him. He jumped to one side, only just avoiding being run down. They turned left, just beyond the mound of rubbish and disappeared into Moors Court. He walked up to a group of men standing to one side of the rubble. "What's going on here?" he asked.

One of the men turned a worried face towards him. "We lived in Moors Court, we were just told to get out," he stammered, "then they came in and started knocking the place down. I barely got the kids out before the roof came in."

Jim looked over at the entrance to Moors Court. It used to be a narrow alley between No. 18 and 19 Essex Street. No. 18 was a narrow house, now it was a gap, clearly the rubble lying outside the Throwstik's was the material of the house. It left a wider entrance to Moors Court. Jim and the man he had been talking with walked over to the gap where No. 18 had been and looked down the length of Moors Court. They both stood in silence and surveyed the devastation in front of them. Several of the houses on the left hand side had been completely demolished, revealing the backs of the houses on the north side of Martins Court, to which they had been attached, including Jim's at No. 5. The men were loading the rubble onto the barrows they had just taken into the court. With a grim expression on his face Jim left the group of dazed residents and made his way into Martins Court. There he found Nell and her family standing with his wife and children in front of Nell's house at No. 1. They were looking shocked

His wife ran over to him. "You seen what their doin'?" she said, a quiver of alarm in her voice.

Jim put his arm round her to comfort her. "there, there, don't take on love."

She pulled angrily away from him, "what do yer mean, don't take on!" she shouted, "can't you see you fool, their pullin' our bloody homes down round our ears!"

He stood there helpless and looked around him, he could see Jeremiah Sullivan with his wife Ann standing outside their home at

No. 2. Their children Mary and John were standing bemused by their side. Ann had her one-year-old daughter, also Ann, clutched tightly in her arms and he was startled to see that the baby had a mass of red spots on its face. He quickly looked away across the narrow court and could see bemused groups of people standing outside the doors of the facing houses. They were talking in whispers, frightened expressions on their faces.

As the demolition work in Moors Court continued, the workmen uncovered deep cellars and privy pits at the far end of the court. It was seen that the privy pits and cellars ran under all the houses at the end of Moors Court and also continued under Nos. 4, 5 and 6 at the far end of Martins Court, to which they had been attached. They cleared out the cellars and privy pits, not realising that, in doing so, they were undermining the end houses, still standing in Martins Court.

Over the next few days, as further houses were knocked down, the area was becoming very dangerous, particularly at night. A heavy, continuous rain had started; there was little lighting to indicate the positions of the deep pits that had been uncovered and there were several accidents, with people falling into them.

Now that the demolition was underway, most of the people in the houses on the north side of Martins Court moved out. Only three families remained: Nell now had the whole of No. 1, the Sullivans' had the whole of No. 2 and the Valentines' the whole of No. 5. The excavations of the cellars and privy pits at the end of Moors Court had caused the floors to crack in the houses at the end of Martins Court, including No. 5. Rain water had seeped through the cracks and pools of evil smelling dirty water were collecting on the ground floor making it uninhabitable. So, as the Mahoneys' had vacated the upper floor and moved out, Jim had moved their mattresses and the furniture, Sarah had bought, upstairs where they now made their home.

Then, on 30 March 1843 there was a tragedy. Ann Sullivan, the one-year-old daughter of Jeremiah and Ann Sullivan at No. 2 Martins Court, next door to Nell, died of the measles. Her parents were distraught and within a few days had moved out.

Shortly after, Jim's daughter, seven-year-old Mary, developed a rash of red spots. His wife and Nell were very worried about Mary, particularly as No. 5, where the Valentines' were living, was becoming waterlogged as the floor continued to split apart. Nell suggested that they should move into No. 1 with her. Nell's house was right at the entrance to Martins Court, at the rear of the Throwstik's and it was not affected by the cellars and privy pits, situated at the end of the court; it was quite dry and seemed to be sound. Jim agreed, but as it was Friday tomorrow, his last working day of the week, he suggested that he move their beds and belongings at the weekend when he would have more time. His wife and Nell were still worried about Mary sleeping in the damp house, so it was agreed that his wife and Mary would move into No. 1 immediately and Jim would put a mattress upstairs for them. Meanwhile, for the time being, he would return to No. 5 with Henry and Caroline, where they would sleep until their beds and all the furniture could be moved on the Saturday.

On the Friday morning, Jim set out early for the docks. It was still raining heavily and he had noticed that further water had seeped into No. 5 through the ever widening cracks in the floor; he was mighty glad that they were only going to spend one more night there. He left Henry and Caroline at Nell's on his way to work.

That Friday evening, during a short respite from the rain, Jim called in The Rose and Crown. The tavern was buzzing with the tales of woe from the people being left homeless. There were also tales of buildings coming down on sleeping or drunken tramps. Their bodies were carted away. Their names were unknown and their identities never sought; they were destined for a mass paupers' grave.

That evening whilst Jim was drinking at the Rose and Crown, John Edmunds's workmen were visiting the houses on the north side of Martins Court asking the residents to get out. They found Nell's family and the Valentines' in No. 1 and told them that they had to be out by the Monday when the houses in Martins Court were due to be pulled down. They found no occupants in the remaining 5 houses; they assumed that they were all vacant.

Following the accidents, under strict instructions from the Board of Works, John Edmunds had intended to use the ballast from the demolished houses to fill in the cellars and privy pits. Unfortunately, the continuous rains had flooded the holes and left the demolition site too deep in mud to allow them to wheel their barrows. They were forced to give up for the day, and left the holes empty.

As Jim left the Rose and Crown that evening, the rain was still falling. He looked up at the sky, it was grey and overcast, made more dramatic by being backlit from a full moon, a sure sign that they were in for a long downpour; he pulled his cap down and his collar up. As he walked up Essex Street the rain intensified and he was soon splashing through growing puddles of water that were gathering on the street. However, his attention was not on the rain, thoughts were racing through his head. He had assumed that his wife and children were removed from the destruction, secure in their court; he was now not so sure. The demolition men were moving inexorably closer. He was troubled and felt a mounting premonition of doom growing within him. He shivered, but not with the cold. It was as if he knew that disaster was imminent. Indeed, he had a right to be afraid. He would be more afraid still if he knew that, before the next 12 hours was up, he would be dead and his family decimated.

After a meagre meal at Nell's house, he collected Caroline and Henry and took them to No. 5 where they all soon fell asleep on their mattresses, on the floor upstairs.

That evening the rain intensified still further, it was coming down in sheets; the houses at the end of Martins Court started to move. They had no foundations, being built straight onto the ground, which was now becoming a sea of mud. Denied the support of the Moors Court houses that had been built directly onto the back of them, they started to tilt backwards, sinking into the mud. There was a jolt; Jim briefly opened his eyes and looked up; there were no upstairs ceilings in these primitive houses, merely the underside of the roof. He heard Henry stirring next to him. There was a second heavier jolt and Jim felt the whole house tilt backwards; roof tiles were falling in on them. Now wide awake, he saw several tiles strike his son's head; he could feel rainwater on his face. Alarmed, he looked up at the hole in the roof, he could see the grey clouds illuminated by the moon. They seemed to be moving rapidly across the sky, then he realised with a fright that it was not the clouds moving, but their house! As the floor tilted to 45 degrees, and beyond, the last thing he saw was his daughter Caroline's frightened face and her wide open, deep brown, eyes. No. 5 Martins Court completed its backward somersault and landed in the exposed open cellar and privy pits, where it was dashed into a thousand pieces.

Early the next morning the rain had thankfully stopped. John Edmunds and his workmen arrived on site to find that Nos. 4, 5 and 6 Martins Court had collapsed. Nos. 1, 2 and 3 were still standing. They immediately cordoned off the area, placing a barrier in Essex Street, just to the north of Moors Court. As an additional safety measure, all of the remaining occupants of Martins Court were rudely awakened and forced out of their houses, barely having time to grab their belongings. They were unceremoniously herded down Essex Street where a further barrier was established by the Rose and Crown Tavern. In all some 80 people had been evacuated and they formed a mass of screaming, crying humanity, crammed into the narrow southern extent of Essex Street.

Sarah's mother was holding tightly onto her daughter Mary and searching the crowds, desperately looking for a sight of her husband Jim, daughter Caroline and son Henry. She looked in vain.

John Edmunds was observing the collapsed houses with mixed feelings. As a result of the accidents, he had been told to fill in the holes left by the excavation of the cellars and privy pits. It had been his intention to use the broken bricks and ballast to do that. He had wanted to salvage all the useable materials for reuse on other building programmes, but the shattered residue of the collapsed houses had filled the holes completely. He briefly contemplated removing the material from the holes to see what could be salvaged, then immediately dismissed the idea, it would take too long. Anyway, on the plus side, the collapsed houses had merely saved him the time and effort of bringing ballast in to fill the holes. So, on balance, it wasn't such a bad thing. He instructed his men to throw earth onto the top of the holes and level it off, completely unaware of the of the Valentines' bodies underneath.

It was early Sunday morning and Sarah Valentine was awakened from her sleep by a furious hammering on the door. She sat up and pulled her curtain aside. She could see Tom Freestone and his wife stirring on their bed. Thomas, lying across the bottom of the bed, was still in slumber. Then a voice shouted from outside.

"Sarah! Sarah! Come quick. There's bad trouble!" It was her brother Jimmy's voice and he sounded desperate.

Sarah jumped off her mattress and rushed to the door. Wrenching it open, she stepped outside, pulling it shut behind her. She saw a distraught looking Jimmy standing there. The fear on his face worried her. "What's the matter?" she gasped.

"Martins Court's down!" he gasped. "It all came down in a bang!" Then his face crumpled. "Dad, Caroline and Henry are gone."

"What do you mean gone?" said Sarah, now very worried.

Jimmy was panting from running all the way. Sarah waited while he regained his breath. "Nell's Beth came to get me yesterday. It took her a while to find me as we was workin' a chimney in Hackney. Anyway she was cryin' her eyes out and I couldn't get no sense out of her. She was sayin' something about the houses all gone. Anyways I went with her back to Martins Court." He paused for a moment before going on more slowly. "My God, It's awful. Moors Court and the top of Martins Court are down. It looked like mum and dad's house is gone."

"No!" interrupted Sarah, "how are they? Did you see them?"

"Mum and Mary are alright. They stayed with Nell on account that Mary's not well. Nell's house and the Sullivans' next door look to be still standin'"

"What about dad?" said Sarah.

"Dad, Caroline and Henry are missing," Jimmy said simply.

A stunned silence settled over both of them. It was broken by the door opening behind them. Tom Freestone was standing in the doorway, sleep still in his eyes. "What's the matter?" he enquired.

Sarah quickly made her mind up. She would go to her mother and help. She dashed back inside to grab her shawl and bonnet telling Tom

Freestone that she had to go, and with that, she and her brother dashed out into the street, leaving Tom Freestone staring after them with a puzzled expression on his face. Sarah and Jimmy hastily made their way back down the Kingsland Road to Whitechapel.

They reached the northern entrance to Essex Street and pushed their way through the narrow alleyway which was full of people trying to get out of Essex Street. Eventually they reached the main street and started to walk down it. They only got as far as Essex Court and could get no further, masses of people were swarming about like headless chickens unsure which way to turn. They linked arms and started to push their way through. After about half an hour, they reached a barrier, formed of barrels with planks of wood across the top. It stretched right across the street; they could get no further. They could see the Throwstik's about 20 yards away and the rubble filled gap that was once Moors Court and the top of Martins Court. Sarah could hardly believe her eyes. The devastation was incredible. The masses of rubble from the demolished and collapsed houses was scattered everywhere.

Jimmy could see that there was another barrier set up across the street further down, with more masses of people beyond. He took Sarah's arm and pointed it out to her. "Mum might be with those people behind that barrier," he said.

"Yes," said Sarah staring intently into the crowd trying to spot a familiar face, "we better try and get over there."

Jimmy made an attempt to climb across the barrier, but a large ugly looking man ran over and warned him not to enter the 'danger area'. With a resigned shrug he turned away and they started to push their way back through the crowds up to the northern exit to Essex Street. It took them nearly an hour to get to the other barrier as it necessitated pushing their way laboriously through several overcrowded streets. They went down Wentworth Street to George Yard, through George Yard to the High Street and back along the High Street to the southern entrance to Essex Street. This was just as crowded as the northern entrance had been and it took them a further half an hour to get into the southern part of Essex Street and reach the barrier that they had seen from the northern end. Slowly they elbowed their way along the barrier, their eyes peeled for a sight of their family; they saw no one they knew. They fought their way down the west side of Essex Street, pushing their way into each of the crowded courts; all to no avail. They were desperate and tears were running down Sarah's face when they reached the entrance to Rose and Crown Court. Then, with a cry of relief, she spotted them. There was their mother holding Mary's hand tightly, so as not to lose her. Nell, with Beth, young Ellen and Margaret were standing beside her; all were looking distraught. They made a pathetic picture of despair. Sarah ran to them, Jimmy close on her heels. Sarah hugged her mother and Mary; both were weeping. Nell was beside herself as her youngest daughter Julia was missing.

Jimmy walked around and questioned everyone he could, but nothing had been seen nor heard of Jim, Caroline or Henry. It was as if they had vanished from the face of the earth. They would never see them again.

Concerning the new street, right up until the eleventh hour it was called Spital Street, Then, in a final twist, it was decided that it should be called Commercial Street, as it still is today. From any viewpoint, the demolition of Essex Street and Rose Lane was a callous and pointless act. 250 houses were destroyed and over 3000 people found themselves instantly homeless. All of these people were regarded, by the establishment of the day, as worthless and hence expendable. The loss of Sarah's father Jim, and siblings Caroline and Henry, was of little significance in the grand scheme of things. Their bodies were never found and their deaths were never recorded.

And, what did it all achieve? In terms of its published objective, to provide a wide new route between Whitechapel High Street and Shoreditch, it spectacularly failed. They ran out of funds half way through the project and the new road ended, just past Spitalfields Church in a tangle of, virtually impassable, courts and alleys, well short of its objective. In fact, at the time it was jokingly stated that its major achievement was in providing a good access for the dock workers to attend Sunday prayers at Spitalfields Church. In terms of humanity, it destroyed the lives of thousands of people, the Valentine family included. In terms of ventilating the area, it also failed. The displaced people had to live somewhere and they did not go far. They merely moved in to the surrounding slums, increasing the population density in those areas to a figure far in excess of what it was before the 'project'. And what of the new 'Commercial Street'? That too was a massive failure. Building plots were put up for sale along the line of demolition. Few sold; many remained empty for more than twenty years.

CHAPTER 28

The Grand House, 1843

SARAH'S MOTHER AND Mary moved in with Jimmy in Pidgeon Court as a temporary measure. It was Nell who finally found them all new permanent accommodation. Some of her family and friends lived just north of Spitalfields Church, in Little Pearl Street, a mainly Irish community. The mass demolitions had stopped abruptly, just short of Little Pearl Street and its houses had been left untouched. But the area immediately surrounding the entrance to it was a mass of rubble and debris.

Nell moved in with some of her family already living in Little Pearl Street and Sarah's mother, sister Mary and Jimmy found lodgings in the house next door. With the demise of his father, Jimmy decided to stay with his mother and Mary. They would not last long on their own; his mother was in a terrible state and sister Mary at seven-years-of-age, could hardly be expected to look after her mother.

Slowly they started to rebuild their life, but none of them would ever get over their sad loss. Sarah's mother was particularly badly hit with the loss of a husband, daughter and young son. She became morose and withdrawn. She took little care in her health or appearance. It was the start of a downhill path for her.

Jimmy focussed on his work. He was now a fully qualified sweep journeyman, with a good earning potential, providing he could secure the work. Sarah's mother, and even Mary, went out with Nell to try and secure cleaning and charwomen's work whenever they could. The survivors of the devastated family struggled on with life.

Sarah spent a few days with her family and when they secured their new accommodation in Little Pearl Street she sorrowfully decided to return to her lodgings with the Freestones. Jimmy tried to persuade her to stay, he was concerned that she had no money. But she was too distraught by the loss of her brother and sister. She was sad for her mother at the loss of her father. But, try as she might, she could not feel as bad about his loss as those of the children. They were far too young for their lives to be taken. She found herself thinking of the day she and Caroline had stood in the deserted Spitalfields market, when they had played their 'little game' to find out how many children Caroline would have. Caroline had blown all the dandelion seeds away; Sarah could not get the vision of her little sister's distraught face staring at the bare dandelion head. Poor thing, she would have no children now, for certain. Sarah knew that she needed time alone to come to terms with her loss.

Despite her refusals, Jimmy forced some money on her, 'to tide her over for a bit', and as she walked up the Kingsland Road she had to smile at his generosity. When she arrived at the Freestones, she found the reception a little cold. Tom Freestone's friend who had employed her as a childminder had been badly let down by Sarah's sudden unexplained disappearance and he had been forced to engage another girl. He had complained to Tom about Sarah's unreliability and it had put some strain on their friendship. Things got a little better when Sarah explained what had happened. Also, she was able to give the Freestones some of the money Jimmy had given her as payment towards the rent. But she was not sure what she was going to do about keeping up any further payments, without a job.

Over the next few days, Sarah made a half hearted attempt to find further employment, but to no avail. It was Thursday 11th May 1843 and she had spent the day trudging up and down the Hackney Road. Her heart was not really in it. All she could think of was Caroline and Henry.

Happy cheerful children, bright and intelligent, with their whole future in front of them. Cut down ruthlessly. It was a cruel world.

As she walked past the northern end of Caroline Street, her mood deepened further, she could not help but glance down it. She could see the outside of No. 9. Her baby Edwin would soon be three-years-old. He would be walking now, he would be starting to speak. She felt a mother's uncontrollable desire to see her child. She wanted to run up to the door of No. 9 and hammer on it, demanding to see her baby. But she knew that all she would get would be the sharp end of Jane Linford's tongue, 'the child is not to be confused at his young age, begone with you'. Uncontrollably, her eyes began to water. The events of the last few days had taken their toll on her morale. She felt at her lowest ebb ever; she continued walking aimlessly.

After half an hour walking, in no particular direction, she looked up and noticed that she was walking past the Nags Head, where she and her brother Jimmy had often drunk. They had got to know the landlord Stephen Standen and his wife Ann quite well. She stopped, she only had a few pence in her pocket left from what Jimmy had given her, but she was in need of some sustenance and so she pushed open the front door and entered the dim tavern. It was not too crowded, so she walked up to one end of the bar and leaned her elbows on it. The landlord's wife Ann and son Billy were behind the bar.

Ann came over to where Sarah was, and started to greet her. Then, noticing the tears in her eyes, leaned over and put her hand on her shoulder. "Hey, my love!" she said, "what's the matter?"

Sarah's face crumpled, and in a sobbing voice, she told Ann what had befallen her family. Ann listened, aghast, as the tale unwound. When Sarah's voice finally petered out at the end of her story, Ann came out from behind the bar and put her arms round her. Whilst Sarah was sobbing into her shoulder, Ann waved to her son. "Get us both a good measure of brandy Billy," she said and eased Sarah into a chair at a table near the bar. She sat down beside her as Billy brought over the drinks.

Sarah was drunk and broke when she walked, with unsteady legs, back home to Edward Street. She collapsed into her corner and fell into a disturbed sleep. She dreamed that she could see her sister Caroline, in the distance, holding her brother Henry's little hand. She kept calling out to them, but they ignored her and walked away into the mist. She tried to run after them, but her legs would not respond. Despite her shouting after them, they disappeared from sight.

She awoke early the next morning. She had few possessions, but she gathered them up and quietly left. She walked down Edward Street into Philips Street and turned right at the end of Philips Street and walked down the Kingsland Road. After 20 minutes of walking she reached Worship Street and was soon standing outside the Court House once again. Two hours later, having appealed to Magistrate Bennet and visited John Coste at the Parish Offices, she was on her way back up the Kingsland Road, with her ticket for the Shoreditch Workhouse clutched in her hand.

So, after only 7 months on the street, on Friday 12th May 1843, she presented herself at the door of Shoreditch Workhouse once again. When the Workhouse Master asked her age she said she wasn't sure but she did remember that he had put down nineteen when she had last been admitted. He looked at the admissions register, grunted and put nineteen down again. She put Freddy's ring deep in her dress pocket and went through the usual admission ritual. Soon, she found herself, attired in the drab Workhouse garb, sitting on a bed in the old familiar womens' working ward 16. There were only a few old and infirm women in the ward, all able bodied inmates being at their allotted work. She did not have long to rest on her laurels. It was wash day and she was soon summonsed to take her part in the monthly wash cycle.

At dinner, she noticed Maggie Orme and Liz Weston sitting next to each other and, further down, Mary Murphy. All three glared daggers at her as soon as they saw her. She sat as far away from them as she could and did her best to ignore them. Fortunately, none of them were working in the laundry and, when she returned to ward 16 after supper, she was relieved to see that they were not in the same ward as her.

The following Wednesday 17th May 1843, Sarah had a pair of visitors. She was taken to the receiving room and was delighted to see her brother Jimmy, accompanied by the Reverend Ratcliffe. She was so pleased to see Jimmy that she cried on his shoulder. When her tears slowed down Jimmy gently raised her head and brushed the tears from her cheeks with his hand. The Reverend Ratcliffe smiled at her. Jimmy had been to see him and explained what had happened to their family. He had been very kind and visited their mother, helping her to cope with her loss. It was he who had discovered Sarah's whereabouts, through his association with the Workhouse Master. He consoled Sarah and encouraged her to have faith in the Lord. He reinforced this by announcing that the Church Wardens had found Sarah a good live-in position, with an esteemed member of the Parish. She could start immediately, if she wished to take it up.

Sarah's mood brightened at this news, and with the encouragement of Jimmy and the Reverend, Sarah applied to leave the Workhouse. With the Reverend's help, her request was granted immediately and her old clothes were returned to her. After changing, and clutching her few possessions, she accompanied Jimmy and the Reverend Ratcliffe outside.

After a few kind words, the Reverend excused himself and strode off up the road back to his church. Jimmy knew where she was to be working as he had cleaned the chimneys there on several occasions and he escorted her down the Kingsland Road to Hackney. Cutting through Union Street, they entered the Hackney Road. After walking for a short while, Jimmy stopped and pointed out a large imposing property, built over several stories and with many chimneys. Sarah looked at it with some trepidation; it was a grand house indeed. Jimmy explained that he would have to leave her as he had only secured a short leave of absence from work and had to return. Sarah clasped his hands, smiled and kissed him on the cheek. With a return smile and a wave, he marched off down the Hackney Road. She watched him go knowing that, as well as being a brother, he was certainly the best friend she had in the whole world; she loved him dearly. Her gaze returned to the grand house, which was to be her place of work, and her home.

Having been a servant in a large house before, Sarah was acutely aware of her lowly position and knew far better than to approach the imposing, shiny front door. So, she walked round the side and soon found the back entrance to the kitchen. The door was open and, from within, she could hear the sound of voices. As she moved closer, she could hear a woman talking; she was complaining to another woman about the poor quality of the vegetables. "These cowcumbers are brown instead of green; this cabbage must be a week old. Look at it! I specifically ordered *fresh* vegetables. And look at these potatoes, they've more eyes than a pack o' rats."

"Why don't you send 'em back?" said the second woman.

"We'll never get fresh ones in time fer dinner," she replied, "but that costermonger will get a piece a my tongue when I sees 'im next. You mark my words!"

Sarah stood at the door wondering if this was a good time to present herself; perhaps she should go away and come back later. Then she was spotted by a tall thin woman, of middling age, wearing a green apron and green frilly bonnet holding two of the offending potatoes in her hands; now it was too late to slip away. "What you doin' there girl?" she shouted at Sarah.

"May it please you ma'am," said Sarah meekly, "I'm the new servant girl."

"God help me!" exclaimed the woman with the potatoes, "not *another* one. As if we don't have enough already!"

"She'll be the new one from the Workhouse," said the second woman, who was of similar age, shorter, fairer and much plumper, but also wearing a green apron with matching bonnet.

"God knows why the Master feels he needs to take in Workhouse girls," said the first woman.

"You knows why," said the second woman, "makes him look big at the Parish Council. Doin' 'is bit to 'elp the local paupers."

All of this exchange was carried out in front of Sarah, as if she didn't exist. She was starting to think that this was not a very auspicious start and she was nervously hopping from foot to foot.

As if suddenly noticing her for the first time, the second woman addressed Sarah. "What yer hopping about fer? You need a pee or summat?"

"No ma'am," said Sarah, then, hoping to change the subject, "what are my duties?"

"Duties!" laughed the first woman, "hark at 'er will yer. Duties! I ask yer. Whatever next, a Workhouse girl askin' what 'er *duties* are, like she's some kinda Chamber Maid or summat." Then, looking directly at Sarah, "your first *duty* is keep out from under my feet!"

Sarah felt her face redden. Clutching her little bundle, she took a step back. Then a door opened at the back of the extensive kitchen and a tall man dressed in fine livery entered and strode with ramrod straight back and military precision up to the women. Both women jumped to attention immediately.

Spotting Sarah standing in the doorway, the man pointed at her. "Who's this then?" he barked out, in a stern, clipped voice.

Both women stood still, rooted to the spot, speechless under his glare.

"Cat got yer tongue has it!" he shouted at the thin woman still holding the potatoes.

"She's the new Workhouse girl," she stuttered, wilting under his glare.

The man's face changed at this knowledge, his mouth curled down at the corners. "I do wish the Master was not so insistent about employing paupers," he stormed, "they are perfectly useless as servants, they just get in the way."

Then, two women walked through the same door that the man had entered by. They were both attired in starched white coveralls, white aprons and white hats. Hearing their entrance, the man turned and addressed the leading woman, a short, stout lady, with a large ruddy face. "Ah cook!" he said, "I need to discuss a change in the menu with you."

"Jesus!" said the cook, "Mistress changin' things at the last knockin's again is she?"

"It's not your place to question the Mistress!" shouted the man sternly.

Then the cook noticed Sarah still standing meekly in the doorway, clinging to her small bundle. "Who's she?" she demanded.

"Another one of those damnable Workhouse paupers!" the man said venomously.

"What on God's earth does the Master expect me to do with the likes of 'er?" stated the cook equally venomously.

Sarah felt all five sets of eyes boring into her; she was now the undivided centre of attention, none of it friendly. She had never felt so alone, useless and unwanted. It was very clear that she was unwelcome here and she felt her eyes moisten under the combined glares. Despite her attempt to prevent it, she felt a tear run down her cheek and she angrily wiped it away with the back of her hand. "I'll go then!" she said fiercely, angry with herself for crying in front of these nasty people, "I can see I am not wanted here!" With that she turned to walk away.

"Stay where you are girl!" ordered the man in a stern bellow. His military parade ground voice stopped Sarah dead in her tracks. She turned round and looked at him, fear etched on her face. "You are certainly not needed here, but it is clearly the Master's wish that you are employed in this household. And it is our duty to carry out his wishes. Come 'ere!" he commanded.

Clutching her little bundle of possessions to her chest she slowly and tentatively advanced into the kitchen.

"Come on girl, I won't bite!" he ordered, showing a set of sharp, yellow, rat-like teeth that made her think he just might do that very thing.

She stopped six feet away from him.

He turned to the cook. "Well what are we to do with her?" he asked.

"She better stay in the kitchen," said the cook, "we'll try and find her some work. She can sleep here with the other downstairs staff. God knows we have little enough room for more bodies." Then she turned to Sarah and pointed to an open archway. "Put your things in the washroom. You'll be sleeping in there."

Glad to get away from their fierce glares, Sarah walked through the arch into a large whitewashed room. It was clean enough and contained sinks and wash tubs. She found several bundles of belongings lined up against a far wall and added hers to them. Looking round, she could see a stack of straw mattresses and folded rough cloth covers, leaning against the wall in one corner. She presumed that they constituted the sleeping arrangements, but there did seem to be rather a lot of them.

She walked back to the archway and stood there looking into the kitchen. The two original women, in green overalls, were busying themselves with the vegetables, whilst the two women dressed in white, one of whom Sarah now knew to be the cook, were in heated discussion with the man in livery about the dinner menu. None of them took the least notice of Sarah; she thought it wisest to remain where she was, and keep quiet.

She looked over the kitchen. It was very large and seemed well appointed; she wondered how many lived in this grand house. A few moments later, more people started to enter the kitchen. Two scruffily dressed lads, a few years younger than her, entered and joined the women cleaning and preparing the vegetables. More women entered, all wearing aprons, and started busying themselves at various benches distributed around the kitchen. As she watched it became clear that each was preparing different food. One large woman, with massive arms, was standing at a butcher's block handling a lump of meat, others were preparing pastries. Each seemed to know what they were about and carried out their tasks in silence; none of them noticed Sarah.

After a final round of shouting, the man in livery turned on his heel and marched out of the kitchen, leaving the cook red faced, standing with her hands on her hips, clearly very angry. The cook then stormed through the kitchen shouting orders to the women, mainly along the lines of instructing them to stop what they were doing and start doing something different. All the women then became angry and started arguing with the cook.

The very large woman who had been trimming the meat stabbed her large knife into the top of her chopping block and faced the cook eye to eye. "You mean they don't want the beef now?" she stormed.

Sarah watched with wide eyes as the two women faced each other off. She stared at them, looking alternately at the women and then at the knife, point down in the wood, handle swinging from side to side, where it had been so fiercely embedded.

No one would get to know what the end result of this confrontation might have been, as at that moment the man in livery stormed back into the kitchen, doubtless alerted by the shouting of the women. He barked out an order for silence, and silence descended on the kitchen. His next shouted order was for them to get back to work, or else!

In silence, they all returned to their tasks. The large woman at the butcher's block struggled to extract her blade. Having done so, she laid it down on the block and picked up the side of beef. She then returned the beef to the cold shelf in the massive pantry and pulled out a large turkey. This she took back to her bench, slammed it down and proceeded to pluck out its feathers with a fury that clearly conveyed her anger to all around her. Satisfied that order had now been restored, the man in livery promptly wheeled round and marched out, closing the door behind him. Silence reigned in the kitchen for several minutes before the women slowly started to talk; at first in whispers, then, as time progressed, louder and louder until they were in full flow jabbering to each other nineteen to the dozen.

Sarah had remained standing in the archway observing this spectacle with growing trepidation. She was still standing there several minutes later, when the large woman plucking the turkey noticed her. "Who's she?" she demanded in a loud voice, pointing at Sarah.

A sudden silence fell and Sarah felt nine pairs of eyes swivel in her direction; she stood there, riveted to the spot, like a rabbit caught in a coach light. She felt a sudden desire to pee, but tightened her legs together, fear showing in her eyes.

It was the cook who broke the silence. "It's only the new Workhouse girl. Someone find her a job ter do, will yer. She's making the place look untidy."

Laughter sprang up at this comment and the tension eased. The large woman went back to ripping the feathers out of her bird and the thin potato woman, in the green apron, that Sarah had first spoken with, called her over. Sarah gratefully ran over to the vegetable station and was soon assigned the job of peeling potatoes with the two young lads. They proved to be an engaging pair and Sarah was soon talking happily with them. They were called John and George and it transpired that they, like Sarah, were from the Workhouse; in their case from the Hackney Union Workhouse. On hearing this, Sarah's face grew a little sad, as this was where she had given birth to her son Edwin, who she had not seen for almost three years. At this thought, she felt the tears welling up again, but she determinedly brushed them aside with the back of her hand and concentrated on talking to the lads next to her. From them, she discovered a little more about the household in which she now worked.

The Master of the house ran a large factory at the back of Paradise Row on the east corner of the Bethnal Green Road. It was a typical 'sweat shop' of the time, where masses of people worked long hard hours for meagre pay, so that he could manufacture goods on the cheap. However, such enterprises often generated massive profits.

His house was typical of the new breed of industrial businessmen springing up in the early part of Queen Victoria's reign. They were frequently born of the middle classes but, taking advantage of the growing industrial revolution, had now found themselves with money. Not having been brought up with money, they did not have the finesse of the nobility, who tended to regard them as rather gauche. In an attempt to prove themselves in society, they bought large houses and often laid on lavish parties. They entertained frequently, inviting all and sundry in the gentry, in an attempt to impress.

In the belief that the more servants you had, the higher would be your position in society, they crammed their houses full of, often superfluous, servants. In keeping with their perceived superior status, they always made a point of membership of their local Church Council or 'Vestry' and had to be seen by all as being most philanthropic; such was the household in which Sarah Valentine now found herself.

Having prepared the food for the Master, his family and guests, the staff themselves were allowed to eat. The cook had ensured that sufficient food was prepared to feed the substantial number of servants; as it was the same food as eaten by the Master, they usually ate very well. The senior among the servants were given plates of food to partake of in their quarters. The more lowly, ate in the kitchen, sitting with the cook and her staff at the table. Sarah and the Workhouse lads, being the lowest of the low, ate theirs sitting on the floor in the washroom. They were joined in the washroom by three men in dirty clothes and muddy, well worn boots; they were introduced to Sarah, by John, as the gardeners.

The food was excellent. To Sarah, it was a veritable banquet and she wolfed it down hungrily. She said it was the best meal she had ever eaten in her entire life; everyone laughed at this.

When all the pots, pans, plates and cutlery had been collected and the Master, family and guests had been catered for that evening, everything had to be washed, cleaned and put away. When this had been completed, the cook prepared a massive pot of tea. Unlike in previous houses, in which Sarah had worked, there seemed to be no limit on the tea consumed. The cook appeared to be free to use as much as she wished; Sarah thought that this must be a very rich household indeed.

The tea finished and everything cleared away, the cook announced that it was time to retire. Everyone jumped to their feet and people were soon milling around. Sarah stood, rooted to the spot, as mayhem went on around her. She soon realised that they were taking the straw mattresses and cloth covers from the washroom and laying them out on the floor. Anxious not to be left out Sarah pushed her way through the crowd of people into the washroom and went to the corner where the mattresses had been stored. When she reached the corner she soon realised what the rush had been about. All that was left of the large stack of mattresses were two poor looking examples, both with very worn covers, torn and threadbare. Most of the straw had fallen out of the holes and was scattered around the floor. She picked the best looking of the two and proceeded to pick the straw up off the floor and stuff it back through the holes. But as fast as she pushed it through one hole, it was falling out of another; it was clearly a pointless task. In the end, she gave up and put one mattress on top of the other to gain a bit of support and looked around for somewhere to sleep.

A tallow candle had been left burning on the workbench in the kitchen, and by its dim light she saw that, whilst she had been busy trying to effect a reasonably comfortable bed, the floor in the washroom had been covered with sleeping bodies. She was astonished to find that the only available space left was where she was currently standing, up against the wall where the mattresses had been stored; there was not an inch of empty floor space to be seen. She lay down on her makeshift bed and tried to get comfortable. Despite her attempts to fill the mattress with straw, she could still feel the hard stone floor under her. She was very uncomfortable and found it difficult to get to sleep. People around her started to snore loudly. She tried to turn over to get more comfortable but was rewarded with an elbow in her eye. Turning the other way she was jammed up against the rough wall. In desperation, she lay on her back and stared up at the ceiling. She saw shadows dancing in the flickering light of the candle; they gradually dimmed as the candle burned down. Finally, giving a last burst of light, the candle flickered out and darkness descended on the washroom. At least the washroom was warm with the residual heat from the kitchen ranges and, after a time, Sarah finally drifted off into a troubled sleep. She dreamed of scrabbling through a mass of bricks and tiles, searching for her family. But, try as she might, fingers cut and bleeding, nails broken, she could not find them.

Sarah startled into wakefulness with the vividness of the dream still in her mind. Her heart was racing, she was dripping with sweat and, at first, she did not know where she was. But then memory flooded back; the multiple, sonorous notes of snoring bodies assailed her ears. She was aware that it was still dark out, but there was a little moonlight and she could just see the room through the half light that her eyes were now accustomed to. Her first impression was a pain in her bladder; she desperately needed to pee. She lay there, thinking what she should do. At first she tried to ignore it hoping to get back to sleep, but it soon became apparent that this would be impossible; it was obvious that the tea she had consumed before retiring was now demanding escape. She carefully rose to a sitting position and assessed her surroundings. She was firmly jammed against the far wall, furthest from the arch leading into the kitchen. Between her and the arch lay at least seven prone bodies, with scarce an inch of space between them. But, even if she could reach the arch, where was she to relieve herself? If there was a privy, she had no knowledge of where it was. However, she did know where the back door was; if she could just get into the garden, perhaps she could find somewhere?

Carefully, she rose to her feet. Taking great care not to step on anyone, she made her way to the arch; this was not without some difficulty as there was scarcely space between the massed beds to place her feet. Eventually, after several gingerly placed steps, she reached the arch. An astonishing sight greeted her; the kitchen was no less densely populated with sleeping bodies than the washroom! The pain in her bladder was now becoming all consuming, if she did not find relief soon, she would wet herself where she stood. Gathering her wits and taking a deep breath she stepped forward. Just at that moment, the body of one of the gardeners, directly in front of her, turned over and her foot caught on his shoulder. She tumbled forward and fell full length onto the next sleeper, the other gardener. She put her hands out to break her fall, but still ended up crashing on top of the prone sleeper, who grunted in response. Worse, her bladder failed her and, with the shock of the fall, she could not prevent herself from peeing over the body underneath her. With a great effort, she stopped the flow and rolled to one side. Her roll was immediately arrested by another sleeper lying right next to the one she had fallen on; she was now jammed between the two of them.

She lay there, rigid with fear that she would be discovered and shamed in front of the whole household. But, after a few grunts and wriggles, both sleepers returned to regular snoring. Sarah very carefully lifted herself up onto her elbow, then slowly got to her feet; this time, she took much greater care in stepping over the bodies. Finally, reaching the back door, she turned the knob and, to her surprise, found it unlocked; she passed through into the garden. She paused for a moment and looked over the extensive back garden. The moon had become obscured by cloud but, by the light of the few visible stars, she spotted some bushes over to her right, about forty feet away, and made her way towards them. As she reached them, she heard a rustling noise and a large dark shape emerged from the bushes just to her left. Startled, she threw herself to the ground and lay still, not daring to take a breath, her heart pounding, squirts of pee escaping from between her legs. The figure loomed tall and dark, blotting out the stars; she could not remember being so frightened in all her life. But, completely unaware of her presence, the figure strode purposefully across the lawn to the back door of the house that Sarah had just exited and, opening the door, entered the kitchen, closing the door behind him. Relief flooded over Sarah and she took several gasping breaths. Having recovered from her shock, she remembered the purpose of her excursion; finding a secluded bush, she relieved herself.

Now, feeling a little more comfortable, although a trifle wet, she made her way back to the house. Reaching the back door to the kitchen, she turned the handle. But the door would not open! With a sudden shock, she realised that the man she had encountered in the bushes had probably left the kitchen for the same purpose as she had. Now he had returned to the house and locked the door behind him. She was trapped outside!

She stood at the door for a few minutes. A fox barked and some hound howled in the distance, she shivered and put her arms round her, her shawl and bonnet were inside the house. She contemplated knocking on the door to gain entry, but decided against it. She did not relish the ridicule she would undoubtedly get for waking the household up, so she sat down with her back against the kitchen door. As the moon came out from behind the cloud and bathed her in its silver glow, she contemplated her situation. After a while she smiled to herself; here she was, locked outside the warm cosy kitchen where she should be sleeping, sitting on cold flagstones, with wet drawers. How Jimmy would laugh when she told him about this; she giggled at the thought. After a while, she looked up at the sky, the cloud was clearing and she could see a multitude of bright stars, unusual for Hackney, which generally had cloudy dismal skies. But, it was the middle of May and not as cold as it might have been; it could have been a lot worse. Resigned, she leaned back against the door and, after a while, she fell into a light sleep.

She was rudely awakened by the kitchen door being pulled open. Not expecting this, Sarah fell backwards into the open doorway and found herself looking up into the startled face of one of the gardeners. "What you doin' out here love?" he asked in some surprise.

Rubbing sleep from her eyes, Sarah mumbled, "I got locked out."

The gardener chucked to himself and held his hand out to help her up. "My you're freezing!" he exclaimed on gripping her hand. As he pulled her to her feet he turned to another man and said, "Alfie, ger another cup o' tea will yer." She felt her face redden as she remembered peeing over him. But he clearly knew nothing of it and Sarah was soon gratefully clutching a cup of strong tea; the hot cup warmed her cold hands and she felt some of the life coming back into her body. She thanked the three gardeners as they walked out the back door into the garden, keeping tight hold of their cups of tea. As she stood there sipping her tea, she became aware of the bodies on the floor stirring.

One of the under cooks walked over to her, rubbing the sleep from her eyes. "My you're an early one ain't yer," she said eyeing Sarah with surprise. "Yer better 'elp us mash some tea."

Over the next few days, Sarah settled into the routine of the household, and as time went by, she became aware of how little she was required to do. The house was full to bursting point with servants, to the extent that they were virtually fighting over the work. She was confined to the kitchen, but the few glances she got through the door into the main body of the house, revealed a constant stream of well dressed servants. Men in smart uniforms and women servants in billowing silk dresses were constantly striding about. Little was said between them and all Sarah could hear was the frou frou of skirts and the clip clop of many shoes.

She found herself scratching around for work and often helped the young Workhouse lads in whatever tasks they were assigned. When she was short of work, which was frequently, she would watch closely at what others were doing. One particular task which greatly intrigued her was the ritual of coffee making. The Master and his household enjoyed coffee after the evening meal and he was very particular about how it was prepared; having visited the houses of the upper classes he was conscious of the fact that the quality of his coffee could mark him down in civilised society if it was not up to a high standard. Under the Master's constant harassment, the cook was at great pains to ensure that only the best coffee should leave her kitchen. She would heat the ground coffee in a saucepan then carefully pour boiling water over it.

Then she would strain the liquid into another pan and leave to stand for a few minutes. One aspect that she struggled most with was its clarity, 'there is nothing worse than a cup full of grounds' she would say to her staff. If it was not clear enough she would add washed egg shells, kept specifically for the purpose. Then it would be strained again to remove the egg shells and re-heated before being decanted into a large silver coffee pot and delivered to the Master. He would always try it first and was not beyond returning it to the kitchen if it did not come up to his exacting standard. At this juncture, the cook would need to start the process all over again; however, the rejected coffee would always be enjoyed by the kitchen staff.

Sarah got on well with the three gardeners and, at midday, she usually prepared them a pot of tea and some bread and cheese. There was a path round the perimeter of the garden, hidden behind a hawthorn hedge that led to their shed; she would put the teapot and food on a wooden tray and carry it round to their shed. The shed was quite large and contained all their tools, several benches and some old garden chairs. With little else to do, she would sit with them, drink tea and chat for an hour or so, before taking the tray of crockery back to the kitchen to wash up.

They were a friendly trio; there were two Alfie's, not related, both about forty. The one who had pulled the door open on her was very large, with a full head of thick black hair, and was called 'big Alfie'. The other one was quite small, slight in build and with a completely bald head; he was called, rather unimaginatively, 'little Alfie'. The third gardener was a younger, skinny, tousle haired man called Tim.

If she had little to do during the day, she would stroll out to the shed to see what the gardener's were up to. It was building up to a glorious summer, and it was here that she got her first introduction to gardening; she had never lived in a home with a garden and it had never occurred to her to try and grow flowers. She remembered when she was younger and living with her parents; they used to scrounge unsold flowers from the street vendors, to brighten their room up. As she watched the gardener's work, she became interested in what they were doing. She helped them thin out the seedlings they had planted earlier, and prepare the hanging baskets that would bring a cheerful façade to the big house. The rows of plants growing in their pots on the benches even brought a cheerful air to the otherwise drab shed. She decided, there and then, that she would have flowers in her next home; they were so cheering and seemed to bring an element of hope and joy into one's life.

She had little to do with the Master and his family. She found out that, apart from the Master and Mistress, there were five children, ranging from thirteen down to a babe in arms and several aunts and uncles, scrounging off the Master's wealth. She had thought that she might get to see the children, but this was clearly not to be. She frequently saw them out on the lawn, on hot summer's days, but they were surrounded by staff. Big Alfie pointed out their tutor, two child minders and a wet nurse for the baby. All of these were under the supervision of a Governess. She was a magnificent woman, tall and elegant, always dressed like royalty. It seemed to Sarah to be rather a lot of staff to look after a few kids.

One afternoon, when she was walking back along the path from the gardener's shed to the kitchen, she could hear the children playing on the lawn; they were shouting and giggling to each other. She paused at a spot where the hawthorn hedge was a little bare; she had a good view of the garden through it. She stood there for a while watching the children throwing a ball to each other. Then suddenly, one of the older boys kicked the ball hard and it shot high into the air. When it hit the ground, it bounced towards where Sarah was standing; there was a little girl hotly in pursuit. It hit the corner of a flower bed and bounced over the hawthorn hedge; Sarah caught it and held it to her chest. The little girl who had been running after the ball stopped dead when she saw Sarah behind the hedge. They were standing, no more than ten feet apart, the hedge separating them. Sarah looked at her and saw a rosy cheeked girl of no more than six-years-old, with light coloured hair, in ringlets, cascading down the sides of her face. Sarah stared transfixed as memories came flooding back; this little girl reminded her of Agnes Clark, the tragic girl Sarah had met in the Workhouse and who had lost her brother and baby sister, before being sent out alone onto the street. Sadness filled her heart, what on earth had happened to poor Agnes.

Her thoughts were interrupted by the little girl's voice. "Can I have my ball back please?" she asked. Snapping out of her trance, Sarah smiled and threw the ball over the hedge. The little girl seized it in her arms and ran back across the lawn to join her siblings. Sarah walked slowly back to the kitchen, her thoughts still on little Agnes.

CHAPTER 29

Susan's Wedding

IT WAS THE beginning of June and, at the Cock and Magpie Tavern on the corner of Worship Street and Wilson Street, the Beadle and the Shoreditch Relieving Officer, John Coste, were sitting at their usual table and nattering on about their usual subject, namely the troublesome girls in the Shoreditch Workhouse.

"So what happened to them then?" asked John Coste.

"You mean Magdalene Orme and Elizabeth Weston?" said the Beadle.

"Yes!" said John Coste, a little irritated, "they attacked one of the attendants at the Workhouse. That big, ugly, scar faced Weston girl damn near killed him. Just looking at that face of hers scares the living daylights out of me."

The Beadle chuckled, "well you won't have to worry about them for a while, they were both dispatched to the Middlesex House of Correction." Then added, "what about those other two, Caroline Copeland and Sophia Crafts?"

John Coste took a sip of his ale, put his glass down on the table and thought for a moment, "it's been a while since we've seen either of those wretches. They are both serious trouble and I certainly hope they stay away from Shoreditch."

But in this wish he would prove to be sadly mistaken.

Back at the grand house, Sundays were exceptionally quiet as the family of the household and the senior servants would all go to St Leonard's Church for morning and afternoon services. Sarah was fascinated by the pomp and ceremony attached to this journey. She would sneak out of the kitchen door and down the side of the house, to the front, where she would hide in the bushes to observe the ritual of departure.

The two carriages would arrive at the front entrance, resplendent in gleaming black paintwork, with brightly polished gold fittings. Each would be drawn by two grand horses, perfectly matched in size and colouring. The Master and elder members of the family would enter the first carriage, the children, under the supervision of the governess, would enter the second. But, the most impressive sight for Sarah were the footmen. They were as well matched as the fine horses; tall, handsome, with massive full calves and perfect ankles, all dressed in white tunics, with starched cravats, impeccably tied, and fine silk breeches. When the family were safely ensconced in the carriages, they would mount one either side at the rear of the carriages and stand, magnificently tall and erect, as the carriages clattered off down the road.

Once all the family had departed for St Leonard's Church and, provided it was not a wash day, Sarah was allowed Sunday afternoon off and she would usually use that day to visit her mother, sister Mary and brother Jimmy. The events surrounding the demolition of Essex Street had brought the remaining members of the Valentine family much closer together.

From the Hackney Road, she would walk down Birdcage Walk, cut left down Turk Street and into Brick Lane. Then, down Brick Lane to turn right into Quakers Street, left into Grey Eagle Street, then right into Great Pearl Street. Half way down Great Pearl Street, Little Pearl Street was a turning off to the left. It was just a little to the north of where the new Commercial Street had ground to a halt as the funding dried up, well short of its intended target. The detritus of the massive demolition was still evident, in mountains of bricks, tiles and dust. Many of the small alleys and courts were impassable due to the piles of rubbish left behind by the departing workmen.

Little Pearl Street itself was bursting at the seams. Thousands of people, displaced by the mass evictions had flooded into the area, creating worse overcrowding than had existed in the original Essex Street and Rose Lane rookery. As soon as Sarah had left Brick Lane, the smell had invaded her nostrils; it grew worse as she approached her family's home. The three story building where her family lived was old and decrepit; it had a distinct lean, as if it was about to topple over. The windows were mainly broken and covered with paper to keep the elements at bay. The residents occupied single sparse rooms; all facilities were shared, which meant that they were no one's responsibility. The cess pits were never emptied; the night soil men never ventured into this area. The raw sewage from the privies ran across the street. The whole area had an appalling stench that the inhabitants did not seem to notice.

Jimmy occupied one of two very small rooms on the ground floor at the back of the main house. The two rooms were contained within what was really just a lean-to shed, cobbled together from cheap materials and built on the back of the house; it looked as if a good gust of wind would blow it down. The second of the small rooms was occupied by two further chimney sweepers: James Green and William Rice. The location was quite convenient for them as it allowed easy access, from the street, for them and their soot, which they stored in the cellar. Sarah's mother and sister Mary lived in the main house, No. 6 Little Pearl Street. They occupied an equally small room on the first floor at the back which overlooked Jimmy's 'shed'. The main house was quite crowded with four further families jammed in.

Sarah went to Jimmy's room first but, finding it empty, apart from a sack of soot, she went up the narrow steep stairs to her mother's room. The walls were damp and covered in mould, the result of no damp-proof course. Reaching her mother's room she heard voices from within and knocked on the door. "Mum!" she shouted, "it's Sarah."

"Come in," replied Jimmy.

Sarah opened the door and walked in. The room was small and sparsely furnished. Little light penetrated the cracked, paper covered, window. Her mother was sitting at the little table, staring at the wall. Sarah hugged her sister Mary. They had been worried about Mary when they moved out of Martins Court as she had developed a rash of spots, but she was a strong girl and had fought off the infection and was now fully recovered. As they stepped apart, they both looked at their mother. Sarah was saddened to see that she was not looking well. It was clear that she sorely missed her husband and the two children. With their disappearance, part of her life had gone and she was starting to deteriorate. Mary had tried to get some servant work, but had not succeeded, she spent most of her time looking after her mother. They were really all living on Jimmy's wages; fortunately, he was doing quite well, but it was very hard work; he was working very long hours and was seldom at home. Having failed to get any servant work, Mary had taken to occasionally helping Jimmy out as his 'climbing boy'.

Their accommodation left a lot to be desired. There was a range out back, but it was broken and, as no one was prepared to pay for it to be repaired, it remained unusable. They did have a small grate in the corner of her mother's room, but were initially unable to light a fire, because the chimney was blocked. Fortunately, Jimmy had been able to clear the chimney and made it possible for them to light a fire. Coal was expensive, but Jimmy often managed to get some cheaply, mainly dust, but it was enough to get a small fire going; it also meant that they were able to cook some food at the grate.

Their friend Nell, and her family, lived in a room in the house next door. On a Sunday, if funds permitted, they all went out. Both families walked up Little Pearl Street to Great Pearl Street, where they turned right into Grey Eagle Street and entered the Crown Tavern, at No. 4. It was a small cosy pub and they usually occupied a table in a quiet corner, where they sat, drinking ale, and chatting amongst themselves.

It was on one of these occasions that Sarah was casually chatting with her brother Jimmy, when, a sudden thought came to her. "Do you know how old you are?" she asked Jimmy.

He laughed, then said, "Yes, I'm twenty."

"Are you sure?" she said

"Yes," he said, "of course I am."

"How can you be so sure?" she asked.

"Well," he said, "'cause of dad really."

Sarah laughed, "but he was terrible with numbers!"

"Well yes," said Jimmy, "but Tom, his friend from the docks, helped him. And he taught me to count as well," he added.

"Dad and Tom never said anything to me about counting," Sarah said sullenly.

"Well, I don't suppose they thought it was important for you to be able to count. You bein' a girl an' all that," said Jimmy. Then immediately regretted it when he saw Sarah's face crumple. He smiled at her. "Sorry Sarah, you have as much right to be able to count as anyone." He tweaked her ear and she grimaced at him. Then laughed.

"Well, I can count a bit now," she said.

"How come?" said Jimmy.

"Well," said Sarah, "I've learned a lot with all the positions I've had as a servant."

"Good for you!" said Jimmy, giving her arm a squeeze.

As she walked back from the tavern, her thoughts were on how old she was. Jimmy seemed to be sure that he was twenty. The last three times she had entered the Workhouse, her age had been entered, in the admission book, as nineteen, but if she was nineteen, then she would be younger than Jimmy. That was ludicrous! She thought back, she could remember Jimmy as a baby, she was always his older sister; she looked after him. But how much older than him was she? Certainly not much older, maybe one, or two, years?

This gave Sarah considerable cause to think. She lay awake for a time that evening, pondering her age. She knew that it would be pointless trying to ask her mother. Then, she fell into a deep slumber, adding her snores to the orchestra around her; it had been a busy day.

At the grand house, she was conscious of her lack of clothing. Every day she wore the same dress. Also, she only had the one set of soiled underclothing; in fact, all she had was basically what she stood up in. Her small bundle contained a shawl, with many patches, a scarf and a threadbare bonnet. She really needed a change of clothes, so that she could at least wash one set whilst wearing the other. She did not relish the thought of standing naked in the washroom whilst she washed her only set of clothes; and those clothes were now becoming very soiled indeed.

So, she approached the cook about being given some money, after all, she argued, she had worked at the house for some weeks now. However, the cook made it clear that having a roof over her head and being well fed was more than good enough for a Workhouse girl; she could not reasonably expect more. Then, seeing Sarah's downcast look, the cook enquired why she wanted money. Sarah rather sheepishly explained her predicament. The cook laughed out loud, then, taking pity on her, said she would see what could be done.

When Friday arrived, the cook gave Sarah two shillings. On the following day, a Saturday, Sarah got leave of absence and made her way to Petticoat Lane. After rummaging around the stalls, she purchased a good condition second hand cotton dress for one shilling, which fit reasonably well. To this she added some patched but serviceable undergarments for four pence and, for a further six pence; she bought a very pretty second hand bonnet. This last was a bit of an extravagance, but she did so like the bonnet. She found a secluded spot behind the clothes stall and changed into her new garments. She took Freddy's poesy ring from the pocket of her old dress, where it had remained since she left the Workhouse. Looking at it she remembered her conversation with Jane Freestone and decided she might as well wear it, so she put it on her right hand. Rolling her old garments up into a bundle, she tucked them under her arm.

Happy with her purchases, she made her way up Petticoat Lane and across to the Spitalfields Church. Everywhere she looked, she saw the evidence of the destruction of Essex Street and Rose Lane. Her eyes filled with tears as she thought of her lost brother Henry and dear exuberant sister Caroline, both so full of life. She walked up the derelict remains of what was once Rose Lane until she reached the point where the demolition abruptly stopped after the project had run out of money. Then, she made her way around a pile of left-over broken bricks and roof tiles, on which a group of scruffy children were playing, and walked up Red Lion Street and Vine Street, to the bottom of Little Pearl Street.

The door to No. 6 stood open and Nell, with daughters Beth, Ellen and Margaret were standing outside.

Sarah shouted a greeting and they waved back. Just as she arrived at the door a young girl bounded out and threw herself at Sarah, wrapping her arms round her neck and her legs round her waist. Sarah staggered back under the onslaught, laughing loudly. "You'll have me over Mary!" she shouted good naturedly at her young sister.

Mary climbed down, but not before she seized Sarah's new bonnet and placing it on her own head marched up and down the street like a high society lady. Everyone laughed and Sarah spent the next ten minutes chasing Mary up and down the street trying to get her new bonnet back, much to the amusement of everyone. Having finally retrieved her new bonnet, Sarah joined Nell and her family and they all stood chatting for a while. Sarah's mother emerged, with her hat and shawl on and they set off down the road. Sarah walked with them to Brick Lane, and when they reached it Sarah turned left to get back to Hackney, whilst the others turned right towards the Whitechapel High Street. Mary was sorry to see Sarah go, but Sarah promised to return on Sunday.

When Sarah arrived back at the grand house, she placed her bundle of old clothes in the corner of the washroom. The next wash day she would finally get to wash her old clothes. This made her feel considerably better.

With little work to do Sarah frequently drank an early morning cup of tea with the gardeners, sitting in their shed. It was at one of these sessions that big Alfie noticed the ring on her finger and commented how nice it looked. Not wishing to recount her experiences with Freddy, she told them that it was her grandmother's and it had been passed to her when she died. When they got up and set to work in the garden, she would sometimes walk out the side entrance and into the Hackney Road, where she would idly walk up and down looking in shops at goods she could never afford to buy. On Monday mornings, if Jimmy was working in the Hackney Road, he would make a point of walking past the house and Sarah would often meet with him. They would stand in the street and chat with each other, for a few minutes, before Jimmy would have to carry on to his work.

Every Monday morning, early on, before any visitors could be expected, was the time to clean both the front door and the, all important, front steps. This task would be accomplished by no less than four maids. Jimmy and Sarah were often standing in the street to witness this ritual. Indeed, they frequently made a point of being there to see the ensuing pantomime. The maids were all dressed in formal attire, with wide silk, fluffed out dresses. There were iron railings on either side of the steps leading up to the door and the maids dresses were so full that it was only with some difficulty, that more than one of them could fit on the steps at any one time. The ritual started with two maids, side by side, pushing their way up the steps, dresses jammed between each other and the railings, the two of them would start on the front door, cleaning the paintwork and polishing the fittings. The second two maids would then push their way up the steps behind them to kneel down and scrub away at the steps, bumping into each other as they worked. The dresses of the maids working on the door would greatly hamper the maids kneeling behind them working on the steps, who would constantly be pushing them out of their faces, shouting abuse up at the door maids.

Next, having finished their work, the door maids would want to get back down. However, unable to turn, they would back, precariously, down the steps. In their attempt to pass the maids cleaning the steps, they would frequently jostle into each other, all four maids shouting and cursing at each other. Sarah and Jimmy found the spectacle of the four squabbling maids quite hilarious. Sometimes, a maid would tumble over, her dress rising up to reveal her drawers. At this sight, Sarah and Jimmy would be in rapturous laughter, clinging to each other for support.

Another thing that Sarah regarded with some curiosity was the regular visits of the dustmen. The deprived courts and alleys where Sarah had lived had not had the benefit of the services of dustmen, indeed any cinders or refuse would merely be tossed into the street to by kicked around and raked through by the masses of scruffy kids roaming about. At the grand house, the dust collectors would arrive early in the morning, ringing their dull sounding bell to alert householders' to their approach. They would arrive with their heavily built, high sided, horse drawn cart to collect the mountain of rubbish and dust that had been deposited at the side of the house the evening before. They would shovel it into baskets, brought with them, which would be carried to the cart where a ladder would be lent. They would mount the ladder and discharge the basket contents into the cart. She looked at the men closely, they wore knee-breeches, gaiters and short, dirty smock-frocks; fantail hats sat on their unkempt heads. But they were all strong, fine looking specimens; indeed, their robust health was notorious. They were usually the ones to cart off the victims of plagues and pestilence, yet it was a known fact that they themselves never suffered such a fate. Having loaded their cart, they would come round the back and harass the cook, who would be compelled to provide them with either money or jugs of ale. Apparently this was needed to supplement their poor wages. Woe betide any household that did not provide the requested sustenance, for it seemed to be a rule among them that, at their next visit, they would scatter the dust, cinders and refuse all over the front of the house and steps.

It was September and, at the Cock and Magpie Tavern on the corner of Worship Street and Wilson Street, the Beadle and the Shoreditch Relieving Officer, John Coste were sitting at their usual table by the hearth. The fire had been lit as the weather was starting to get a little chilly of an evening. John Coste was staring into his ale with a grim expression on his face. "You know," he said, "I'm at my wit's end with these girls. I had hoped we had seen the back of Caroline Copeland and Sophia Crafts."

"I take it that it was Magistrate Benett that let them back in," said the Beadle.

"Damn that man!" said the Relieving Officer with some venom, "he does not have to suffer the consequences of their behaviour."

"Did you speak with the Master of the Workhouse about what they did?" asked the Beadle.

"Yes," said John Coste, "and a sorry tale it is too. That Caroline Copeland had been in the House barely three days before she was caught stealing medicines from the infirmary. She was dispatched to the Magistrate and sent to the House of Correction. Then that awful Sophia Crafts arrived with her summons from Magistrate Benett. She had barely been admitted before she started trouble with the attendants. She is too big and aggressive to control."

"But they did send her to the House of Correction as well, didn't they?" said the Beadle.

"Yes," said John Coste, "but they were both back in the Workhouse after their time in prison." He took a sip of his ale, then continued, with some anger, "two days!" he exclaimed, "they had only been in for two days before they caused mayhem again!"

"What happened?" asked the Beadle.

"Don't think we'll rightly know exactly what happened," replied John Coste, "but they were the root cause of it. I told the Workhouse Master that it was not wise to put them to work in the kitchen after the last trouble they caused."

The Beadle swallowed the last of his ale before replying, "How's the cook?"

"Badly beaten," said John Coste, "they wanted revenge for that trouble last February; took three big male attendants to get that Sophia Crafts off her."

"But the Magistrate sent them to prison for three weeks this time," said the Beadle as he rose to go to the bar to refill their glasses.

"Yes," said John Coste, "but they will be back. Count on it!"

Winter arrived with cold winds and snow flurries. At the grand house, Christmas was celebrated in the main household by a huge party with many guests. For once, Sarah was very busy helping in the kitchen and by the time evening arrived, was thoroughly exhausted. Before retiring, the kitchen staff were treated to a drink by the Master of the household who sent down bottles of wine, rum, port and gin. Sarah joined in with the other staff to polish off the unexpected booze. Soon, they were all singing at the tops of their voices. She danced with the gardeners, crashing into everyone in the crowded kitchen.

Eventually, one by one, they started to fall down; no one bothered to get a mattress, they slept where they fell. Sarah did not remember falling asleep. However, she did remember waking up the next morning; she was cuddling big Alfie, who was snoring loudly. Her head was throbbing with pain, her throat was dry and she was dying for a pee. She tried to get up, but the room started to spin and she fell back on top of big Alfie. Giggling to herself, she tried again; this time she managed to get to her feet and staggered to the door, just about avoiding treading on any of the sleepers scattered about the floor. After struggling with the lock, she finally got the door open and fell through it onto the paved patio, grazing her knees. Gingerly rising to her feet she swayed unsteadily towards her favourite bush; squatting behind it, she relieved herself. Returning to the kitchen, gasping for a drink, she busied herself brewing the morning tea. Bodies started to stir as the staff began waking up. Big Alfie was first to get up and walked over to Sarah who immediately pored him a cup of tea. Sarah then busied herself pouring out cup after cup of hot tea from the enormous pot she had brewed. Suddenly, she was everyone's favourite, as they greedily supped the hot refreshing beverage. And so, with much celebration, 1843 drew to a close.

The New Year of 1844 started with a heavy snow fall and the garden was knee deep in snow; the children of the household were overjoyed. They were soon out in the garden, making snowballs and pelting everyone they encountered. Making her way to the gardener's shed with the midday tea, Sarah found herself ducking and dodging numerous snowballs chucked over and through the hawthorn hedge. Laughing and shaking the snow from her hair, she barged into the shed nearly dropping the tray on the floor. The gardeners had little to do in the winter and spent most of their time in the shed, drinking tea and chatting.

Sarah met with Jimmy on Monday morning, on the 12th February and he had some news for her. He had been cleaning chimneys opposite the tailor's shop and he had chatted with George Linford. Jimmy bumped into him from time to time and always enquired about Sarah's son Edwin. She was always eager for news; Edwin would be four this year. But, it was not her son that George Linford had been talking about. It seemed that George's son Edwin Linford had finally arranged to marry his sweetheart Susan Smith. The wedding was arranged for next Monday, 19ᵗʰ February, at the Stepney Parish Church. Sarah felt a wry smile touch her lips as she realised it was the self same church that she was to marry Freddy Linford in, some five years ago. She had always been fond of Edwin and Susan and both she and Jimmy decided that they would try to get to the church to see the wedding. When Sarah returned to the house, she asked the cook if it would be possible for her to take a little time off next Monday to see her friends get married. The cook looked at her and said she could do as she pleased as, 'her presence, or absence, from the house would not be noticed'.

On the Wednesday 14ᵗʰ February, Valentine's Day, Sarah was enjoying her early morning tea with the gardeners, in their shed. It was a cold blustery day, but they had a fire going, in an iron stove, and it was nice and warm in there. In a lull in the conversation Sarah announced that today she was celebrating her birthday. They all congratulated her and big Alfie asked her how old she was. Much to her embarrassment, she felt her face flush. She was about to mumble that she was not very sure when, realising her plight, little Alfie put his hand on her shoulder and admitted that he did not know his own age and it was nothing to worry about; red faced, she nodded.

The Sunday found Sarah walking through the deep snow to Whitechapel to visit her family. After chatting together for a while, they all decided to go round to the Crown for a little tipple. They were welcomed by landlord Bob Bowyer and wife Jane, who were lighting a massive log fire. It was while they were warming themselves at the flames that Jimmy turned a frowning face towards Sarah.

"What's the matter Jimmy?" she said, noting his dark look.

After a moment's hesitation, Jimmy blurted it out. "I talked with George Linford again, about Edwin's wedding."

"And?" said Sarah.

"Well," said Jimmy, "not only are we not invited, but we are positively not welcome."

"What!" exclaimed Sarah, "why?"

"Oh it's definitely not Edwin and Susan's doing. It's that wife of George's. She wants you well out of the way. In fact George was most apologetic about it, but there's little he can do, she rules the roost in that house."

Sarah remained silent for a time, then spoke out again. "Right!" she stormed, her eyes blazing, "that madam may well be able to keep me out of the church, but she can't keep me off the streets! I intend to be outside that church and if she wants to start a scene I will be happy to oblige her!"

Jimmy kept his peace, but had a worried expression on his face; he thought it best that he turn up at the church as well, to keep an eye on his sister.

Mid-morning on Monday 19th February 1844 found Sarah standing in the High Street, on the corner of Totton Street, just over the road from St Dunstans Stepney, where she had a good view of the magnificent structure. It was the oldest church in the area, by a long chalk, pre-dating St Mary Matfelon at Whitechapel by many years. St Dunstan was made Bishop of London in the tenth century and was reputed to have pinched the Devil's nose with iron tongs, hence the carving over the right hand side of the doorway into the church. On the left hand side, Sarah could just make out the carving of a ship, for this was a sailor's church and, in times past, a light was lit in the substantial tower to help to guide ships into the port of London. Her mind drifted back nearly five years, to when she and Freddy Linford came here to arrange the banns for their wedding, which never took place. She briefly wondered what had become of him; would he turn up to see his brother's wedding?

She had been standing there for nearly an hour, when she felt a presence at her side. She wheeled round, startled, to see a smiling Jimmy standing beside her; she elbowed him in the ribs. "You startled me!" she accused him, "what are you doing here?"

He smiled, "I thought we both said about commin' 'ere?"

She shrugged and continued to watch the church.

It was another hour before people on foot began arriving and going into the church. Then, a while later, two coaches turned up and disgorged a varied group of people. Sarah looked intently at them as they walked up the pathway to the church entrance. She immediately spotted

George Linford and his son Edwin, both smartly dressed in dark frock coats. She recognised the younger daughter Caroline, walking arm in arm with a tall man dressed in a police uniform. Then, she saw what she had been waiting for, it was Jane Linford emerging from the second coach with a small boy. She knelt down in front of him to make sure that his coat was done up, then rose up and held his hand tightly as they walked to the church. From time to time she looked down at him and smiled. Jimmy looked at the boy, his hair had darkened and his eyes had gone from blue to hazel, making him look a little more like a Valentine than a Linford now. Then, Jimmy looked at Sarah, she was staring intently at her son, tears streaming down her face. He put his arm round her to comfort her, but she seemed not to notice, instead she started to walk across the road towards the church. Jimmy followed, he wondered if she would call out to them, but instead, she stopped at the entrance to the church grounds and watched them go inside.

They had been stood their, in silence, for a few minutes, when another coach pulled up beside them. Sarah looked at it and recognised it as the one Susan Smith had pulled up in outside the tailor's shop, but the driver was different, a much younger man. Then an older man got out of the coach and Sarah recognised him as the original driver, Susan's father. He stood on the pavement and helped a young girl out of the coach; it was Susan in a beautiful dress. She locked arms with her father and they made their way to the church. As they passed Sarah and Jimmy, Susan gave them a weak smile and her father gave them a quizzical look; but as Susan walked away, Jimmy could see that she had a worried expression on her face.

They remained standing there for the duration of the service. Of Freddy Linford, there was no sign.

The first to emerge from the church were the bride and groom, others crowded out after them and followed them down the path, these were added to by passers-by stopping to see what was transpiring. As they passed Sarah and Jimmy, Edwin waved and Susan gave them a sad smile. They climbed into the coach that Susan had arrived in and with a flick of his whip, the driver got them under way amidst much cheering and shouting from the expanding mass of people. Last to emerge, were the close family members, who had presumably been seated in the front pews. George Linford, his daughter Caroline and her policeman friend came out of the door and started to walk up the path. Then came George's wife Jane holding Sarah's son Edwin's hand. At the sight of her son Sarah started to move forward but, at that instant, she was spotted by George Linford, Caroline and her policeman. All three walked determinedly towards her. This was what Jimmy was afraid of and he quickly stepped between them and Sarah.

Being younger, taller and with a greater stride, the Police Officer was the first to reach them. He attempted to get past Jimmy to Sarah, but Jimmy was having none of that and he remained in front of him, barring his path to Sarah. "Get out of my way!" he shouted at Jimmy.

"Not until I know your intentions towards my sister!" Jimmy answered, now chest to chest with him. Although shorter in height, Jimmy was strong and firm muscled, gained from his strenuous job. It was clear that the Police Officer would not easily get past him. Meanwhile, others in the crowd had noticed the confrontation and heads were turning their way.

George Linford and his daughter reached them, both panting with their exertions. George Linford put his hand on the Police Officer's shoulder. "It's alright Bill," he said, "we don't want any trouble. Let me handle it."

But Bill was not finished yet, "This is that troublesome Workhouse dollymop isn't it. Caroline has told me all about 'er. She's not wanted here." Then to Sarah, "be on your way tramp!"

Sarah glared at him from behind Jimmy. "You have no right to order me away!"

Jimmy glared at Bill and added, "she's right, you can't stop her from standin' on the public highway. You don't 'ave the right!"

"I'll show you what right I've got," Bill said and tried to push past Jimmy again, reaching his hand out and grabbing at Sarah.

This was too much for Jimmy and he placed both his hands on the Police Officer's chest and pushed hard. Bill shot backwards, lost his footing and fell to the floor.

George Linford took his opportunity and stepped in front of Jimmy. He put both his hands on Jimmy's shoulders and looked him in the eye. "Don't do this Jimmy, please!" he said, "It will only cause bad trouble for you and Sarah. You know you can't get away with attacking the police."

"Well, you better make sure he doesn't lay a finger on my sister then!" replied Jimmy.

Whilst this was happening, Sarah had moved from behind Jimmy and was now walking towards her son. Jane Linford and young Edwin had drawn level with Sarah and she looked down at her son with tears in her eyes. He looked up at her with surprise on his face.

Jane Linford stepped between them. "You were told not to come!" she stated.

"I am standing on a public highway, you have no right to say I cannot be here!" Whilst they were thus arguing staring at each other, eye to eye, Caroline Linford had taken young Edwin from her mother's grasp and led him off to one of the coaches. Suddenly, seeing her son being led off, Sarah tried to get past Jane Linford, but the woman stood firm and blocked her way. She looked at her son over Jane Linford's shoulder. As she watched, he turned round to look at her. "Edwin!" she called out. But she saw not a glimmer of recognition in his eyes. Distraught, she just stood there the tears streaming down her face.

Jane Linford took one more look at her, turned and walked towards the coach that Caroline and young Edwin had just entered. Just before she got in, she turned and shouted at Sarah. "Keep away! You are *not* welcome!"

Meanwhile the Police Officer, Bill, had got to his feet, dusted himself off and decided that he would have better luck with Sarah than he had with her tough brother and started to push his way through the crowd towards her. When he reached her, she was just standing there crying, he grabbed her and started shaking her; she ignored him, far too distraught to care what happened to her. He pushed her to the ground and she just lay there sobbing. Then the crowd started to turn ugly. The police in uniform were not much liked by the Stepney populace and they were not too enamoured at seeing one of them ill treating a young woman. Bill started to reach down to grab Sarah again, when he felt strong arms grab him and jerk him backwards. He turned round to his assailant and started to say something when he was punched in the side of the face. He staggered sideways and felt another punch in his kidneys. Now very worried, he pushed his way towards the coach, with the crowd kicking and punching him on his way. Finally, he reached the coach and climbed up with the driver who he instructed to go quickly. George Linford had just got in the coach, having left Jimmy looking for his sister. It pulled sharply away and was soon lumbering off down the road back to Hackney.

Jimmy had reached his sister, who had been helped to her feet and was being comforted by an elderly woman. He stood there looking sadly at her tear stained face as the crowd, grumbling amongst themselves, slowly melted away. They walked in silence back to Hackney, where Jimmy saw her safely to the grand house. When she got there, she went round the back and entered the kitchen. It was too early to start preparations for the evening meal and the kitchen was empty. She was glad that there was no one there to see her watery eyes and tear streaked face. She went into the wash room and sat down in the corner next to her little bundle of belongings, her back resting against the hard, rough wall. She opened her bundle and pulled out two pieces of paper that she had kept; both were creased where they had been folded and unfolded many times. She opened the first one and looked at it; it was the birth certificate for her son Edwin. She could not read the exact words, but she knew from what the Reverend Ratcliffe had told her that it had no name recorded for her son, only the single word 'Bastard' which was underlined. She unfolded the second piece of paper; this was her son's baptism certificate. The Reverend Ratcliffe had shown her the words on this paper as well. She looked closely at the document and ran her finger over the words that she knew spelt 'Edwin son of Sarah Valentine'. She knew the document also recorded her as 'single woman' and her abode as 'Workhouse', but she ignored those. As she ran her finger over the words again, her eyes were drawn to the poesy ring, still on her finger; the two crumpled pieces of paper and the ring were all that she had of her son. Her head fell forward and her tears started to fall again; her shoulders were heaving. All that kept running through her mind was the look in her son's eyes as he had beheld her; she was a complete stranger to him.

Winter turned to spring and Sarah spent much of her time helping the gardeners with preparing the plants for the summer. She helped to plant bulbs and seeds in pots to grow and be transferred later into the garden beds. She was learning all about growing plants and was happy in her work. But, it was while she was helping in the garden shed one day, that big Alfie imparted some worrying news. The Master's factory was doing very well, boosted by the Victorian industrial revolution that was taking hold on the Country. He had opened another factory and was now earning even more money. He wanted to move into a bigger property more befitting his rising station in society. However, it was the case that many of the grand houses in the Hackney Road were no longer inhabited by individual rich families. Some of them were falling into disrepair and others were being seized by unscrupulous landlords who were turning them into ragged tenements which they let to the poorer classes. The area was rapidly declining and the Master was anxious to move out to the country. Sarah had become accustomed to the grand house and good food, she was now worried that it was all going to come to an end.

Then, her worst fears were realised. On the morning of Tuesday 23rd July 1844 all the lower level servants, including Sarah, were summoned into the grand reception room. The Master of the household appeared and after demanding silence explained that the house would be closed tomorrow as it had been sold and they were moving to the country. All the lower servants must pack their bags and depart first thing in the morning. Following this announcement the lower servants, Sarah included, were milling about jabbering and shouting. It soon became clear that the Master only intended to take the senior servants, in livery, with him to his new house in the country, all the rest were to be dismissed. Sarah and her companions spent a restless night on the floor of the washroom. It was sometime before Sarah finally fell asleep, wondering what was to become of her; despite an inauspicious start, she had quite liked her time at the grand house.

CHAPTER 30

Trouble With The
Police, 1844

I<small>N THE MORNING</small>, Sarah gathered up her small bundle of possessions. Counting the coins in her pocket, she found two pennies, all that was left of the two shillings that the cook had given her to buy her clothes with. This would not go far and so she decided that she really had only one option left to her. So, after 14 months at the grand house, Sarah found herself walking back down the Kingsland Road to Worship Street, the Court House and the Parish Offices. Four hours later, on the afternoon of Wednesday 24th July 1844, having gone through the, now familiar, routine, she found herself standing in the Shoreditch Workhouse Master's office. She handed over the admission note from the Shoreditch Relieving Officer, John Coste. This time, when the Workhouse Master asked her how old she was, she tried to think clearly about the question. But no immediate figure, for her age, presented itself to her, so she shook her head. With a grunt of displeasure, the Workhouse Master looked back in the admissions register and noted her age at last admission. He looked up at her. "When you were last admitted on the 12 May 1843, you were recorded as being nineteen years old. It is now one year on, so you must be twenty," he said.

Sarah thought about this for a few moments. "No," she said, "I can't be twenty, 'cause my younger brother is twenty."

The Workhouse Master considered this for a short time. Then said. "Well let us say you are twenty one shall we?"

Sarah nodded meekly.

She was admitted to ward 16 and was set to work in the kitchen. She looked around and saw some familiar faces, but no one she knew well. Over the next few weeks, Sarah soon found herself fully established in the Workhouse routine once again. The first thing she noticed was the food. At the grand house she had been drinking copious quantities of tea and eating high off the hog. The Workhouse was a very different kettle of fish with no tea and tough gristly meat. She also had to get used to the much harder work in the kitchen; her duties in the grand house had been light to non-existent, in the Workhouse kitchen it was long hours and endless toil. She recognised many of the kitchen staff, including the cook with the broken nose, courtesy of Sophia Crafts fists; she had taken great care to look for any of her old enemies, but saw none of them. One new thing she did notice was the intense activity at the corner of the fever block and sick wards, where her friend Sarah Murray had died of Consumption and she herself had spent some unpleasant periods. There were masses of workers toiling away: Bricklayers, labourers and carpenters. Horse drawn carts were making deliveries, sometimes many during the course of a day: bricks, tiles and lengths of timber. The nurse Eliza Ribnall was still there and Sarah questioned her about the activity. Eliza told her that it had been decided to build a new fever block. She was evidently quite proud of the fact that it was to be the newest and most modern fever block in the area, with a new infirmary and beds for 168 patients. Sarah was suitably impressed, although she was a little confused by the figure of 168. It sounded to be a mighty number, but her counting ability had not quite extended that far yet and she was not too sure precisely how many it represented.

It was the middle of August when Sarah got her first shock. As soon as she entered the dining hall at dinner she saw her sitting there; it was Kate Copeland! Sarah immediately realised that she had not been seen by her, so she walked quickly to the back of the hall and sat down, feeling a little worried; throughout the meal she looked at the back of Kate Copeland's head willing her not to turn round and see her. She delayed leaving the dining hall for as long as possible, to ensure that she did not encounter her outside. When she returned to ward 16 after supper, she was very relieved to find that Kate Copeland was not in there.

Over the next couple of weeks she tried to ensure that she was always hidden in the middle of a cluster of women and managed to avoid being spotted by Kate Copeland. Then, towards the end of August, she got her second shock. Whenever she entered the dining hall she always looked for Kate Copeland, this time, seated next to her, was Sophia Crafts! Sarah was careful to mingle with the crowd of girls entering and slunk away to the back of the room, now very worried; she knew that if they ever spotted her, she would be in for a lot of trouble.

Then, a few days after Sophia Crafts arrived, Kate Copeland disappeared. Although Sarah felt some relief at only having one nasty girl to steer clear of, she was still very worried, as the remaining girl was by far the biggest and worst of her antagonists. However, three weeks of nerve racking days later, Sophia Crafts also disappeared. Sarah breathed a huge sigh of relief.

Sarah had been in the Workhouse for almost three months and it was Sunday 13th October. She, together with the other girls from her ward, were attending the Sunday service at St Mary's Haggerstone. She had been taking only slight notice of the service, having heard it many times before. She was engaged in her usual pastime, namely looking round at all the other people attending the service. Many of them, like her, were from the Workhouse, but others were local residents, and it was these that interested Sarah the most. Some wore old clothing and clearly had little money, but others were in newer clothes, with fancy lace shawls and pretty bonnets. One girl sitting near the front drew her attention, she seemed very familiar. However, Sarah could not get a clear view of her face from behind; sitting next to her was a young man in dark clothing. The way that they were leaning into each other suggested that they were not brother and sister and certainly more than just friends. Sarah was intrigued, and continued to stare at them.

Then, two things happened simultaneously, the Curate started to read out the Banns for forthcoming marriages and the girl that Sarah had been staring at turned her head towards the man next to her and he turned his towards her, giving Sarah a better view of both their faces. Recognition dawned on Sarah immediately, just as she heard the Curate's words announcing the forthcoming marriage, of Caroline Linford to William Maynard; the girl Sarah had been staring at was the younger sister of Freddy Linford, the father of her baby. She could now clearly see that the man next to her was wearing a Police Officer's uniform and was the one who had accosted her outside the Stepney Parish Church. They had clearly come to the church to hear their Banns.

The service ended and they all started to make their way out of the church. As they had been at the back, the Workhouse inmates were the first out. As Sarah looked back at the church entrance, she saw them emerge. At that point, Caroline Linford looked up and her eyes met Sarah's; for a second, Caroline's face screwed up in puzzlement. Then, her eyes widened as recognition dawned, her eyes drifted down to Sarah's distinctive Workhouse uniform and she quickly turned away, put her face down, clutched her man more tightly and pulled him off to one side, away from Sarah. Startled by the sudden change in direction, the Police Officer looked round to see what had triggered Caroline's sudden anxiety. He immediately saw Sarah staring at them, his eyes locked with Sarah's then, observing her attire, his mouth curled in distaste. Then Sarah saw the distaste change to something else that she immediately recognised as hostility.

The following Tuesday, Sarah was still pondering over her encounter with Caroline Linford and her prospective husband, when she was summoned from the kitchen by a burly woman with huge arms and a sour expression on her face; she was led to the reception area. Asking why, she was told that she had a visitor; she wondered who it might be. When she reached the reception area, she saw three elderly tramps in filthy clothing who were clearly trying to gain entry to the tramps' ward of the Workhouse. Sarah was well aware that this often happened when a cold spell struck and life on the street became difficult.

Looking round, she suddenly stopped dead in her tracks. Standing just inside the entrance was the uniformed Police Officer she had seen with Caroline Linford the previous Sunday, at the church. Seeing her enter the reception area, he walked briskly up to her and taking her firmly by the upper arm led her forcefully over to a quiet corner of the room; taken unawares by his action, Sarah allowed herself be led. Once in the corner, still gripping her arm firmly, he put his face close to hers and openly glared at her. She looked into his eyes and saw a mixture of anger and hostility. His lips curled back from stained teeth as he growled at her. "Listen to me you worthless tramp, Caroline's told me all about you. How you tricked her brother and brought shame on the family, causing him to run off. Don't think you are going to cause me and Caroline any trouble. If you try, I'll fix you good and proper, see if I don't!"

Sarah was so aghast at his comments that she was frozen to the spot. She looked away from his glaring eyes and saw the burly woman who had escorted her staring at them intently. He clearly took her turned head as an act of defiance on her part and shook her roughly, pushing his face even closer to hers. His eyes were blazing and she could smell his foul breath. "Look at me, and listen to my words you worthless strumpet!" he shouted, his saliva splattering her face.

Suddenly, galvanised into action by his harsh, unfair words, Sarah wrenched her arm free from his grasp and struck him on the cheek with all her might. She was only a slightly built girl, but the blow came with the force of all the anger pent up inside her. He staggered back surprised by the force of the blow. But Sarah wasn't finished yet. She had been brought up in the roughest area of London and had learned well how to deal with the undesirable attentions of men, she kicked him hard between his legs and screamed out. "How dare you call me such names!"

Police Constable William Maynard doubled up with a howl of pain and collapsed in a heap on the floor, writhing in agony. The situation was not improved by the sudden cheering of the three tramps who, drawn by Sarah's outburst, were clearly enjoying the spectacle of the Police Officer rolling around the floor in pain. They started shouting at Sarah to 'finish the Crusher off. Give him a good kickin'. But, she was spent, she put her hands to her face and tears streamed down her cheeks.

The Workhouse Master, obviously alerted by the noise in reception, pulled his door open and surveyed the scene. He shouted some instructions, and Sarah found herself grabbed, on one side, by the burly woman who had escorted her to the reception area and, on the other, by one of the male reception staff, who had been interviewing the tramps.

The Workhouse Master ordered Sarah taken into his office. She was dragged, then pushed, none to kindly, over to his door and thrown inside with such force that she was unable to keep her footing and fell full length onto the floor. Constable Maynard staggered to his feet and, amidst the taunts from the three tramps, limped to the door and exited the Workhouse. The Workhouse Master stared down at Sarah, lying in a heap on the floor in his office, and demanded an explanation for the fracas.

After a few moments Sarah climbed to her feet and responded with. "He dragged me across the room and shouted at me, calling me a tramp and a strumpet."

The Workhouse Master looked towards his staff. The burly woman gruffly stated that this was indeed what had happened. Somewhat confused by this explanation, the Workhouse Master ordered that Sarah be taken back to her work. As she was being escorted back to the kitchen, Sarah thought to herself that this was not going to be the end of the matter; in this, she was quite correct.

The following day, the Wednesday, further trouble descended on Sarah, in the shape of Kate Copeland, who had just been admitted and this time there was no avoiding her. When Sarah returned to ward 16 from supper, Kate Copeland was sitting on a bed just inside the door and spotted Sarah immediately. Sarah looked at her in dismay; Kate Copeland's face was a mask of fury. Sarah's bed was further down the ward, she walked down to it and sat on the end, casting furtive glances along the ward, towards the entrance. Each time she looked, Kate Copeland was staring straight at her, venom in her eyes. Now quite worried she lay back on her bed and stared at the ceiling.

A few minutes had passed when she felt a sharp pain in her arm. She whirled round to see Kate Copeland standing beside her bed. Looking down at her arm she could see that it was bleeding and that Kate Copeland was holding a piece of wood sharpened to a deadly point. Sarah clutched her injured arm and looked into Kate Copeland's beady eyes. "You hurt me in front of all these people and they will send you to prison!" she gasped out.

"Your dead meat!" Kate Copeland hissed, "you won't get away this time. I'm gonna finish you off!" With that she turned on her heel and stormed off down the ward back to her bed. She sat down on her bed and fixed Sarah with a malignant glare.

Sarah's heart was pounding and she was clutching her bleeding arm tightly. She was now very afraid. She felt that she was relatively safe whilst the candles were alight and witnesses would see any attack on her. Her problems would come after the night bell and darkness descended. She sat on her bed petrified about what the night would bring.

Shortly after the night bell sounded, the burly woman entered the ward to ensure that all the women were in their beds and the candles were extinguished. As she walked past Sarah's bed, Sarah called her over and told her that she feared that she would be attacked by the new girl and asked if she could change wards. The woman looked at her for a moment and could see the genuine fear in her eyes and the blood on her arm. She had been informed by the Master about the troublesome girls and knew Kate Copeland to be one of them, but she told Sarah that there was nothing she could do right now as it was night time. She said she would speak with the Master in the morning and turned away. Sarah was desperate, pleading to her retreating back, but she ignored Sarah's pleas and continued on her way. She extinguished the candles and exited the ward, locking the door after her.

Sarah lay in her bed, in the dark, trembling with fear. She could hear beds creaking, snores, coughs; then she felt she could hear footsteps, slowly getting closer. She realised that if she stayed in her bed she risked being stabbed where she lay, so, slowly and very quietly, she slipped out of her bed and crawled across the floor. She reached the other side of the ward and leaned back against the wall between two beds. She could still hear the soft stealthy footsteps, they stopped opposite her, across the ward, where her unoccupied bed was. She listened carefully, heard nothing, then there was a furious thumping sound coming from her bed, it sounded like someone was hitting the bed, then it stopped and she heard a whispered voice, thick with menace. "Where are yer bitch?"

She stayed where she was, frozen in place, trying hard not to make a sound. Then she heard the footsteps again, moving down the ward; Kate Copeland was trying to find her! She was trembling with her fear as the footsteps returned. But the ward was pitch black and after a while the footsteps stopped. Sarah lay still, back against the wall. She wondered if she should try and get back to bed, but decided against it. She stayed where she was and after a while fell into a fitful slumber.

She was startled awake by the woman in the bed beside her stirring. As awareness hit, fear and panic rose in her, she felt her heart pounding in her chest. She looked up, there was a faint, first light in the sky. She rose to her feet slowly and made her way back across the ward to her bed. She stopped at the foot of her bed; it was occupied! Someone was in it! She stared down and recognised the face of Kate Copeland! She took a step back, fear making her heart pound even more heavily in her chest. Then she realised that Kate Copeland was asleep; she had crawled into Sarah's bed in the hope that she would return to it and be ambushed. Carefully, Sarah walked away from her bed. Now it was getting light, she needed a hiding place until the morning bell sounded. But where? She was locked in the ward.

Kate Copeland stirred, opened her eyes; she cursed, she had not intended to fall asleep. But it was light now, all the women were still asleep in their beds. If she could find that Sarah Valentine, she would rip her face to pieces and stab her to death; she slowly and quietly slid out of bed. She walked slowly down one side of the ward to the end, carefully looking at the occupants and around and under each bed, She repeated it down the other side; no Sarah Valentine! She checked the door, it was firmly locked. She must have missed her, she couldn't get out of the ward. She set off down the ward again, this time she took more care with her search, even pulling covers back to make sure that

Sarah was not hiding in one of the beds with someone else, but there was no sign of her.

Kate Copeland was standing in the middle of the ward, with her hands on her hips and a puzzled expression on her face, when the morning bell sounded and the burly woman unlocked the door to take the roll call. It was then that she saw Sarah emerge from the privy, where she had been hiding and follow closely behind the burly attendant back to her bed. The expression on Kate Copeland's face was a picture of rage.

The burly woman told Sarah that she would spend the rest of her stay in ward 15 and, as Kate Copeland was not working in the kitchen, Sarah would only encounter her at meal times, where there would be many witnesses if she chose to attack her there. This however, would not deter Kate Copeland. Her anger at Sarah was all consuming, but it was two weeks before she got her chance. Sarah was late leaving supper as she had met her old friend Mary Caddy whom she had met in the lunatics ward 14, and chatted with her in the corridor on her way back to ward 15. Her friend was still in ward 14 with the lunatics and they paused for a moment outside the entrance. When Mary Caddy entered ward 14, Sarah was alone in the corridor as she walked towards ward 15; as she reached the entrance to her ward a figure emerged from ward 16, next door. It was Kate Copeland! She leaped at Sarah, who backed away. Kate Copeland produced the piece of sharp pointed wood from under her Workhouse uniform and stabbed at Sarah's face with it. Sarah put her hand up to protect herself and the sharp pointed end of the wood pierced her forearm. Sarah shrieked in pain and blood poured from her arm. Kate Copeland pulled the wood out and made to stab Sarah again, but she turned and ran down the corridor, yelling at the top of her voice, blood dripping from her arm; Kate Copeland set off after her. Sarah turned a corner and dashed down the stairs where she crashed into two male attendants attracted by her screams. She ran behind them and they saw the blood dripping from her injured arm. She pointed her finger and they turned and stared at a wild looking Kate Copeland running down the stairs with a bloodstained pointed piece of wood gripped in her hand and murder in her eyes. The confrontation was fierce, but short. Kate Copeland was nowhere near as big as her friend

Sophia Crafts and the two men soon overcame her and disarmed her, sustaining only a few scratches and bruises in the process.

Sarah was sent to the Matron to tend to her wound. Kate Copeland was dragged, kicking and yelling, to the Court House, where the Magistrate sent her to The Middlesex House of Correction, once again, for 14 days.

The two weeks passed without further incident. Sarah's arm was healing nicely, the new infirmary and fever block were completed and opened with much pomp and ceremony. Kate Copeland was returned to the Workhouse in the middle of November and placed in ward 14 with the lunatics. She was not permitted to leave the ward and took her food with the lunatics. She was furious, but there was little she could do about it.

Sarah, meanwhile, was still wondering about her altercation with Police Constable Maynard. Nothing had been said and she was hoping that the incident had been forgotten. However, in this, she was quite wrong.

It was a late November evening and a cold wind was blowing down Worship Street. The Shoreditch Relieving Officer John Coste and the Beadle were warming themselves in front of the roaring fire in the grate of the Cock and Magpie Tavern on the corner of Worship Street and Wilson Street, supping their ales.

"So," said John Coste, "what is the substance of this complaint from Constable Maynard?"

"Hah!" said the Beadle, with a smile on his face, "he seems to have been assaulted by a girl from your Workhouse."

"With all the troublesome females we have in the House, I am not surprised," said the Relieving Officer, "which one was it; no let me guess, Sophia Crafts, or Liz Weston."

"No neither," said the Beadle, "it was a Sarah Valentine. She doesn't appear to have been in much trouble in the past, but we did have her in the Station House for a week, though that was over two years ago." He paused to sip his ale, then continued, "She was attacked herself quite recently by that Caroline Copeland. Sustained an injury as I recall. Copeland was then sent to prison."

"Best place for that Copeland wretch," said John Coste, then, "this Sarah Valentine doesn't sound to be too bad, and I certainly don't recall her as a persistent troublemaker."

"Maybe not," replied the Beadle, "but he is a Constable and we must take this seriously. And there is another more concerning issue."

"Oh," said John Coste, "what is that?"

"The wife of our esteemed leader of the Board of Guardians," said the Beadle, letting his statement drift on the air.

"Oh my God!" exclaimed John Coste, "what has that dreadful woman got to do with it? She pokes her nose into Workhouse business on the back of her husband's position. She is of the opinion that women should be allowed on the Board of Guardians. Over my dead body I say!" he stormed.

"Yes," agreed the Beadle, "she behaves as if she already is on the Board of Guardians. And no one dares argue with her lest they attract the wrath of her esteemed husband. But she has got her teeth into this matter."

"In what way?" asked the Relieving Officer.

"She has discovered that this Sarah Valentine has been in and out of the Workhouse at least 12 times in her short life and wants her sent out on the basis that she is cheating the rate-payers by being in the House when she has no need of relief. Furthermore, she has cajoled her husband into sending a letter to the Master of the House instructing him to meet with her and stating that she has his full authority in this matter. He will have little choice but to bow to her demands, whatever they may transpire to be."

"Oh dear," said John Coste," I pity this Sarah Valentine. I would not like to incur Agatha's wrath."

"Will you get involved?" asked the Beadle.

"Mmm," said John Coste, his mind racing, "no," he finally uttered. "I will stay well clear of our dear Agatha."

It was Monday 25th November 1844 and Sarah was in the kitchen of the Workhouse, washing the dishes from breakfast, when she was summoned to the Master's office. Once again, she was escorted by the burly woman. When she entered the Master's office, he was sitting behind his desk, opposite him, sitting in a straight backed chair, was a stout, well dressed, middle aged woman, wearing a black silk dress, black bonnet and a stern expression; Sarah was not invited to sit down. Without ceremony, the Workhouse Master stated that the woman was a representative of the local Board of Guardians, elected by the community of rate-payers to run the Workhouse. The tone of his voice left no doubt in Sarah's mind of the high stature of the lady in question. The woman looked Sarah up and down in a disdainful way and proceeded to explain that they had received a formal complaint from one of the local Constables, accusing her of an unprovoked attack on him. At this, Sarah started to protest, but was shushed into silence. The woman went on. "This is a very serious matter young woman. You will likely go to prison or be deported to the colonies."

Sarah was stunned. To be deported was everyone's worst nightmare. The thought of never seeing her family again brought tears to her eyes. "No ma'am!" she wailed, "he handled me roughly, for no good reason, and called me bad names. I couldn't help myself. What he said was wrong and unfair."

The woman looked closely at Sarah. "What did he call you?" she asked.

Sarah looked down at her feet.

"Speak up girl!" said the woman.

"He called me a tramp and a worthless strumpet," she meekly replied.

The woman turned to the Master. "Is this true?" she asked.

"I believe it to be the truth ma'am," the Master replied, "we have reliable witnesses to the altercation," he added, looking at the burly woman standing next to Sarah. Then he continued in a pompous voice, "I am not happy with this accusation. If this Police Officer had some official reason for his visit, then he should have consulted with me first. I am the Master of this Institution and it is not proper for him to assault the paupers without recourse to me."

The woman sat thinking for a while before she spoke. "This does change things slightly," she eventually said, "we were not appraised of these circumstances." Then she went on, "but it does not materially effect the committee's decision to expel this girl from the Workhouse. It merely means that we will not be sending her for prosecution, since her actions were clearly provoked."

"What do you mean, expel me from this Workhouse?" asked Sarah, in some alarm.

"You should learn to hold your tongue in the presence of your superiors!" said the woman, addressing Sarah directly in a sharp voice, her eyes blazing, "looking at the records, it seems clear to us that you are merely using this Workhouse as a free hotel, coming and going as you please. You seem to be young, fit and healthy, which means that you are well able to work and maintain yourself. It is not the purpose of this Workhouse, nor the wish of the rate-payers, to provide you with free lodgings and meals as and when you desire. This Institution is solely for those in desperate need. We do not see you as in desperate need."

Sarah had no immediate response to this, so she remained silent.

"Do you have family?" the woman asked.

"Yes ma'am," Sarah meekly replied.

"Then I suggest that you go to them," she said.

Then, the woman turned away from Sarah and addressed the Master. "You will discharge this girl immediately," she said. Then added, "I think my work here is done, so I will bid you good day. I will see myself out." With that she rose and exited the office, sweeping through the door like a departing dowager. The Master merely nodded at the burly woman, who grabbed Sarah by the arm and led her out.

Some twenty minutes later, Sarah was standing outside the Workhouse, clutching her small bundle of possessions, wondering what to do and where to go. This had all happened so suddenly that she was quite at a loss and started to wander slowly down the Kingsland Road. It was a bright sunny day, but the sun was weak in the sky with a chill wind blowing down the road from the north. She clutched her shawl tightly round her shoulders to keep out the biting cold. Searching the pockets of her dress, she found some coins buried in the folds, together with Freddy's poesy ring. Taking them out, she counted two pence on her fingers. Then she remembered that this was what was left of the money she was given to buy clothes. She looked closely at Freddy's ring;

momentarily she wondered what it was worth. Should she sell it? Then she dismissed the thought and put it on her finger; it was a reminder of her son Edwin and she was unwilling to part with it.

She spent the day wandering aimlessly, trying to work out what to do. As the afternoon wore on and the sky darkened, she found herself in the Hackney Road. Putting her hands in her pockets, her fingers brushed the two pennies; she made a decision. She crossed over and walked down to the Nags Head Tavern, where she and Jimmy had often met. She walked in the door and found the place quite empty, it was still a little early for the evening crowd. She had expected to see the publican Stephen Standen, his son Billy, or his wife Ann, but there was a young girl behind the bar that she did not recognise, the girl looked up from a glass she was wiping and smiled at Sarah. Sarah looked at her closely, she was quite pretty, with long golden hair, and she wore a very low cut cotton dress that seemed rather thin for the winter weather, but it did give a generous view of her ample cleavage. For some reason, Sarah took an instant dislike to her. Hiding her dislike behind a forced smile, Sarah walked up to the bar and ordered a halfpenny glass of ale, then took a seat in the corner facing the door; she was hoping that her brother Jimmy would come in after his work.

Several hours later and she was nursing the last dregs in the bottom of her fourth glass of ale; she had no money left and was aware of the barmaid watching her. She knew that she could not reasonably remain here without buying another drink. With a sigh, she rose up, sank the last mouthful and placed her glass on the battered bar top. Just as she turned to walk to the door, it opened, and in walked Jimmy, whistling happily to himself; Sarah had never been so pleased to see anyone in her life. She ran across the room and flung herself at him. Laughing, he grabbed her and swung her round, lifting her feet clear off the ground. Regaining her feet, she kissed him on his, ever sooty, cheek and they walked, arm in arm, up to the bar.

The young barmaid had observed this scene with a wry grin on her mouth. As Jimmy got to the bar, she stood with her hands on her hips and addressed him. "Well Jimmy, here's me thinking that I'm the love of your life!"

Jimmy reached across the bar and pulled her to him, kissing her full on the lips. Sarah's mouth fell open; this was a side of Jimmy she had not seen before. The barmaid pulled back, grimacing at Jimmy, he took hold of her hand and said. "But you still are Lizzie, this is my big sister Sarah, and I haven't seen her for, what, it must be at least four months."

At this, the barmaid's face softened considerably; she leaned on the bar, putting her head closer to Jimmy's, giving him a good view down her full cleavage, which was clearly not lost on him. Sarah was now the one wearing the wry grin, clearly there was something going on between her little brother and this young lady. She pushed the little tang of jealousy to the back of her mind, after all, her brother was a grown man now, and she herself had said he should be looking for a wife, although she had rather hoped for a more respectable choice on his part.

Jimmy bought drinks for the three of them and they returned to the table that Sarah had just vacated. As there were still no other customers as yet, Lizzie, the barmaid, joined them at the table. Jimmy guessed that Sarah had been in the Workhouse yet again and would probably not welcome a discussion on that issue in front of Lizzie, so they engaged in small talk. Lizzie completely ignored Sarah and busied herself playing up to her brother. He was soon buying her drinks, not cheap ones either, she liked brandy, and preferred the better, more expensive brands. She also seemed to have a bottomless stomach, knocking them back with a flourish. Sarah looked at her brother in dismay; the words, 'a fool and his money are soon parted' sprang immediately to her mind.

Lizzie had already sunk three large portions of fine brandy, to Sarah and Jimmy's single ale each, when three men walked through the door, shouting for drinks. With a sigh, Lizzie rose up, threw down her forth brandy, and walked behind the bar to tend to her customers. Jimmy and Sarah both watched her waltzing away in her high hemmed dress, showing a shapely ankle, but with entirely different eyes. Sarah watched her leaning forward, showing herself to her best advantage to the three men, who were soon plying her with drink. She looked back at her beloved brother sitting opposite her, his lovelorn expression told her that he did not see a money grabbing harlot at the bar; his was a much more rosy perception. Sarah coughed to attract his attention.

Jimmy turned away from the bar and took Sarah's hands in his grubby ones. He looked into her eyes. "Well big sister," he said, "and what have you been up to?"

Sarah appraised him of her last four months in the Workhouse, including the scene with Constable Maynard.

At this Jimmy's face clouded over. "The bastard," he said, "he deserves a smack in the mouth."

"Don't you dare!" said Sarah fiercely, "I don't want you gettin' in no trouble with the police."

Jimmy continued to glare into his drink.

"The thing that really worries me Jimmy," Sarah was continuing, "is what they are telling my son Edwin. He's only four now, but if they are telling him bad things about me, when he grows up, he's going to hate me!" At this last comment her eyes started to water.

Jimmy squeezed her hands. "Nothing they can say will ever alter the lovely person you are," he said, "he will love you when you meet him."

"But when on earth will that be?" she wailed.

They sat there for a while clutching hands. Then Sarah pulled herself together, took her hands away from Jimmy's and took a large swig of her drink.

He smiled at her. "So, what are you going to do? Where will you stay?" he said.

"I really don't know," she said.

"Well," said Jimmy, "you'd better stay with us until you get yerself fixed up."

"What will mum say?" Sarah asked.

"I'm sure she will be very pleased to see you," said Jimmy.

Sarah was not so sure about this, but she had very limited options at this moment in time.

After their drink, Sarah accompanied Jimmy back to Little Pearl Street. The rubble and devastation resulting from the destruction of Essex Street and Rose Lane was still all too apparent. They found their sister Mary sitting on the step outside the tenement building where her family lived. She was overjoyed at seeing Sarah and they embraced warmly. Arm in arm, the two girls walked into the tenement, followed by Jimmy. When they entered her mother's room, she looked up from where she had been tending the hearth, filling it with wood and paper, seeing Sarah, she stood up.

"Hello mum," said Sarah tentatively.

"We haven't seen much of you lately," her mother said, staring at her with no warmth in her eyes.

Sarah was struck by the gaunt look on her mother's face, she seemed to have aged a lot in the few months since Sarah had seen her last. She walked over and embraced her. Her mother did not respond, simply standing still, with her hands down by her sides. Stepping back Sarah smiled at her.

It was Jimmy who spoke. "Sarah will be staying with us for a while. Until she gets on her feet," he said.

"Oh will she," said her mother simply.

"Only if it's all right with you mum," added Sarah quickly.

"You better ask 'im," her mother said pointing at Jimmy, "he's the breadwinner now."

Sarah realised that her mother was still bitter about the loss of her husband and children; she couldn't really blame her for that. "Let me help with the fire mum," she said, "I'm quite good at it now. I've had a lot of practice," she added wryly, kneeling down to attend to the grate.

Whilst Sarah got a fire going, Jimmy walked round the corner to the Crown in Grey Eagle Street and, after a few minutes commiserating with the proprietor, Jane Bowyer, who had buried her husband Robert some two months ago, brought back a large jug of ale. When it got dark, Jimmy lit some tallow candles, Mary was sent to get four penny pies, a pint of shrimps for two pence and some winkles. Jimmy produced some strips of meat from his pocket that he had obtained from a butcher in the Hackney Road on his way home from work. He then proceeded to hang the strips of meat from lengths of string mounted in front of the fire; he turned them round from time to time. When Mary returned and the food had been arrayed on the small table, the meat was ready. They sat at the table and enjoyed their food, washed down with a mug of ale. That evening, Mary was happy to share her bed with Sarah, cuddling into her back to keep warm.

CHAPTER 31

The Last Of The Workhouse

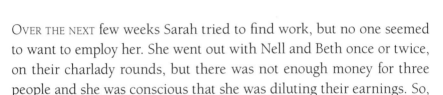

OVER THE NEXT few weeks Sarah tried to find work, but no one seemed to want to employ her. She went out with Nell and Beth once or twice, on their charlady rounds, but there was not enough money for three people and she was conscious that she was diluting their earnings. So, she politely said no to any further excursions, and allowed them to share their meagre earnings between them.

If they had a lot of work on, Mary would go out with Jimmy and the Ricketts to help with sweeping the chimneys, Liz Ricketts was training her up, she was small, lithe and strong and, according to Jimmy, she was getting quite good at it. Sarah would laugh when they both returned home with matching sooty faces.

She was very conscious that, with her in the house, Jimmy had to support an extra mouth to feed. To his credit he did not complain, but his earnings were not great and she was certainly a drain on his resources. In addition, her clothes were getting rather threadbare and she could hardly expect Jimmy to clothe her as well as feed and house her. She thought about trying to get back into the Workhouse, but knew better than to attempt it just before Christmas. So, she decided to wait until the New Year and try her luck then. She had a momentary thought about what the woman from the Board of Guardians had said to her about relying on the Workhouse too much, but she quickly dismissed it.

As Christmas day grew closer, Sarah managed to get a part-time job with a local trader in the Whitechapel High Street. It did not pay much, but it did help cover the cost of her food and she was able to get herself a better second hand dress down Petticoat Lane.

She spent Christmas day with her family and thoroughly enjoyed it. On Boxing Day, Lizzie, the barmaid from the Nags Head, called round to see Jimmy and they all went round to the Crown with Nell and her family. The tavern was packed to bursting point and they spent most of the day laughing and singing along with all the customers. The landlady, Jane Bowyer, took a break, leaving the busy bar to her staff, and came over to join them; her two daughter's, Emma age-sixteen and little Sarah, only three-years-of-age, were following her with sad expressions on their faces. Their fun loving father Robert had died only a short while ago and it was their first Christmas without him. Sarah Valentine, her sister Mary and Nell's girls all did their best to cheer them up.

It was quite late on when they decided to leave; some of the local costermongers started rowing with each other and a fight broke out. They fled out the door to the sounds of angry voices and breaking glass.

Jimmy offered to walk Lizzie home as she was more than a little tipsy and, with a sly wink at Sarah, took Lizzie's arm and led her off to the Hackney Road where she had lodgings near the Nags Head. Sarah glared at him, wagging her finger warningly, but he just laughed, cuddling Lizzie a little closer. The rest of the party walked arm in arm back to Little Pearl Street still singing at the tops of their voices.

The day after Boxing Day was a Friday and Sarah turned up for work a little late, to be told that it would be her last day, she was no longer required. She knew from the outset that the job was only temporary, just over the Christmas period, but she had hoped to be employed until the New Year. That evening, she returned home with a heavy heart; she realised that, with no money coming in, she could not reasonably stay any longer. She had already taken far too much advantage of her brother's hospitality, she could not expect him to keep her any longer. Over the weekend she told Jimmy that she would be leaving. He said that she was welcome to stay and her sister Mary begged her to stay, but Sarah was adamant, she would leave next week.

So, after a month on the street she decided to try her luck at getting back into the Shoreditch Workhouse. She knew better than to approach the Relieving Officer, who would be aware of the Board of Guardians ejecting her. She knew that she could gain direct admission from the Master, if she presented a good case. So, on New Years Eve, Tuesday 31st December 1844, with some trepidation, she presented herself at the Workhouse. She had put mud on her dress and some pig's blood on her face, she intended to say that she had been assaulted and needed aid; however, she was lucky. Indeed, she was lucky on two counts: in the first instance, when she walked through the door, she was startled to see her old enemy Liz Weston who was struggling in the grip of a Police Constable; in the second instance, the Workhouse Master, William Thomas, was away and his wife, Ann Thomas, was seeing to the admissions in his absence. The Police Constable was stating that he had brought Liz Weston to the Workhouse as she claimed to be destitute and there was no room for her at the Robert Street Station House. Liz Weston was clearly very drunk, shouting and yelling at everyone in sight. She was a considerable distraction to the Workhouse staff, who might otherwise have devoted more attention to Sarah. Ann Thomas remembered Sarah from her past admissions, but was clearly not fully aware of her previous history with the Governors. Seeing the blood on Sarah's face and hearing her tale of assault, she saw Sarah as being the most easy to deal with and quickly agreed to admit her on her husband's behalf. So, within the hour, Sarah was safely ensconced in the Workhouse. She was taken to the familiar womens' working ward 16. At her own suggestion, claiming previous experience, she was set to work in the kitchen.

The following day, the 1st January 1845, she was pleased to note that Liz Weston had not been placed in ward 16, however, at breakfast she was startled when she saw Liz Weston sitting with Kate Copeland. She very carefully avoided them seeing her, she did not want another confrontation with either of them.

She spent the next few days maintaining a low profile. Not only did she need to avoid being seen by the two girls, but the Workhouse Master had returned and Sarah needed to give him a wide berth as well.

If he was about, she made sure that her face was always turned away from his direct sightline. The burly woman was still there and gave Sarah some curious looks, clearly surprised to see her back again, but nothing was said.

On 11th January Kate Copeland was thrown out by the Board of Guardians. On the 18th January, a new girl, Mary Robinson, was admitted and put in the bed next to Sarah. In the evenings, before the final bell, Sarah and Mary Robinson started talking and soon found that they liked each other.

On the 31st January Liz Weston, unhappy with the small amount of food on her plate, attacked one of the servers at dinner and was dispatched to the Magistrate and sent to the House of Correction for 14 days.

Over the next few weeks, Sarah continued to maintain her low profile and the monotonous routine began to make an automaton of her once again. As time marched on, the memory of her previous expulsion grew dim and Sarah became less observant in maintaining her low profile.

On the 18th February, Liz Weston returned from the House of Correction and Sarah noticed her in the dining hall, but managed to keep out of her sightline. On the 5th March Liz Weston no longer appeared at meals, so Sarah assumed she had left the Workhouse; she breathed a sigh of relief. But this only lasted a couple of weeks, when she saw Kate Copeland appear in the dining hall. Fortunately, she was not in Sarah's ward or working in the kitchen and Sarah managed to keep out of her sight for a few days. But then, one dinner time, as the girls were leaving the dining room, she was spotted. On seeing Sarah, Kate Copeland gave an angry screech and started to push her way through the throng of girls to get at her. Seeing her advancing on her, Sarah tried to get away, but Kate Copeland caught up with her and started to punch her in the back, shouting at her to turn round. The burly woman grabbed hold of Kate Copeland and tried to restrain her. Whilst the two of them were struggling with each other, Sarah took advantage and sped away back to the kitchen. She was a very worried girl as she laboured away cleaning the crockery from the dinner. She still had the scars from her previous attacks by Kate Copeland and knew that she was a very real danger.

It was some hours later and Sarah was still working in the kitchen when one of the cooks grabbed her by the shoulder and told her to go and collect some fresh drying cloths. On her way back from the laundry room, she was walking round a corner in one of the Workhouse corridors, her mind on Kate Copeland, rather than where she was going, when she ran straight into a man. Her sightline was partly obscured by the mountain of cloths she was carrying and initially she did not see who she had run into. She started to apologise, then saw who it was. It was William Thomas, the Master of the Workhouse! He was staring at her in disbelief. Her eyes widened in fear.

"What are you doing here?" he said in an angry voice.

"Please sir," Sarah stammered, "I was admitted at the beginning of the year."

"Who admitted you?" he stormed.

"Please sir," she said again, then a little weaker, "Misses Thomas sir."

Clearly surprised, and wrong footed by this answer, he brushed past her and marched off down the corridor.

'Oh Hell!' thought Sarah, 'that's done it'. And she walked off to the kitchen with the cloths, a very worried girl. However, over the next couple of days nothing happened, and Sarah began to think that she might have got away with it.

The Shoreditch Parish Relieving Officer, John Coste, was sitting behind his desk in the Parish Offices in Worship Street, staring at the man seated opposite. Both wore worried expressions on their faces.

The man opposite was William Thomas, Master of the Shoreditch Workhouse and he started to speak. "I will have to inform that wretched woman of Sarah Valentine's return to the Workhouse. Her husband has the power to dismiss me on the spot if I were to incur her wrath! As it is I will have to go down on my bended knees about my stupid wife allowing her back in."

"Of course you will," said John Coste, pursing his lips. Truth to tell he was less concerned about William Thomas's future, than with his own. His fervent desire was to keep out of this mess.

"Oh what am I to do?" bleated the Master of the Workhouse, "what do you suggest?".

"I will tell you what we will do," said John Coste conspiratorially, "I will speak with the Reverend Ratcliffe. He is probably the only person in the Parish who can stand up to Agatha and get away with it. I will ask him to intercede in this matter. Though I know not what the ultimate outcome will be."

The Master of the Workhouse clasped his hands together. "Thank you John, thank you very much!"

John Coste smiled, this was a good outcome indeed. He would stay completely out of this difficult matter, let the Reverend sort it out.

Back at the Workhouse, Sarah was now convinced that the matter was going no further. But then came the inevitable summons to the Workhouse Master's office. Once again she was escorted from the kitchen by the burly woman. When they entered the Master's office, the burly woman was dismissed. Sarah looked round, apart from the Master, there were two other people present, and she knew both of them. One was the woman representing the Board of Guardians, who had previously thrown Sarah out of the Workhouse, the other was the Reverend Ratcliffe. The atmosphere was a little tense in the room and Sarah got the distinct impression that an argument had just taken place. It was the Reverend who asked Sarah to sit in the one remaining vacant chair; his was the only face in the room that did not wear a frown, but it was the woman from the Board of Guardians who spoke first. "I thought that I had made it perfectly clear that you should not abuse the services of this Institution. What are you doing here?"

"May it please you ma'am," started Sarah, "I could not get work and was destitute."

"Well it does not please me in the least!" said the woman glaring at Sarah.

"Now, now, Agatha," said the Reverend, "I thought we had agreed that this is not the way we are going to do this."

At this, the woman made a loud 'hurrumph' sound and folded her arms over her ample bosom.

The Reverend continued, in a kindly voice "Sarah, how old are you?"

"I think I'm about twenty-two, or twenty-three sir," she said uncertainly.

The woman 'hurrumphed' again.

"Well no matter," said the Reverend patiently, "I think we can agree that you are old enough to make your own way in the world. Are you ill or unfit in any way?" he continued.

"No sir," said Sarah, fully aware of where this conversation was heading.

"Well," said the Reverend, "This Institution is really only for those who are desperately in need; those who are too old or too sick to work. If fit and healthy young people like you come in here, you take up a bed that could be better used by someone more in need of help. They could die on the street as a result of you taking up the bed they need."

Sarah looked down at her feet, suitably chastened. Then, looking up at the Reverend. "I'm sorry sir," she said, "but I really have nowhere to go and no prospects of work."

"It is not our intention to throw you out on the street," said the Reverend.

At this the woman representative from the Board of Guardians 'hurrumphed' even louder, invoking a dark look from the Reverend. It was quite clear to Sarah that throwing her bodily out into the street was exactly what the woman had in mind.

However, the Reverend was continuing, "the Church Wardens will find you a position, and you will remain here until that is done." He looked sternly at the woman, who made no comment. Then, he looked directly at Sarah, "but you will not return here. Is that understood?"

Agatha's face was bright red with her anger, she could restrain herself no longer. She stood up and took two paces towards Sarah, bending down to look directly into Sarah's face. "If you attempt to return to this establishment, I will personally see that you are removed to the Magistrate's Court *forthwith!*" she stormed.

"Agatha!" said the Reverend.

Agatha reluctantly sat back down. But her face was a mask of fury. All directed at Sarah.

"I understand sir," Sarah said, directing her comment at the Reverend and trying her best to ignore the daggers coming from Agatha.

Up until that point, the Workhouse Master had said nothing. Then, obviously uncomfortable with the atmosphere in his office, he cleared his throat and spoke. "Well," he said, "that just about clears it up. That will be all Sarah, you may return to your work now."

With that, she was dismissed. She stood up, smiled at the Reverend, nodded to the Master and ignored Agatha; then, she opened the door and departed. As she walked back to the kitchen, she thought that it could all have been so much worse. She was astute enough to realise that it *would* have been much worse, if it wasn't for the presence of the Reverend.

The Reverend was true to his word and a few days later Sarah was informed that she had been offered a position with a shoemaker in the Hackney Road. When she told her friend Mary Robinson, she found out that her friend had also been given an opportunity of employment and would be leaving the Workhouse on the same day. So, on Saturday 29th March 1845 they both left the Shoreditch Workhouse. For Sarah, it would be the last time. She knew full well that she dare not return, she was on her own from now on.

The position Sarah had been found by the Reverend Ratcliffe was not a live-in one, so she needed to find somewhere to live. Bidding her friend Mary Robinson goodbye, Sarah set off up the Kingsland Road. She had decided to try the Philips Street and Edward Street area, by the Regent's Canal, where she had found accommodation before. But after walking up and down all the surrounding streets for several hours, she had found nothing suitable. She had even tried the room she had stayed in before, where her friends the Freestone's had lodged, but they were not there any more.

She was just about to give up when she spotted a familiar face walking down the street towards her, it was Sarah Chamberlain, her old friend from her early Workhouse days. She was carrying a small bundle under her arm; Sarah stopped to talk with her. After a few minutes chatting about what they had been doing since they last met, Sarah explained that she needed to find lodgings. It transpired that her friend had just left a room in a local doss house, just down Philips Street, and her space should still be vacant. Thanking her for the information, Sarah walked round to Philips Street, to the building her friend had told her about and walked in. After a brief discussion with the landlord, Sarah was led to a room at the end of the dark narrow hallway. It had the same arrangement as the room she had shared with Ann Pluckrose, some thirteen years earlier, in that it was divided into four small sections by means of three dirty sheets pinned across the walls. She was directed to the left hand end section and when the landlord pulled back the screening curtain, Sarah noted a small straw filled mattress which almost completely filled the diminutive space. The floor was covered in dirt and grime; she could see black beetles scurrying about, but she could not see any rats. The rent was three pence a night and if she rented by the week, Sunday was free. With no other alternative available to her, she agreed to take the space. The landlord initially wanted some money 'up front', but Sarah explained that she was just starting work the next day and proposed to rent by the week. She begged to be allowed some time to get the money. Grudgingly, the landlord agreed to a few days grace and so she settled in to her new home.

A few days later, Sarah had started work at the shoemaker's and things were going reasonably well; she was beginning to feel much better about her life. Her lodgings in the old doss-house left much to be desired, her close neighbours, sharing the room, behind their curtains, were filthy and noisy and she kept herself to herself. The straw mattress she slept on was crawling with bugs and black beetles were everywhere at night, frequently crawling across her face, but she was quite used to enduring such minor irritations and she put them to the back of her mind. She was finding that she did get some enjoyment from her days, in fact, she had found that she quite liked working at the shoemaker's.

She got up bright and early in the morning. It was a clear bracing spring morning and she had a skip in her step as she walked down the Kingsland Road towards Bethnal Green. She was happy to be free and in the open air, she cocked a snoot at the Workhouse as she walked past and made a mental promise to herself that she would not return to that Institution ever again, no matter what may transpire in her life.

She cut through Union Street on to the Hackney Road and set off at a brisk walk. Her destination was almost at the far end of the Hackney Road, a distance of just under a mile, but she didn't mind the walk. The Hackney Road was full of interesting shops to look in and it was a bustling thoroughfare, even early in the morning. She had developed an interest in people watching, fostered by her time in the Workhouse and attending St Mary's Church; she was always observing passers by. She amused herself by trying to guess what they did and where they were going.

Her eye caught one girl, with golden hair and low cut dress, she knew exactly what she did and where she was going, it was Lizzie from the Nags Head. Fortunately, she was on the other side of the road, clearly heading towards the tavern, presumably to prepare the place for opening time. Sarah had no wish to talk with her and turned her back towards her, dawdling in a shop doorway. She watched Lizzie's distorted reflection in the rippled surface of the glass in the shop window. Sure enough, reaching the Nags Head, she disappeared down an alleyway at the side of the tavern, probably heading for a rear entrance.

Once Lizzie had gone from view Sarah turned from the shop doorway and continued her walk down the Hackney Road. She had gone only a few steps when she was brought up short by the sight of a woman emerging from a side road next to the one Lizzie had just gone down, she was pushing a perambulator and had a small boy walking alongside her; Sarah recognised her immediately and crossed the Hackney Road. Just as she reached the other side of the road Sarah shouted out and waved her arms.

The woman with the perambulator turned round and looked at her. "Sarah Valentine!" she exclaimed, "fancy meeting you here!"

"Jane Freestone!" Sarah mimicked her, "well, well, fancy seeing you here!"

They both laughed. Sarah looked down at the little boy, who was smiling up at her. "My, aren't you getting big Thomas!" she said, and knelt down to ruffle young Thomas's hair. She immediately collected a pinched nose from him, laughing, she stood up whilst Jane told her son off for tweaking Sarah's nose. It transpired that it was something his father always did to him, so, he was naturally copying it. "And who's this?" said Sarah, looking in the perambulator.

"This is my new baby daughter Jane," she said proudly. "We moved from that small room we shared with you in Edward Street as soon as we knew I was expectin'. We live down there now," she pointed back down the side road she had emerged from, "Wellington Place," she continued, "number six, if you ever want to call on us. You're more than welcome."

The two women chatted for a while, catching up on each other's lives, since they had last lodged together. Then Sarah bade her goodbye, saying she mustn't be late for work. Waving goodbye, she re-crossed the Hackney Road and trotted on her way, now hurrying a little faster.

After a few minutes, Sarah arrived at No. 16 Gwynn's Place, her new place of work. In layout, it was much the same as the tailor's shop she had worked in, where she met Freddy Linford, but with the exception that this premises dealt in footwear rather than clothing. There was a shop front with a small glass window, which was decked out with a wide range of footwear, and a small entrance doorway to one side, it was here that the customers off the street were received. Her Master was the owner, one Samuel Cleare, in his mid fifties, a shoemaker of some renown. His wife Martha was also experienced in shoemaking, and ran the workshop girls with a rod of iron. They had two grown up son's living with them, Henry and George, the eldest, George Cleare, had a wife Hannah and four children, also living there.

Sarah made her way round to the back of the premises and let herself in through a double width doorway, she entered a dark hallway which led to the workroom. As with the tailor's shop, she knew that the workroom would be full, even at this early hour. A row of women boot and shoe closers would be struggling to earn a pittance, it would be precious little reward for the many hours they put in.

She was not going to enter the workroom just yet. Off to one side, there was a set of narrow stairs to the upper floor and her first chores were upstairs. She mounted the steep wooden stairs which creaked ominously at every step.

"That you Sarah?" Came a woman's voice from the landing above.

Sarah recognised the strained voice of Hannah, wife of the eldest son of the Master of the house. "Yes," replied Sarah.

"Get the children ready," said Hannah.

Although Sarah's main job was downstairs in the shop and workrooms, she was also assisting upstairs. Hannah had recently given birth to a baby girl called Martha and was still recovering from a difficult childbirth; she was quite weak and unable to do very much. They did have a live in servant called Mary Meek, but she was quite old and a little unsteady on her feet. Although she could handle most of the simple chores, she was not able to cope with some of the more arduous tasks. In particular, she was not up to supervising the boisterous older children of the household, so part of Sarah's job was to look after the three of them. Her first task was to get them up and dressed; the two older boys, George who was eight, and John who was six, attended a local school. The youngest, four-year-old Hannah, would usually spend the day getting under Sarah's feet.

Having got the children up, Sarah collected some money from Hannah and ran down the stairs, exiting the rear of the shop and trotting into the Hackney Road. She was destined for the baker's shop, just a few yards down the road; the shoemaker's shop was No. 16, the baker was 3 doors down at No. 13. There she purchased some bread, pausing a while to chat with the proprietor, John Carter and his garrulous wife Sarah; they were a local couple, always ready for a chin-wag, and Sarah frequently found it difficult to get away from them. Returning to the shoemaker's, she fed some breakfast to the children, then she would take the two boys to school, this was not a difficult task as the school was only a short walk down the Hackney Road.

It was still bright and clear when Sarah ushered the boys out of the rear door of the shoemaker's shop, young Hannah usually accompanied them, chattering constantly. Fortunately, the school was on the same side of the road and so it did not require a hazardous attempt at crossing the busy main road. After a few minutes walking they passed the local pond and were soon at the tall block of buildings known as Matthews Place.

The school was the fifth building in the block; it was run by Schoolmaster Joseph Stansbury and his wife Catherine. They tutored boys from the age of six up to fifteen and could accommodate some live-in students. Sarah opened the door and followed the children in, where they were met by Sophia, one of the two assistants, she greeted Sarah and took charge of the boys. Waving them goodbye, Sarah and young Hannah exited the building.

On the way back to the shoemaker's, they stopped at the pond. Hannah usually brought a piece of bread with her, taken surreptitiously from the breakfast table and hidden in her dress. They stood at the side of the pond and Hannah pulled crumbs of bread from her dress pocket and tossed them into the water. Very quickly, ducks swam across and started devouring the bread voraciously. More and more of them kept arriving and splashed as they fought with each other to reach the bread first, this thoroughly delighted young Hannah who was giggling and squealing at the antics of the ducks. All too soon, the bread ran out, Hannah pulled out her pocket and shook it to get at the last remaining crumbs. Seeing no further bread arriving, the ducks started to drift away and soon they had migrated to the other side of the water. The morning's entertainment now at a finish, Sarah took Hannah's hand and they walked back to the shoemaker's shop.

During the day Sarah would first help Mary Meek clean and tidy the upstairs. She would take on the heavier tasks, such as cleaning out the fire grates removing the ashes and filling the scuttles with coal for the evening; Sarah also made herself useful by doing most of the shopping for the family. The shoemaker's shop was in Gwynn's Place and next door was Howard's Place. Together they formed a row of about 30 premises, which included the Cambridge Heath Brewery, the Adelaide Tavern and many shops. Also within easy walking distance were: a butcher, greengrocer, fishmonger and an oilman from whom she could buy candles and matches.

After her chores upstairs had been completed and the shopping delivered to Mary Meek, she would report to the Master Cordwainer downstairs for further instruction, this would usually involve keeping the workshop and shop areas clean neat and tidy. Having previously worked in a tailor's shop, doing much the same work, she was very familiar with the tasks and soon got up to speed. This gained her much favour with the Master Cordwainer, one George Mason. He ran a tight ship and kept everyone on their toes, he was well trained in the profession, a member of the Cordwainer's Guild and a master craftsman.

Over the course of the next few months Sarah gained quite a familiarity in the work of the shoemaker's art. The first thing she learned was acquired the hard way. She made the mistake of saying that she had once met someone, in Whitechapel, who was also a cobbler. George Mason corrected her immediately. "I am a Cordwainer Journeyman, not a cobbler. A cobbler," he said in a derisory voice, "works with old leather to repair old shoes. They will sometimes tear apart an old shoe and re-cut the leather to make a totally different shoe, but we, on the other hand, work only with the best new leather, to make new shoes, to the highest standards."

Sarah was very conciliatory and decided that the best course of action was to humour him and ask him to enlighten her. To her chagrine, he did so at great length.

"The finest leather in the world is made in Cordoba. This leather was called cordouan in French which is now called cordwain in England. Since we only make shoes with this new leather, we have adopted this name for our profession. We serve strict apprenticeships and only when we have completed seven years of learning are we accepted into the Master Craftsman's Guild, as a Journeyman."

Sarah was suitably impressed, and thanked him. She quickly realised that he was very proud of his profession and treated her better if she expressed an interest in it. She did not want to upset him and she was acutely aware that she could no longer rely on the Workhouse as a backstop if she found herself out of work; she was also aware of how difficult it was to find work. It was suddenly dawning on her that she desperately needed to hang on to this job. For the first time in her life, she was facing up to the reality of the importance of being able to make her own way in the world. Accordingly, she decided to take more note of what went on in the establishment and use this knowledge to make herself a better, more highly regarded worker. This, she believed, would help her to keep her job.

She soon realised that, much as with the tailor's shop, there were off-the-shelf customers that came into the shop and bought boots and shoes that they tried on. Then, there were the more important customers that had personal fittings for their shoes. These would have their feet measured and examined, with meticulous notes taken on the precise statistics of each foot. These specific measurements, tracings and notes were then used to create a mould of each foot, called the 'Last', this was a wooden foot-shaped form used to stretch and shape the leather. A pair of Lasts would be individual to the feet for which they were designed, allowing further pairs of shoes to be made for the same customer. Measurements were also taken to produce a pattern specific to each customer's required 'design'. This pattern would include all the intricate details and information needed to make the shoes look and feel just right. The back room contained shelves with rows and rows of these Lasts, so that an important customer could request a new set of shoes that would be made quickly to fit his, or her, feet perfectly.

Regarding the manufacture of the shoes themselves, the higher level tasks were usually undertaken by the Master Cordwainer, but the manufacture of the shoe required much skilled work by lower paid minions, mostly women, who worked long hours for little money. These each had their designated task and functional name: the 'Clicker' would use information from the pattern to select the correct grades and flexibility of leather to suit the shoe and then cut the pieces that would go to form the upper part of the shoe to the shape of the pattern, the 'Closer' would then make the upper part of the shoes out of the cuts from the Clicker: the sides, tongues, aprons, saddles, back strips, and many others, according to fashion, sewing together all the various pieces and adding stiffeners as necessary; she would also ensure that the lining and final shaping worked around the Last. Next, by working the Closer's uppers around the Lasts, the 'Maker' would stretch the uppers and add the soles and heels, and line the inner part of the shoe. The job of the Maker was by far the most skilled and was usually performed by George Mason himself. Sometimes, for the very important customers, they would leave the uppers on the Last for up to seven days, to ensure that the leather would better take the shape of the Last, to give a more accurate fit. At this point, before finally adding the heels and soles, an appointment would usually be made for a second fitting, allowing the Maker to carry out final adjustments before completing and producing the shoes. Finally, the 'Finisher' would dye, clean and polish the shoes, ready for the customer to collect.

Sarah was particularly taken by the tools used by the people in their various tasks. While many of the tools seemed fairly common, such as some of the hammers used by the Closers, there were many others, of different sizes and odd shapes; some had longer handles and larger striking surfaces. The Clickers used knives but, again, there were different types of knives; the most unusual of these knives was the half-moon knife, this had a half-round blade used for cutting the leather. Sarah asked George about its unusual shape. He went into some detail, explaining why it was thus shaped to better cut the leather. He told her that shoemakers' had been using such a knife for thousands of years and that Archeologists had discovered very old half-moon knifes almost identical with those in current use; she was suitably impressed.

On her own initiative, she observed the shoe manufacturing process carefully and, if her other duties were completed, she would help out in the workshop. She had no skills to carry out any of the manufacturing jobs, but she helped move the materials to the workers benches and transport part finished shoes from one bench to the next. On particularly hectic days, George Mason greatly appreciated Sarah's help in the workshop and thanked her accordingly. She glowed with his praise and was beginning to feel that she would really be able to keep this job.

CHAPTER 32

Surprise, Surprise, 1845

PROVIDING THERE WERE no rush jobs, or backlog of shoes to be filled, Sarah was usually given Sunday afternoon off. On these occasions, she would often take the opportunity to visit her family. She would find these visits quite distressing as her mother was looking more gaunt and haggard with each week that passed; she seemed to be fading away and Sarah was quite concerned about her.

Her sister Mary, although only nine-years-of-age, was growing more adult in her ways and was assuming more responsibilities, both in working with Jimmy and around the home. When Sarah visited, it was often Mary that was cleaning out the grate and tidying the place up, while her mother sat with a vacant expression on her face, staring into space. Jimmy was frequently absent, 'visiting his fancy piece' as Mary succinctly put it; it seemed that Mary shared Sarah's instant dislike of the buxom barmaid Lizzie.

Sarah was sad that she was seeing less of her brother, she had even stopped meeting him of an evening in the Nags Head. Although she passed it every day on her way home from work, she really couldn't face seeing him leaning on the bar drooling down the barmaid's cleavage. The last time she called in to meet with him he barely heard a word she was saying, he was so distracted by the effervescent Lizzie.

With the arrival of September, came a spell of fierce rain showers. It was one evening as she was walking home from work, that she was caught in a particularly heavy shower. The rain was bouncing back up off the pavement, almost to eye level, and rivers of water were gushing down the road. She was soaked to the skin in seconds and found herself splashing through the puddles seeking shelter; she was only some twenty yards from the Nags Head, so she decided to run towards it. Reaching the door, she pushed it open and dashed inside. She was drenched, she took off her bonnet and shawl, both were ringing wet, she dripped her way across the room to the bar. There was a fair crowd of people congregated there, many of whom had also taken shelter from the rain. The floor was soaking wet, leaving the bare wood quite treacherous and Sarah nearly slipped over as she pushed her way through the crowd. Reaching the bar, she saw her brother Jimmy in his usual spot at the end and elbowed her way towards him.

As she reached him, she noticed that he had an unusually downcast expression on his, usually cheerful, face. Sarah squeezed his arm and he jumped, startled out of his solace. "What's the matter Jimmy? Why the long face?" Sarah inquired with a worried expression.

"Oh nothing really," he said, then shouted for a drink for Sarah.

It was then that Sarah noticed that the landlord's son Billy was serving behind the bar, there was no sign of the buxom Lizzie. Billy came over with her drink and whilst Jimmy handed the coins over, Sarah spoke with Billy. "Haven't seen you for a while Billy," she said.

"Naw," said Billy, "me an' mum been over me Aunt Bessie's, she was taken bad an' someone had to stay with her to look after 'er."

"Oh!" said Sarah, "how is she?"

"Dead," said Billy simply, "buried her last Friday."

"Oh!" said Sarah again, "I'm sorry to hear that Billy."

"Thanks," said Billy. Then, "gotta go an' serve John." With that he turned and walked down the bar.

A thought was germinating in Sarah's head, but she was not quite sure how to express it. Then she turned towards Jimmy and decided to take the plunge. "Lizzie not on tonight I see," she started.

There was no response from Jimmy.

"Er, how is she?" Sarah added.

"Look!" said Jimmy, a little too abruptly, "she's gone!"

Sarah paused and pondered this for a short while. "What do you mean. Gone?" she said.

"Just that!" said Jimmy, clearly upset. "Here one minute, gone the next."

With that he lapsed into a sullen silence. This was so unlike the Jimmy she knew that Sarah was stunned into silence herself. Then, seeing that Billy had finished serving his customer and that Jimmy was still lost in his own thoughts, she sidled up the bar to where Billy was standing polishing some glasses with a dirty cloth. As she moved up in front of him, it occurred to Sarah that he was wiping more dirt onto the glasses than he was removing from them, but that was not her primary concern at the moment. "Billy," she started.

"Yes Sarah," Billy replied.

"That barmaid. You know. What was her name now? Yes, Lizzie wasn't it?"

"Oh her!" Billy said meaningfully, "what about 'er?"

"Has she gone then?" Sarah enquired in her sweetest voice.

"Booted out on 'er arse!" he said, "and good riddance, thieving tramp!" This last with venom.

Now thoroughly curious, Sarah contemplated her next question carefully. She had just opened her mouth to voice it, when a raucous voice shouted from down the bar.

"You servin', or just standin' round doin' nothin'!"

"Just commin'," said Billy, and moved off down the bar.

Sarah spent a frustrating ten minutes standing there whilst Billy served several customers. When he was finally free, she walked up to him. "What was she thieving then?" she asked him.

"Who?" said Billy.

"Lizzie!" said Sarah getting more frustrated.

"Oh 'er!" he said. "Yea! Had 'er fingers in the cash draw alright. Dad caught 'er red 'anded. Came out into the bar unexpected like, just at closing time. There she was putting money down the front of her dress. He had suspected that money was going missing, stock didn't tie up with takings see. So he caught 'er out."

"What happened?" asked Sarah.

"Dad grabbed her and I went and got the watch. Found the money in her dress and they took her to the Station House. She'll be deported, like as not." With that he moved off down the bar to serve someone else.

Sarah could not help a wave of smug satisfaction creep over her. Then she saw the distraught look on her brother's face and felt a little chastened. Jimmy had clearly liked the girl; even if she was a thieving harlot. Rejoining Jimmy, Sarah put her arms around him and cuddled him tightly. "Come on sweetheart," she said softly, "cheer up, there's plenty more fish in the sea." Jimmy looked up at her fresh face and deep brown eyes and smiled a little crookedly, she squeezed him again and shouted to Billy. "Two brandies down here Billy! Come on Jimmy, let's drown your sorrows."

It was quite late in the evening when they left the Nags Head, both a little unsteady on their feet. They parted company at the end of the Hackney Road, Jimmy went left and Sarah right. She fell asleep with a smile on her face at the demise of buxom Lizzie and slept very well that night; even the black beetles crawling across her face did not disturb her.

The next Sunday afternoon, having got the day off, Sarah was just turning the corner from Great Pearl Street into the entrance of Little Pearl Street, on her way to visit her family. There was a scrabbling of feet behind her and her arm was grabbed tightly. Swinging round in alarm, she faced her laughing sister Mary. "God help me girl!" she shouted, "you scared me to death coming on me like that!"

"Sorry," said Mary. Not meaning a bit of it.

Mary was a very precocious nine-year-old coming on sixteen. She had the Valentine brown eyes and dark complexion but, as she grew older, her eyes were becoming a lighter brown and her hair, when not covered in soot, was not quite black. Circumstances, mostly bad ones, had made her old beyond her years, but she still had a playful streak in her. As they walked up to Sarah's mother's lodgings, arm in arm, Mary spitefully regaled Sarah with the news that the hated Lizzie had been deported to the colonies. "And good riddance to her!" she yelled gleefully, "that doxy was no better than she aught to be!"

"Mary!" shouted Sarah, aghast at her little sister's language. But, more importantly, she was worried about how Jimmy was taking it.

As it turned out, she need not have worried, Jimmy seemed resigned to the fact that he would see no more of Lizzie. In conversation with him she realised that he had latched on to her words, 'there are plenty more fish in the sea'. He had already eyed up one or two prospective young maidens and certainly did not intend to let the grass grow under his feet. 'God help us!' thought Sarah, 'I do hope they are a bit better than that awful Lizzie'.

Now that Lizzie had departed these shores, Sarah had taken to calling in the Nags Head more often, to meet up with her brother after work. It was now October, and the rainy spell had given way to a cold snap. Sarah and Jimmy were huddled together in the Nags Head, supping their ales. Jimmy was staring at the wall behind the bar, something was obviously on his mind.

"What's the matter with you?" said Sarah.

"Er what," he said.

"I'm not daft," said Sarah, "leastways not yet anyway. You've got summat on your mind. I can see it clear as day, so, spit it out!"

"I was thinking about Lizzie" he said cautiously.

Sarah looked at him. "Don't tell me that awful woman's come back?" she said.

"No she hasn't!" he said then, deciding to change the subject, added, "I was speaking with George Linford yesterday."

Panic filled Sarah. She grabbed Jimmy's arm. "Nothing's happened to my son Edwin has it?" she shouted.

"No, no!" said Jimmy firmly, "he's fine. Growing good and strong."

"Have they heard from Freddy then?"

"No," said Jimmy, "he has completely vanished," then, "it's about Edwin and Susan."

"What's wrong with them?" Sarah asked.

"Sarah!" said Jimmy, "stop lookin' on the black side of everythin'. There's nothin' wrong with them."

"Sorry, I guess I just expect things to go bad these days."

"Well this is good news," said Jimmy.

"That's nice," said Sarah, "what is it?"

"Well," Jimmy said, "George said that they, that's Edwin and his wife Susan, are now living just over the road from him, at No. 30 Caroline Street." He paused, then went on, "It seems that Susan has just given birth to their first baby, a girl they are also calling Susan."

"That's wonderful news Jimmy! I'm very happy for them, this calls for another drink," and with that Sarah jumped up and walked over to the bar. But, as she reached the bar, her mood changed, she could not help but be reminded of her son Edwin. She was still haunted by the blank unknowing look he had given her outside the Stepney Church at Susan and Edwin's marriage; that was the only time she had been able to see him. She was clearly of no consequence to him in his little life and she felt her eyes moisten over. She paid for the drinks and dawdled a little at the bar, composing herself, in the process noting that Lizzie's replacement was an older man. Then, she brought the two drinks back and they sat in an awkward silence for a time. Sarah was still trying to come to terms with her feelings when the landlord, Stephen Standen, and his wife Ann walked into the bar from a door at the back. Seeing Jimmy and Sarah sitting at their usual corner table, Ann walked over, whilst her husband joined their son Billy and the new barman behind the bar, ready for the late evening rush.

Reaching their table Ann looked down at them. "Mind if I join you?" she said, "I could do with a quick drink before the evening crowd gets in."

"Sure," said Jimmy, "What can I get you?"

"That's all right Jimmy," said Ann. Looking up, she shouted to her son, "Billy, bring me a glass of Port will yer!" Then, she looked at Sarah and observing the downcast expression on her face, "what's the matter with you, got wet drawers or summat?"

At this Ann and Jimmy burst into raucous laughter, recalling the story Sarah had told them about her first night at the grand house; Sarah glared at them. Then, infected by their belly laughs, started to smile. Finally, she was laughing with them, her brooding mood broken. She was soon joining in the conversation and, several hours later, left the tavern in quite a merry mood and made her way home.

That evening though, lying on her bed behind the screening curtain, listening to the snores of her neighbour's, she pulled out her son's baptism certificate and, by the dim light of her fading candle, ran her fingers over the words, 'Edwin son of Sarah Valentine'. She glanced at Freddy's poesy ring, which had now become a permanent fixture on her right hand, her thoughts drifted to her son. She loved him dearly and, although she had only had him for a short time, she realised that she missed him terribly. Sleep was a long time coming.

When she finally drifted off, she dreamed of the day of her son's baptism, some five years ago, at St John's Church in Hackney, her delight at the whole of her family being there. Her eyes sprang open in the morning, the dream still fresh in her mind. Of course, she thought, families attend baptisms. This thought was still rattling round in her head as she walked to work.

She could hardly wait for the day to finish. Finally, she was bidding the workshop girls goodbye and hurrying down the Hackney Road. Reaching the Nags Head, she hurried inside, bought herself a drink and settled at their usual table to await her brother Jimmy. After an hour, she was getting anxious. They had not arranged to meet, she was there on the off chance that he would turn up. Then, to her relief, the door opened and in he walked.

Spotting Sarah, his usual cheerful grin spread across his face. He bought two drinks and walked across to the table. Sitting down opposite her he smiled. "Well, well!" he said, "this is getting to be a habit. I hope your not getting into your cups?"

"No I'm not!" said Sarah testily, then lowering her voice, "I've a small favour to ask you."

Jimmy looked at his sister's smiling face and fluttering eyelashes and immediately got the distinct impression that she was up to something. He took a slow sip of his ale before answering. "And what would that *favour* be then?"

She hesitated a little before saying, "you see George Linford from time to time, don't you?"

Not sure where this conversation was going, he nodded to her.

"Well," she continued. Jimmy could see her mind racing as she chose her words. "I was wondering if Susan and Edwin Linford were going to have their new baby baptised?" she flashed a beaming smile and her eyelashes fluttered again.

"Er, I don't know," Jimmy replied.

"I would like so much to congratulate them, do you think that you could find out from George Linford?"

"I suppose so," said Jimmy.

"Thank you," said Sarah, putting her arms round him. "Oh, and don't tell him I asked, just make it a casual enquiry." Then, standing up, "let me get you another drink Jimmy."

It was a slightly confused Jimmy who left the Nags Head later that evening, to walk back home to Whitechapel. His sister Sarah had a smile on her face as she made her way back home.

The following evening, Sarah was waiting at their usual table in the Nags Head when Jimmy walked in. He saw two drinks on the table in front of her, so he walked up to the table and sat down. Sarah smiled sweetly at him and asked him how his day had gone.

He looked her straight in the eye, a serious expression on his face. "I spoke with George Linford today," he said.

"Oh did you?" said Sarah, still smiling sweetly.

"You remember, you asked me to," he said, his expression unchanging.

"Oh yes, so I did," she replied.

"Come on Sarah, don't play games with me," he said, looking intently at her.

"I don't know what you mean Jimmy," she said, dropping her eyes.

"Oh yes you do! George Linford was a bit smarter than me and asked straight away if it was you wanted to know about the baptism."

Sarah looked downcast and said, "what did you say to him?"

"The truth," Jimmy replied, "that you wanted to know about the baptism."

They sat in silence for a few minutes, then Sarah said, in a low voice. "He wouldn't tell you would he?"

"No, he guessed immediately that you wanted to know so you could turn up to see your son Edwin and create another scene like the one at Susan and Edwin's wedding. He said you are not going to be allowed to ruin their child's baptism as well."

Sarah's face fell at that statement and tears started to roll down her cheeks. Jimmy's serious expression faded as he saw his sister's tears. "Look Sarah, I know you want to see your son, but creating deliberate trouble is not the way to go about it, George Linford is right, you caused a bad scene at their wedding and you now plan to repeat it at their baby's baptism. They don't deserve it, they are good people. I thought they were your friends."

"Oh but they are Jimmy," Sarah blurted out between sobs.

Another silence ensued. After a while Jimmy got up and went to the bar to replenish their drinks. When he returned to the table Sarah had gone. He looked down at the two drinks he had just bought; with a shrug of his shoulders, he made a start on the first of them.

It was two weeks before Sarah ventured into the Nags Head again. During that time she had not been sleeping well and was growing increasingly upset at the way she had tried to use her brother. She had come to the conclusion that her effort to see her son Edwin was causing trouble to her friends, who were in no way responsible for the situation in which she found herself; she resolved to offer her apologies.

When she entered the tavern, she saw Jimmy at their table talking with the Landlord's wife Ann Standen. She walked over to the table and, looking sheepishly at Jimmy, asked if he and Ann would like a drink. He accepted and Ann declined, saying that she must now take her position behind the bar. Sarah followed her to the bar and returned with two drinks which she placed on their table. She sat down and looked at Jimmy. She reached across the table and took his hands in hers, they felt rough and, looking down, she could see that they were black with soot. She lifted one up and pulled it to her mouth, kissing the back gently, she looked into his eyes. "I'm sorry Jimmy. I've been very selfish, thinking only of what I want, not how what I do effects other people. Please forgive me."

He smiled at her sad face. "Nothing to forgive," he said, "I know how you are feeling, it's only natural that you would want to see your son." Then he continued, "It's that wretched Jane Linford at the root of all this. I saw Susan Linford in the Hackney Road, with her new baby. She was going to meet her husband at the tailor's shop, we stopped and talked for a while."

"Oh I do so hope she doesn't hate me for what I did at her wedding!" Sarah exclaimed.

"No," said Jimmy smiling, "Now she has her new baby, she knows more than anyone how you are feeling; she bears you no grudge. In fact, it was her told me about Jane Linford."

"What did she say?" asked Sarah.

Jimmy took a long pull at his ale whilst he mustered his thoughts and considered what to say to his sister. He had no wish to heap further distress on her. "She feels that Jane Linford is being unreasonable in denying you a sight of your own son. She says that Jane has become obsessed with him. As each day goes by she seems to become more convinced that he is her son and not yours," he paused before continuing, "she has also started to call him Freddy, not Edwin,"

"What?" Sarah screamed. Her shout was so loud that everyone in the tavern turned to look at her.

Jimmy held her hands in his and watched in dismay as the tears streamed down his sister's cheeks. Without another word, she pulled her hands gently from his grasp, rose and walked to the door, all eyes following her. Reaching the door she opened it and passed out into the street, closing it softly behind her. Jimmy looked down at the table, at his drink and Sarah's untouched one. Another two drinks to finish; this was getting to be a habit!

The baptism of Susan Linford took place on Sunday 19th October 1845 at the Church of St John the Baptist, in Hoxton. The venue had been chosen, and the ceremony arranged, by Jane Linford. Susan had wanted her daughter baptised at the church they were married in, but Jane Linford was violently in disagreement with this and was supported by Edwin's sister Caroline and her policeman husband, neither of whom wanted a repeat of the disruptive performance, by Sarah Valentine, at the wedding. Susan was angry at this; indeed, she would have been happy to invite Sarah and was not supportive of Jane Linford denying her access to her son. But, she was only supported by her husband who, to her chagrin, was unable to stand up to his mother. However, she learned something at the baptism that set her mind racing. Perhaps there was something that she could do after all.

The following Saturday, Sarah Valentine had just left the shoemaker's at the end of her day's work. She was walking down the Hackney Road on her way home. Her eyes were cast down at the pavement in front of her and she was feeling very low. She had not been in the Nags Head since she had left in tears and felt no desire to be in the raucous atmosphere of the tavern.

She was so absorbed in her maudlin mood that, for a time, she did not notice the woman keeping pace, stride for stride, beside her. Then a voice sounded in her ear. "Hello Sarah."

Startled she looked across at the young woman keeping pace with her. Then recognition dawned and she stopped walking, it was Susan Linford. She also had stopped and was looking at Sarah with a sad expression on her face. "How are you keeping?" she asked.

Sarah was silent for a while, unsure what to say. Then she blurted out. "I'm sorry Susan. I'm really sorry for what I did at your wedding. It was unforgivable."

"That's alright," said Susan, gently putting her hand on Sarah's shoulder, "that's water under the bridge now." They both started to walk again. Silence reigned for a while. It was broken by Susan speaking again. "Are you working tomorrow?"

"No, not on Sunday," Sarah replied.

"Can you come round to see me tomorrow?" Then a pause, "it's really important to me."

"I'm not sure Susan," Sarah said uncertainly, "what about the Linfords?"

"Don't worry about them, they have an important engagement. It'll just be you and me. We can have a good chinwag over a cup of tea. Come on! We haven't had a good talk for quite a while."

"All right," said Sarah smiling, "if your sure they won't be there."

"I'm sure," said Susan reassuringly. They walked on for a while in silence. Sarah was about to ask Susan where her baby daughter was, when she stopped. They had reached the corner of Caroline Street and Susan was speaking. "I live just there," she said, pointing out a house with a red door, part way down Caroline Street, opposite to where she knew George and Jane Linford lived with her son. "Call on me after 10 O'clock." Then, with a cheery wave she was gone.

Sarah continued on down the Hackney Road, deep in thought. After a while she started to smile, it would be nice to see her friend Susan again and have a natter over a cup of tea.

On Sunday morning Sarah walked down Philips Street, crossed the Kingsland Road and made her way down Haggerstone Lane to the Church of St Mary's. She could not go this way without remembering the many times she had made the same journey in her distinctive striped Workhouse garb and ill fitting mismatched shoes, enduring the ridicule of the local kids. Thankfully that was now behind her, she had a nice dress on, a smart bonnet and a fine shawl with no patches or rips in it. She even had a good, serviceable pair of matching boots on her feet. Reaching the church, she walked idly round the square at the front, glancing up at the clock tower from time to time. At 10 O'clock she made her way down Brunswick Street to the Hackney Road. Reaching the Hackney Road, she looked across at the imposing frontage of Norway Place at the top of Caroline Street. She crossed over and walked down Caroline Street to the house Susan had indicated to her yesterday evening. Gingerly looking around her, she knocked on the red door. It was opened immediately by a smiling Susan. After a brief embrace, Sarah followed Susan down a narrow hallway to a door at the back, it was open and led into a small parlour. It was bright and airy, a window looked out onto a small rear garden, there was a small table and chairs in one corner and in the other corner was a cushion on which a baby girl lay asleep. Next to the sleeping baby was a toy doll and a pile of wooden bricks. Sitting right in the middle of the bricks was a little boy trying to place one brick unsteadily on top of another. At the sight of him Sarah's mouth fell open, she was unable to utter a word, for it was her son Edwin. Her hand went to her open mouth and she turned to look at Susan who was smiling widely at her.

"Why don't you go play with him, while I make us some tea," she said, walking out of the room.

Sarah stood looking at her son for a full minute, unable to move, her eyes filling with tears. He was clearly fit and healthy, chubby even, she could see that he had rosy cheeks and bright clear eyes. She was startled to see that his hair and facial features were remarkably like Freddy Linford's, he had his womanly full pouting lips and slanting eyebrows. Slowly, she walked over to him, he looked up at her approach and frowned. She smiled at him and slowly got down on her knees; she did not want to frighten him. Gently, she took one of the wooden bricks and placed it on top of another, then a third one on top of that. As she placed the fourth brick on the very top, he reached out his hand and knocked them to the ground. He looked at Sarah's startled expression and burst into a fit of giggles. "More!" he said, "more!" Smiling, Sarah repeated the process. She got no further than four bricks high before he dashed them to the ground again. When Susan returned with the pot of tea on a tray, they were both laughing at the little game.

Susan put the tray on the table, set up the cups and poured out the tea. "You'll be doing that all day," she said, "He loves to knock them down."

Sarah got up and moved to the table, they both sat down, drank their tea and watched Edwin play with his bricks. "How did you manage this?" Sarah asked in wonder, "won't you get into trouble with Jane Linford?"

Susan laughed, "she'd kill me if she saw this!" Susan then went on to explain that at her daughter's Baptism, a relation had told Jane Linford that her brother was very ill with a fever, he was in the London Hospital on the Whitechapel Road and not expected to last long. Jane wanted to visit him, so it was arranged that the family would visit the Hospital on the Sunday; her husband Edwin had gone with them. Susan told Jane that she wanted to stay with her daughter and offered to look after baby Edwin. Jane was very reluctant to leave Edwin, but she was also not happy about him entering a hospital full of sick people. In the end she had decided to leave him with Susan.

"So you planned this then?" Sarah exclaimed.

"Yes I did!" said Susan, with a wide grin on her face. "I think it's scandalous that Jane Linford is doing this to you, and no one seems able to stand up to her!"

They sat and watched Edwin play, Sarah thought that she could just pick him up and take him away with her. But, it was a fleeting thought, where would she take him to? Her small space in a grubby room. How would she look after him? She was just able to fend for herself, let alone bring up a small child; the thought passed. Although she hated Jane Linford with a vengeance, looking at the plump healthy young boy in front of her, she could not deny that her son had a much better future in the Linford household.

Her tea finished, Sarah got up and walked over to Susan's new baby girl. She was lying on her cushion sleeping peacefully. She looked so small and frail, but all Sarah said was. "What a lovely baby, she looks just like you." Susan smiled at the complement.

Sarah spent over an hour playing with her son. Then Susan said she had better leave before the Linfords' returned. Sarah kissed her son goodbye and hugged Susan warmly thanking her profusely for giving her the time with Edwin.

Sarah had very mixed emotions as she walked down the Hackney Road. On the one hand she was overjoyed at being so close to her son, but on the other, she was sad to say goodbye to him. Susan had promised that she would let Sarah know if another similar opportunity presented itself in the future. They both agreed that it would be safer to keep this a secret between themselves, Susan was not even going to let her husband know, lest Jane Linford somehow wheedled it out of him.

The weather grew colder as Christmas approached. Sarah heard no more from Susan and no further opportunities arose for her to see her son. The Valentine family had a simple Christmas day. Sarah joined them and although Mary was happy and playful, Sarah's mother was quite morose, clearly still missing her husband and her lost children: Caroline, Henry and both of the Joseph's. Nothing further was heard of her missing sister Charlotte and snow was falling as the year drew to a close.

The New Year of 1846 found Sarah trudging down the Hackney Road to work through thick snow. She was getting on quite well at the shoemaker's shop. With the knowledge that she could no longer rely on the Workhouse as a refuge if she was destitute, her attitude to work had shifted markedly, she had come to realise the importance of regular paid employment. With the onset of winter, business was booming at the shoemakers and she was helping out in the workshop more and more often as they struggled to fill all the orders for shoes. In recognition of this, she had been given a small pay rise and was now better off than she had ever been before in her life. Indeed, her wages had enabled her to buy a thick top coat and heavy boots, things she had never previously owned; the boots were a godsend in the winter weather. Over the preceding months, she had cemented a good relationship with the shoemaker's shop owner and the senior cordwainer George Mason. Her showing a real interest in the profession had impressed her Masters and she was more confident than ever at keeping this job.

It was Saturday February 14th 1846, Valentine's Day. Sarah Valentine was up bright and early, for her celebratory day. She had arranged to meet her brother Jimmy, after work, in the Nags Head, for a drink.

She was in a happy mood as she trotted up the Hackney Road to work that morning, she had a strange premonition that it was going to be a special day; she arrived at work early. She let herself in at the back door and, as she was a little too early to wake the children who had no school that day, she decided to go into the workshop and chat with some of the women; over the months she had got to know many of them quite well.

As soon as she entered the workshop, she knew that something was afoot. For a start, George Mason was there, he would not usually arrive so early. He was with another man and they were standing in the far corner. The other man had his back to Sarah, and they were talking with the senior closer. Also, standing with them, she could see George Cleare, eldest son of the owner of the shop; something was definitely happening. Sarah quietly made her way to one of the women shoe binders, Mary Ann Bean. She was just a little younger than Sarah and they got on together quite well. "Mary," she said quietly, "what's happening over there?" She pointed to the three men.

Mary cleared her throat with a raucous cough. Then said, "new man starting. Trade seems to be picking up and they need Martha in the shop, to help George Mason with the ladies, so, they've got a new man in to run the workshop. He's being introduced to us all, actually, he's George Mason's son would you believe!"

Sarah looked over at the group of men. Just at that moment George Cleare looked up and spotting Sarah, he called her over. As she walked across the room towards them, the new man still had his back to her. "I'd like you to meet our new workshop Master, Edward Mason," said George Cleare to Sarah, "actually, he's George here's son," he added. Then, addressing the new man, "meet Sarah Valentine, she's our general factotum, keeps the place ship shape; and you will find her very helpful in the workshop."

Staring at the new man's back, Sarah felt a sudden jolt, this man was familiar in some strange way. Then he turned round and her mouth fell open. Her heart skipped a beat.

It was the man she had seen three years ago, outside St Leonard's Church, at the wedding. The man with the shiny shoes!

Edward Mason looked at Sarah and a curious expression crossed his face, he seemed to be trying to remember something. For some odd reason, Sarah could feel her heart pounding in her chest, she felt her face start to redden. It was at this point that she somehow knew that she would never need to seek the sanctuary of the Shoreditch Workhouse ever again. In fact, from this moment on, things would never be quite the same again for her.

She instinctively knew that it would be the end of Sarah Valentine and maybe the beginning of Sarah Mason!

THE END OF PART 2

To be continued in Part 3